Blair Hoffman was a judicial staff attorney with the California Supreme Court for many years, until his recent retirement. History, and especially medieval English history, has fascinated him since his youth. In addition to his work as an appellate attorney, he authored a murder mystery, *Murder for the Prosecution*, and has written various legal articles. This is his first foray into writing about history since his university days. He lives in Moraga, California, with his wife of over four decades, Peggy. His daughter and son have blessed him with three cute and adorable grandchildren.

To my two children, Stephanie and David, who love history as much as I do.

Blair Hoffman

THEY NEVER REIGNED

Heirs to the British Throne Who
Never Became the Monarch

to the Ringlees

Blair Hoffman

AUSTIN MACAULEY PUBLISHERS™

LONDON * CAMBRIDGE * NEW YORK * SHARJAH

A CIP catalogue record for this title is available from the British Library.

ISBN 9781398419476 (Paperback)
ISBN 9781398419483 (ePub e-book)

www.austinmacauley.com

First Published 2023
Austin Macauley Publishers Ltd®
1 Canada Square
Canary Wharf
London
E14 5AA

I would like to thank the following:

My wife, Peggy, for her encouragement and putting up with my monopolising the home computer for long periods at a time.

The history department at the University of California, Santa Barbara, for helping me learn how to study and write about history.

The professors and amazing library (among the largest in Germany) at the Georg August University in Göttingen, Germany, where, in 1971, I was able to write an independent study paper on King Richard III (in German), which whetted my interest in medieval English history. (Georg August, after whom the university was named, was the Elector of Hanover and, simultaneously, the English King George II—and the father of an heir who never reigned. [Chapter 15])

My son-in-law, Paul Verbanszky, himself a history teacher, for his encouragement and helpful comments.

The research librarians at St Mary's College of California, the college in my hometown of Moraga, California, for giving me, a non-alumnus, unsparing research advice and help.

The librarians at the Moraga Public Library, for helping me learn about and gain expertise in using a wonderful inter-library loan system that gave me access to the resources of a multitude of large libraries, including those of numerous colleges and universities.

Readers, including especially those in the United Kingdom, for overlooking any errors, which I hope are few but are probably inevitable despite my best efforts and which are exclusively my responsibility.

And, finally, the United Kingdom itself, for having such interesting history.

Table of Contents

Introduction   14

Chapter 1 Off Crusading: Robert of Normandy   20

Chapter 2 A Royal Tragedy: William the Atheling   37

Chapter 3 The Anarchy: Matilda (Maud) and Eustace   44

Chapter 4 The Sons of Henry II: Henry and Geoffrey   71

Chapter 5 The First Non-King Arthur   82

Chapter 6 Edward, the Black Prince   89

Chapter 7 The Wars of the Roses, Part I:

      Richard, Duke of York and Edward of Lancaster   111

Chapter 8 The Wars of the Roses, Part II: Two More Edwards   133

Chapter 9 The Second Non-King Arthur   151

Chapter 10 Mary, Queen of Scots   160

Chapter 11 Henry Frederick   189

Chapter 12 James, the Old Pretender   193

Chapter 13 The Children of Queen Anne, Including

      William of Gloucester   204

Chapter 14 A Distant Branch: Sophia of Hanover   208

Chapter 15 Frederick, Son of King George II   213

Chapter 16 Princess Charlotte of Wales   221

Chapter 17 Prince Albert Victor, Known as Eddy   237

Conclusion   248

British Monarchs from 1066 to the Present and Heirs Who Never Reigned (marked with *).

William I, the Conqueror (c. 1028-1087, reigned 1066-1087).
      Robert of Normandy (c. 1051-1134).*
William II (c. 1056-1100, reigned 1087-1100).
Henry I (c. 1068-1135, reigned 1100-1135).
      William the Atheling (1103-1120).*
      Empress Matilda (Maud) (c. 1102-1167).*
Stephen (1092/1096-1154, reigned 1135-1154).
      Eustace (c. 1127-1153).*
      Henry II (1133-1189, reigned 1154-1189).
Henry, the Young King (1155-1183).*
Richard I, the Lion Hearted (1157-1199, reigned 1189-1199).
      Geoffrey (1158-1186).*
      Arthur of Brittany (1187-c. 1203).*
John (1166-1216, reigned 1199-1216).
Henry III (1207-1272, reigned 1216-1272).
Edward I (1239-1307, reigned 1272-1307).
Edward II (1284-1327, reigned 1307-1327).
Edward III (1312-1377, reigned 1327-1377).
      Edward, the Black Prince (1330-1376).*
Richard II (1367-1400, reigned 1377-1399).
Henry IV (1367-1413, reigned 1399-1413).
Henry V (c. 1386-1422, reigned 1413-1422).
Henry VI (1421-1471, reigned 1422-1461, 1470-1471).
      Edward of Lancaster (1453-1471).*
      Richard, Duke of York (1411-1460).*
Edward IV (1442-1483, reigned 1461-1470, 1471-1483).

Prince Edward, aka Edward V (1470-c. 1483, nominally king April-June 1483).*

Richard III (1452-1485, reigned 1483-1485).

Edward of Middleham (c. 1473-1484).*

Henry VII (1457-1509, reigned 1485-1509).

Arthur Tudor (1486-1502).*

Henry VIII (1491-1547, reigned 1509-1547).

Edward VI (1537-1553, reigned 1547-1553).

Mary I (1516-1558, reigned 1553-1558).

Elizabeth I (1533-1603, reigned 1558-1603).

Mary, Queen of Scots (1542-1587).*

James I (1566-1625, reigned 1603-1625).

Henry Frederick (1594-1612).*

Charles I (1600-1649, reigned 1625-1649).

(Commonwealth, 1649-1660.)

Charles II (1630-1685, reigned 1660-1685).

James II (1633-1701, reigned 1685-1688).

James, the Old Pretender (1688-1766).*

William III (1650-1702, reigned 1689-1702) and Mary II (1662-1694, reigned 1689-1694).

Anne (1665-1714, reigned 1702-1714).

William, Duke of Gloucester (1689-1700).*

Sophia of Hanover (1630-1714)*

George I (1660-1727, reigned 1714-1727).

George II (1683-1760, reigned 1727-1760).

Frederick, Prince of Wales (1707-1751).*

George III (1738-1820, reigned 1760-1820).

George IV (1762-1830, reigned 1820-1830).

Charlotte of Wales (1796-1817).*

William IV (1765-1837, reigned 1830-1837).

Victoria (1819-1901, reigned 1837-1901).

Edward VII (1841-1910, reigned 1901-1910).

Albert Victor ("Eddy") (1864-1892).*

George V (1865-1936, reigned 1910-1936).

Edward VIII (1894-1972, reigned 1936).

George VI (1895-1952, reigned 1936-1952).

Elizabeth II (1926-2022, reigned 1952-2022).

Charles III (1948-present, reigned 2022-present).

      William, Prince of Wales, Heir Apparent (1982-present).

Introduction

The English, later British, monarchy is famous and some of its kings and queens are among the most familiar names of history—William the Conqueror, Richard the Lion-hearted, Henry VIII, Elizabeth I, Victoria, Elizabeth II. But what about those men and women who at one time were in line to become the king or queen but, for a variety of reasons, never did? This is the story of the heirs who never reigned. It begins with the oldest son of William the Conqueror, the Norman duke who seized the English throne in 1066 by defeating the last Saxon King, Harold, at the Battle of Hastings. No effort is made to sort through the often chaotic times before the Norman Conquest.

During the Middle Ages, the French monarchy had a remarkable three-century run of royal stability, with father following son in an unbroken line, beginning with Hugh Capet in 987 and continuing until Phillip V succeeded his nephew, John I (who died at the age of five days), in 1316. The English never came close to such a record. Since the Conquest in 1066, essentially the same family dynasty has reigned in England, then Great Britain, then the United Kingdom. But there have been many ruptures and fissures, with the throne shifting from one family branch to another. Many luckless heirs failed to become king or queen. The vicissitudes of history—or life, many simply died too soon—deprived them of the chance to become the monarch. As a group, they obviously are less famous than those who did become the monarch, although a few, such as Edward, the Black Prince (chapter 6) and Mary, Queen of Scots (chapter 10), did become famous.

This book is about them, the ones who did not become the monarch. It involves some of the most famous episodes of world and English history. The First Crusade, the Magna Carta, the Hundred Years' War, the Wars of the Roses and the so-called Glorious Revolution, all provide material for this book. Those so inclined can find ample opportunity to ponder the imponderable "what ifs" of history:

What if the White Ship, England's medieval Titanic, had not hit a rock and sunk in 1120, drowning some 300 souls, including the sole male heir to the throne? (Chapter 2.)

What if King John's older brother had not been killed in a jousting tournament in Paris, opening the way for John to become king in his place and eventually be forced to sign the Magna Carta? (Chapter 4.)

What if Henry VIII's older brother, intended to become a second King Arthur, had not died unexpectedly young and Henry—he of the six wives—had therefore never become King? (Chapter 9.)

What if King James I's oldest son, Henry, raised from birth to become a king, had not gone swimming in the Thames and contracted typhoid fever, from which he died at the age of 18, with the result that his younger brother, Charles—who had not been raised from birth to become a king—became king instead and went on to be overthrown by the Long Parliament and Oliver Cromwell during the English Civil War and meet his end on the executioner's block? (Chapter 11.)

What if either Queen Mary II or Queen Anne had produced an heir and the British throne had never passed over to the Hanoverian branch of the family? (Chapter 13.)

And what if the beloved nineteenth-century Princess Charlotte, who appeared destined to preside over Britain's "Charlottian Era," had not died in childbirth at the age of 21, but instead had lived a normal life span and reigned as queen for several decades, with the result that the actual Queen Victoria, whose name instead designates an era of British history, would probably never have been born? (Chapter 16.)

The names in this story include several that never become those of a British monarch—Robert, Matilda, Sophia, Frederick, Charlotte, Albert, even Eustace. Two heirs, who never reigned, were named Arthur. England has never had a second King Arthur after the fabled Arthur of Camelot, but it came close twice. Several of those who never reigned were strong women; three had sons who became king. The ultimate fates of two of the heirs who never reigned—the first non-King Arthur (chapter 5) and the youth called King Edward V, also famously known as one of the "Princes in the Tower" (chapter 8)—present two of the enduring mysteries of English history. They were undoubtedly murdered, but how and when is unknown and, today, probably unknowable.

It is not always clear who does and who does not belong in this story and the author had to make choices. Readers may decide for themselves whether they agree with the choices. This book does not include everyone who was ever heir but never became a monarch. Several heirs died in infancy or early childhood. King Henry II's first son, William, was the heir until he died at the age of three in 1156. King Edward I's three oldest sons were each the heir for a short time but died young—John at the age of five in 1271, Henry at the age of seven in 1274 and Alphonso at the age of ten in 1284. Edward, the Black Prince's oldest son and first heir, also named Edward, died aged five in 1370, allowing his younger brother to become King Richard II. King Henry VIII had two sons born to his first wife, Catherine of Aragon, who died in infancy—Henry, who died in February 1511 when less than two months old and another Henry, who died in 1515, also less than two months old. Because these heirs died so young, they have no real story to tell.

This book also generally excludes those who were merely the heir presumptive and then lost their position in the natural course of events when the monarch produced an heir apparent. An heir *apparent* has always been the oldest son of the king or queen, who could not be supplanted by an heir born later and thus would expect to become king when the reigning monarch died. An heir *presumptive* is usually a person who is next in line to a childless monarch but would be supplanted when the monarch produces an heir apparent. For example, King Henry III was nine years old when he became king in 1216 and, obviously, he had not yet produced an heir. His younger brother, Richard of Cornwall, was the heir presumptive and would have become king had Henry died childless. But Richard lost his position when Henry's son, the future Edward I, was born. Edward, the new heir apparent, supplanted Richard in the line of succession.

Until recently, when the rules have been changed in many monarchies for the sake of equality, a woman could never be considered an heir apparent. Theoretically at least, even if not in practical fact, the monarch might produce a male heir, who would supplant her. For example, until her father died and she actually became Queen, Elizabeth II was considered the heir presumptive, not heir apparent, because her father could, theoretically, still have had a son who would have become the heir apparent. Sometimes the heir apparent to an heir apparent (i.e., the grandson of the monarch whose parent is the heir apparent) is also called an heir presumptive on the theory that there can be only one heir apparent at a time. But such an heir cannot be supplanted; he (or now possibly she) merely needs to outlive both the grandparent monarch and the parent monarch-in-waiting. Most heirs presumptive, such as Richard of Cornwall, had no strong expectancy of becoming King. This book does not include those who simply lost their position when the monarch produced an heir to supplant them. But it does include heirs presumptive if they never reigned for a reason other than merely being supplanted, such as an early death.

Whether the first person in this story, Robert of Normandy, William the Conqueror's oldest son, belongs here is debatable. Primogeniture (the oldest son inheriting the father's kingdom) was not fully established in the eleventh century. When William the Conqueror died, Robert became Duke of Normandy, but not King of England. His younger brother became King of England as William II. This result was what the Conqueror intended. But Robert probably had legitimate expectations of becoming King of England when William II died without an heir. Unfortunately for him, Robert was in Italy, returning from being one of the heroes of the First Crusade when William died. Robert's youngest brother took advantage of Robert's absence to seize the throne as King Henry I. Accordingly, Robert reasonably can be counted among those who never reigned.

Another Henry, the oldest child of King Henry II to survive into adulthood, known as the Young Henry, was actually crowned King. But he was only crowned during his father's lifetime and was never king on his own. He never had any personal authority and he is not included in the numerical listing of kings. (King Henry III was the son of the Young Henry's brother, who became King John.) So, the Young Henry is appropriately considered an heir who never reigned.

The so-called King Edward V presents a closer question. If he was called Edward V, how can we say he never reigned? But this Edward, although technically king for a very short time, was never crowned nor permitted to act as a king. The title does not reflect the reality of his life. Edward's uncle, Richard, famously seized the throne and became King Richard III in his place. It is reasonable to say that this Edward never actually reigned. Additionally, his story is fascinating.

This book focuses only on the English and later British, crown. It includes Mary, Queen of Scots. Mary did reign, but only over Scotland, not England. She was never officially recognised as Queen Elizabeth's heir. However, as a practical matter, she was the heir presumptive at a time when it was obvious that Elizabeth would never produce her own heir. It appeared that Mary would succeed Elizabeth if only she outlived her. Her son did, in fact, succeed to the throne when Elizabeth died. So, it seems reasonable to include Mary among the heirs who never reigned. Her story is also fascinating, which made the decision to include her an easy one.

The first five chapters tell essentially one continuous story. Chapter 1 involves the first generation after William the Conqueror (Robert of Normandy), Chapter 2—the second generation (William the Atheling), Chapter 3—the same second generation (Matilda, also known as Maud) as well as the third generation (Eustace), Chapter 4—the fourth generation (Henry the Young King and Geoffrey) and Chapter 5, the fifth generation (the first non-King Arthur). William the Conqueror had been the Duke of Normandy when he conquered England and he continued to possess these lands after he became king. So, to a large extent, did his successors. Thus, a common theme in these five chapters is that the kings of England and their heirs, both those who did and those who did not reign, possessed many territories in what is today France, although which ones continually shifted over the years. Sometimes these kings spent more time in France than in England and were more interested in their French possessions than in England itself. During these times, the kings of France sought any opportunity that presented itself to cause trouble for the English kings.

In Chapter 6, we come to the opening stages of the Hundred Years War and the oldest son of King Edward III, also named Edward, known to history as the Black Prince. This Edward, who died a year too soon to become king, was heroic in war and exemplified chivalry at its best and, arguably, its worst. Then we come to the chaotic time of the Wars of the Roses in the latter half of the fifteenth century. The Wars produced four heirs who never reigned, one named Richard (heir by an act of Parliament) and three named Edward. (Chapters 7, 8.) Chapter 9 tells the story of the second non-King Arthur, a Tudor prince. Chapter 10 is about Mary, Queen of Scots A short chapter follows, talking about a Stuart prince who died young but old enough to have a story to tell. (Chapter 11.)

Chapter 12 speaks of James, the Old Pretender. This James spent most of his life as a mere claimant to the throne, just as did his son, Charles, the Young Pretender. But James was born to King James II. When the Old Pretender was an infant, his father was overthrown in the Glorious Revolution and he lost his position as an heir. But, for a short time in his infancy, this James was heir apparent to a king and (had he been aware at the time) could have expected to succeed his father in due course. So, he belongs in this book. Charles, the Young Pretender, was a mere claimant and never a recognised heir to a king. So, he is not included as an heir who never reigned.

Chapter 13 tells collectively the story of the children of Queen Anne, who was pregnant 17 times but left no heir. Indeed, only one child of hers survived infancy. This child was the heir to Anne before she became queen and would have succeeded to the throne if he had lived longer. Chapter 14 tells of the German Electress, Sophia of Hanover, a Protestant who was made heir by an act of Parliament when it became clear that Anne would never produce her own heir. Sophia died some two months before she would have become queen. Her son became King George I in her stead.

Chapters 15 and 16 tell of two more heirs (Frederick and Charlotte) who died too young to become the monarch, Charlotte heartbreakingly. Finally, chapter 17 tells the story of Albert Victor, the oldest son of Queen Victoria's oldest son— Edward (later King Edward VII). This prince's sexual orientation and mental state have been the subject of speculation and dispute. Long after his death, some even claimed, based on speculation and pure imagination—and despite actual facts that prove them wrong—that he was Jack the Ripper. This prince also died too soon to become King.

One difficulty in writing these stories is that often, especially during medieval times, it is uncertain exactly what happened. Sometimes the sources are silent, unclear, or contradictory. Some sources are, or might be, unreliable; they might be based on hearsay of questionable value, or they might be biased. Sometimes, the chronicler might simply have wanted to tell a good story whatever may actually have occurred. For example, it is unknown whether Prince Edward, the son of King Henry VI, was killed *during* the 1471 Battle of Tewkesbury or *afterwards*. (Chapter 7.) All too often, the author has had to use words and phrases such as "probably", "it is likely (or unlikely)", "apparently", "reportedly" or "might have." The author regrets the necessity but wishes to avoid expressing unwarranted certainty.

Chapter 1
Off Crusading: Robert of Normandy

The Duchy of Normandy—a region in the far north of France and thus closest to England—was founded in the tenth century by Rollo, a Viking adventurer from what is today Norway, who became the first Duke of Normandy. It was named for the Normans (North men), Viking invaders from Scandinavia who later intermarried and mixed with the native population. One of Rollo's descendants, William, later called the Conqueror after becoming King of England, was born around 1028, the illegitimate son, but also the only son, of the Duke of Normandy. Despite his illegitimacy, a significant stigma in those days, he became the Duke of Normandy himself in 1035. He married Matilda of Flanders, who bore him four sons. Robert, called Curthose, was the oldest. Next was Richard who, however, died young in a hunting accident. William, called Rufus (probably because of his ruddy complexion), was the third son, followed by Henry. William Rufus and Henry became kings of England after their father's death. Robert, despite being the oldest son, became the Duke of Normandy, but never King of England. He is, thus, the first of the heirs who never reigned.

Robert was born in Normandy. His birth might have occurred in 1051. It might have occurred in 1054. Or it might have occurred sometime in between. We do not know for sure. The lack of certainty in the records—typical of those times, even among the nobility—might reflect the lack of interest in the birth of children in an age of high infant mortality. Robert got his nickname, Curthose, from his father because of his short legs and, accordingly, short leggings. In his youth, he often acted as the king's regent in Normandy alongside his mother. Robert did well in military exercises and was considered courageous. William of Malmesbury, a twelfth-century chronicler, said he was "already a young man of established prowess…his courage was proven, although he was small in stature and pot-bellied."[1] According to Orderic Vitalis, another twelfth-century chronicler, "He was talkative and extravagant, reckless, very courageous in battle, a powerful and sure archer with a clear, cheerful voice and a fluent tongue."[2] But he was also considered lazy and weak. Regarding him later in life, Orderic said that Robert "exercised no discipline over either himself or his men. He was prodigal in distributing his bounty and lavish in his promises, but so thoughtless and inconstant that they were utterly unreliable."[3] As time would show, he could also be rebellious.

As a child, Robert often quarrelled with his younger brothers, something that, as will be seen, continued with a vengeance later in life. He was betrothed as a child to an heiress named Margaret of Maine, but she died long before the marriage could actually take place. As it turned out, Robert was not to marry until late in life. His future prospects took a considerable turn for the better in 1066. Before his father left to conquer England that year, he declared Robert, his heir, as Duke of Normandy. Then his father won the Battle of Hastings and became King William I of England. Robert, then a young teenager or close to it, could expect to inherit big things, probably including a kingdom. Unfortunately for him, he had a younger brother, William Rufus, and would soon have another brother, Henry. William and Henry would also be ambitious and would prove to be more capable or, at least, more devious than Robert.

In 1073, King William campaigned in Normandy and conquered the province of Maine. Robert fought alongside his father and did well, so well in fact that he pointedly suggested that the king return to England and let the son rule over Normandy. This might have been the first time Robert's rebellious nature surfaced. It would not be the only time Robert would chafe under his

---

[1] R.A.B. Mynors, ed. and transl., *William of Malmesbury: Gesta Regum Anglorum, A History of the English Kings, vol. I*, Oxford University Press (1998), p. 701 (hereafter, *William of Malmesbury, vol. I*). William, who lived around 1095 to 1143, was a monk at Malmesbury, an Abbey in Wiltshire. He is a highly regarded source.

[2] Marjorie Chibnall, ed. and transl., *The Ecclesiastical History of Orderic Vitalis, vol. II*, Oxford University Press (1969), p. 357. Orderic, who lived from 1075 to around 1142, was a Benedictine monk who lived in a monastery in Normandy. He is generally considered reliable.

[3] Marjorie Chibnall, ed. and transl., *The Ecclesiastical History of Orderic Vitalis, vol. IV*, Oxford University Press (1973), p. 115 (hereafter *Orderic Vitalis, vol. IV*).

father's rule. William refused to give his son autonomy in Normandy or any other significant independent rule.

Robert's quarrels with his brothers reached a crisis in 1077. It appears that, as a prank, William Rufus and Henry poured the contents of a well-used chamber pot over his head. A chamber pot was the medieval equivalent of a toilet, so the prank was quite unpleasant for Robert, to say the least. Robert was furious and, egged on by his friends, he assaulted his brothers. They fought fiercely until their father intervened and stopped the fight. Robert became angry with his father for what he viewed as the father's lenient treatment of his brothers. He thought the king was taking his brother's side when he considered himself the aggrieved party. He thus began his first rebellion, one that, as with most of his endeavours in life (with one notable exception), ended badly for him.

Some of Robert's friends, as well as discontented Norman lords, supported Robert. The lords believed that encouraging conflict between him and his father would further their own ends. Robert and his young supporters tried to capture the castle in Rouen. The attempt failed and William ordered their arrest. They fled. Robert eventually went into exile in Flanders, where he lived with his uncle, the Count of Flanders, also named Robert. There he continued his rebellion. Orderic wrote that he "foolishly rebelled against his father in his youth and, as an exile leading a great band of robbers, disturbed Normandy with raids and many outrages."[4]

Money concerns also seemed to contribute to Robert's disaffection. In his view, the king never supplied him with enough. Robert played one parent off against the other. Queen Matilda, Robert's mother, "feeling a mother's affection for her son, often used to send him large sums of silver and gold and other valuables without the King's knowledge."[5] When William learned of this, he became furious with both her and Robert. Their quarrels soon escalated. Robert rebelled again, this time seeking to rule Normandy while his father was still alive. In the winter of 1078-9, William besieged the fortress at Gerberoy, in the North of what is now France, where Robert had assembled his forces. The two sides fought a significant battle in front the fortress in January 1079. During the battle,

---

[4] Marjorie Chibnall, ed. and transl., *The Ecclesiastical History of Orderic Vitalis, vol. V*, Oxford University Press (1975), p. 283 (hereafter, *Orderic Vitalis, vol. V*).

[5] Marjorie Chibnall, ed. and transl., *The Ecclesiastical History of Orderic Vitalis, vol. III*, Oxford University Press (1972), p. 103 (hereafter, *Orderic Vitalis, vol. III*).

Robert "clashed with the father, wounded him and cut down his horse."[6] When he recognised his father's voice, he stopped the attack. William, humiliated, cursed his son and possibly never forgave him.

In early 1080, the king's army and that of Robert and his supporters were posed to fight another battle in Normandy. But then father and son were reconciled—for a while. Members of the church convinced the warring parties to make peace and a battle was averted. Over Easter of that year, Queen Matilda, frustrated with the interminable quarrels and finding it difficult to remain loyal to both her husband and her firstborn son, arranged a more lasting informal truce between the two. The truce lasted until the queen died in 1083.

In the summer of 1080, during this period of reconciliation, Robert, who mostly resided in Normandy, came to England, possibly for the only time while his father was alive. William entrusted him with an army to invade Scotland, whose King, Malcolm III, was causing trouble in the northern regions of England. The parties made peace without much effort on Robert's part and Robert visited the Scottish royal court. There he met the Scottish Queen, Margaret, later canonised as St Margaret. This Margaret had a daughter who later married Robert's brother Henry and was destined to become a queen consort of England. (Chapter 2.) Robert remained in England for several months.

After the death of Robert's mother, Queen Matilda, relations between Robert and the king deteriorated again. Orderic reported that "the peace between the king and his son which had taken so long to achieve was soon clouded. The stubborn young man contemptuously refused to follow or obey his father; the quick-tempered king continually poured abuse and reproach on him in public for his failings."[7] It was probably not chance that these events occurred soon after the queen was no longer alive to mediate between them. Robert left his father's court and once again went into exile. What he did during the next four years is poorly documented, but he probably travelled through the Low Countries, France, Germany and Italy. In Italy, he unsuccessfully sought to marry a rich heiress, Matilda of Tuscany. During these years of wandering, he reportedly fathered several illegitimate children.

Robert's period of wandering ended in 1087. In September of that year, in the city of Rouen, William the Conqueror died of injuries suffered when he fell off his horse during a battle two months earlier. Even though Robert was

---

[6] *William of Malmesbury, vol. I*, p. 477.
[7] Orderic *Vitalis, vol. III*, p. 113.

William's oldest son, he did not succeed to William's English throne. Instead, as he was dying, William summoned his younger sons, William Rufus and Henry. Robert was not present; he was probably at the French court. The king was tempted to disinherit Robert, his rebellious son, entirely. But, as he told his younger sons, Robert had been named and recognised as his heir to the Duchy of Normandy back in 1066, before the Battle of Hastings, something that could not, or at least should not, be undone. So, William divided his possessions between Robert and William. Robert received Normandy and became the Duke of Normandy, which he remained until 1106. One reason Robert did not inherit the English throne was that he was barely known in that country. He had lived most of his life in Normandy. William Rufus, the non-rebellious son, became King William II. The youngest son, Henry, received money to buy his own lands. Later, when Robert found it difficult to live within his means, Henry used the money to purchase the County of Cotentin in the west of Normandy from Robert.

After their father's death, William Rufus, who never married, and Robert, also not yet married, agreed to be each other's heir. However, this agreement did not last long. William the Conqueror's decision to divide his lands between his two sons caused grave difficulties. The barons with lands both in Normandy and England, and they were many, owed feudal allegiance to both William Rufus and Robert. They found the situation difficult, if not intolerable, given the hostility between the two brothers. They feared that if they served Robert well in Normandy, they would lose favour with William, their English overlord; and if they served William well in England, they would lose favour with Robert, their Norman overlord. Many wanted the realm reunited. Many also welcomed Robert's becoming their overlord. He was considered weak and pliable and the lords believed they would have considerable autonomy under his rule. Thus, Robert had supporters, at least in Normandy, who wished him to become king in William's place.

In 1088, several Norman lords, led by the powerful Odo, Bishop of Bayeux, a half-brother of William the Conqueror, rebelled against William Rufus with the intent of replacing William with Robert. They invaded England and established several rebel strongholds. But, to their surprise, William's English lords remained loyal to him and William was able to crush the rebellion. Part of the reason the rebellion failed was that Robert never appeared personally in England with his own troops. He claimed bad weather prevented him from crossing over to England, but Orderic stated that he "was delayed through his inertia and love of ease."[8] William treated the rebel lords leniently in the hope and expectation that, because he had been lenient, they would remain loyal to him in the future.

The struggles between William II and Robert continued. In 1091, William invaded Normandy and forced Robert to agree to a treaty that divided the duchy between them. The two then joined forces against their youngest brother, Henry, to deprive him of his lands in Normandy. Henry retreated to a castle where, after a 15-day siege and with water running low, he was forced to capitulate and abandon any claims to Normandy. After that, Robert went to England with William for a few months, returning to Normandy in December 1091. Over the next few years, Robert struggled, with limited success, to maintain control over the Norman barons and administer the duchy. In 1094, Robert renounced the previous treaty with William. William returned to Normandy with troops in February 1094 and the conflict continued without a decisive outcome. During this time, William formed an alliance for a while with Henry against Robert. By 1096 a stalemate had arrived and the struggle promised to continue, seemingly interminably. Then came an interruption, one that Robert probably welcomed. History called.

At the Council of Clermont in 1095, Pope Urban II called for a military expedition to aid the Christian Byzantine Empire against Islamic incursions. For most of its history, the Byzantine Empire had controlled Anatolia (roughly the Asiatic part of modern-day Turkey). But at the disastrous Battle of Manzikert, fought in eastern Anatolia in 1071, the Seljuk Turks, followers of Islam, decisively defeated the Byzantines. As a result, the Turks occupied most of Anatolia, threatening the nearby Byzantine capital of Constantinople, as well as the land route for pilgrims going to Jerusalem. In this crisis, the Byzantine Emperor Alexios Komnenos (Latinised as Alexius Comnenus) requested assistance from the West. The Pope was persuaded and called for the expedition that was later called the First Crusade. The Crusade's immediate goal was to help the Byzantine Empire recover Anatolia. It is unclear whether, in the beginning, the goal was even more ambitious: recapturing the Holy Land, including Jerusalem, from the "infidel." Yet that is what the Crusade ultimately accomplished.

The Crusade was to become a humanitarian catastrophe, as, among other atrocities, the Crusaders massacred most of the population, civilian and military,

---

[8] *Orderic Vitalis, vol. IV*, p. 127.

of Jerusalem, slaughtering Christians, Jews and Moslems indiscriminately. But, from the perspective of those who called for the Crusade and the Crusaders themselves, it became a spectacular success. Against all odds, the Crusaders did, indeed, capture the Holy Land, including Jerusalem. For a while, the Holy Land was under Christian, primarily Frankish, control. Future Crusades, and there were several, merely sought to defend and consolidate what the First Crusaders had won. Some of the later Crusades were utter failures, some were partial successes, some were diverted to other ends, none was a total success. Unlike later Crusades, no king or emperor participated in the first. But many high nobles did. Robert of Normandy was among those who heeded the call. In contrast to most of his endeavours in life, which generally ended in failure, he was to play a substantial part in the crusade's success.

As with most major life decisions, there were undoubtedly many reasons Robert took up the Cross and risked all in an uncertain military expedition to places far away. The perpetual wars with his brothers and restless barons must have worn on him. He simply could not rule peacefully over his duchy. He had an adventurous spirit, courage and military experience. He seemed to have had a love for travel, as his wandering years attested. Unlike many of his fellow Crusaders, Robert was unmarried, so he had no wife or family to worry about. Indeed, separation from the life he was then living and from his family might have been welcome. Maybe, he sought glory and renown as a warrior for Christ, which, he could hope, would help him regain control of his realm on his return. That is, *if* he returned, something that, given the vagaries of the enterprise, the distances involved and the unknown nature of the enemy, was far from certain.

Religious fervour certainly played a role in Robert's decision to go crusading. Most people, in those days, were religious, or purported to be, and emissaries of the Church whipped up support for the Crusade among nobles and commoners alike. Orderic states that Robert "resolved on the advice of certain men of religion to hand over the administration of his duchy to his brother and, himself taking the cross, to go on pilgrimage to Jerusalem to make amends to God for his sins"[9] But before he left, he needed to ensure, to the extent possible, that he would have a duchy to return to. He also needed money to finance the expedition.

To protect those who left their homes and domains to go crusading, the Pope ordered the local barons to cease, for the duration of the Crusade, the petty local

---

[9] *Orderic Vitalis, vol. V*, p. 27.

wars endemic in the region. This order promised to bring a period of peace to Normandy. Members of the Church helped negotiate a truce between Robert and William. William gained control of Normandy in Robert's absence in exchange for a payment of 10,000 silver marks that Robert sorely needed to pay for the enterprise. The truce was no guaranty that William would actually cede Normandy back to Robert when he returned. Nothing could be a firm guaranty. But Robert accepted the truce (and money) as the best he could do.

Robert did not go on crusade as a mere pilgrim but as one of the leaders. Many of his comrades joined him, including his uncle, Odo, Bishop of Bayeux, who had supported Robert in his earlier attempt to seize the throne from William Rufus. Odo died on the way and thus never made it to the Holy Land. Robert joined forces with two other major French nobles. One was Stephen of Blois, Robert's brother-in-law, the husband of his sister Adela. (This Stephen was the father of another Stephen of Blois, who became England's King Stephen and is a key figure in chapter 3.) The other was Robert's cousin, Robert of Flanders. With the money acquired from William, Robert gathered and equipped a substantial army. It is difficult to determine how large his army was, probably a few thousand strong. Historians believe it was roughly the same size as the army of Godfrey of Bouillon, who was to play an even more glorious role in the Crusade than Robert. Having created a crusading army, Robert set off for far-off Anatolia.

The French armies, including Robert's, left France around September 1096, going first to Rome. Pope Urban received them in Italy. Because of inclement weather, they did not attempt to cross the Adriatic until spring and spent the winter of 1096-7 in Italy. During this time, Robert probably met his future wife, the wealthy heiress Sybilla of Conversano, a town in southeast Italy. He might have begun negotiations to marry her should he return from the Crusade.

In the spring, the armies crossed to Durazzo, a city in modern-day Albania. They then continued on towards the lands of the Byzantine Empire. They were late joining other crusader armies, arriving in Anatolia around May 1097. Up to this point, they had been in friendly territory and, unlike other crusading armies, had seen no hostile action. But Robert would soon be put to the test.

By June 1097, crusading armies had captured the key city of Nicaea, which was only 50 miles from the Byzantine capital of Constantinople. Thereafter, to ease problems of supply, the crusaders divided their forces in two. One force, led by Robert and others, marched towards Dorylaeum, a city to the southeast of

Nicaea. The leader of the Turkish forces, Kilij Arslan, knowing he could not defeat the combined crusading armies, chose to attack and try to annihilate this isolated force. He planned an ambush on 1 July 1097. That morning, Robert and his allies were horrified to observe several thousand Turkish horsemen in their way. No one knows for sure the size of the opposing contingents, but Arslan's forces probably outnumbered the Crusaders substantially. The Battle of Dorylaeum ensued. The First Crusade had arrived at a crossroads. Defeat meant almost certain annihilation. If Arslan's planned ambush had succeeded, the remaining crusading armies would probably have returned home and the crusade would have failed. The later crusades would never have occurred.

But Robert and the others were up to the test. The Turkish forces attacked ferociously and in large numbers. The Crusaders formed a defensive line and held firm. A historian of the First Crusade wrote, "In a moment of extraordinary courage and composure, Bohemond [another crusading leader] and Robert kept their heads and stayed the pulse of panic rushing through their forces." Despite heavy losses, the Crusaders held off the Turks until reinforcements from the second crusader army arrived in the afternoon. "Through five dreadful hours, the Franks waited,…inspired by Bohemond's and Robert's immutable stance. This was an extraordinary feat of martial discipline, the product of inspired General-ship…Bohemond's and Robert's achievements in the battle near Dorylaeum were of the highest order."[10]

When the second crusader army arrived, Alp Arslan, unable to defeat the single isolated army, gave up and fled the battlefield. Despite suffering some 4,000 casualties, it was a complete Crusader victory and it opened the door to Jerusalem. Robert had much to do with it.

Robert participated in the subsequent siege of Antioch, south of Anatolia on the route to Jerusalem, and the capture and siege of Jerusalem itself in June and July 1099. His forces besieged the north side of Jerusalem. But his most famous exploit occurred after the July 15 capture of Jerusalem. An army from Egypt led by al-Afdal Shahanshah, the vizier of Egypt's Fatamid Caliphate, with perhaps 20,000 troops, invaded to try to recapture Jerusalem. An army of Crusaders, with around 10,000 troops, led by Godfrey of Bouillon, but including Robert and his forces, left Jerusalem to confront the threat. The opposing forces met on August 12 1099, near the city of Ascalon, southwest of Jerusalem. Badly outnumbered,

---

[10] Thomas Asbridge, *The First Crusade: A New History*, Oxford University Press (2004), p. 135-6.

the crusaders, consisting now of only the toughest and most battle-hardened of troops, decided to attack. An early morning attack achieved total surprise. The vizier's army was routed. Another historian of the First Crusade wrote, "The hero of the day was Robert of Normandy, 'a fearless warrior,' who spotted the standard of al-Afdal by the golden apple at its tip. The duke charged at the vizier, drove away his men and thus broke the entire enemy's will to resist. Robert later presented the standard before the Holy Sepulchre [in Jerusalem]."[11] The Battle of Ascalon is considered the last battle of the First Crusade.

After accomplishing what they had set out to accomplish, most of the crusaders who survived the lengthy military campaign left the Holy Land to return to their former homes. A few—too few, as subsequent events were to prove—remained behind, some to carve out small Frankish principalities for themselves and some to establish and try to defend the new Christian Kingdom of Jerusalem. Godfrey of Bouillon, Robert's comrade in arms, became the first ruler of the new kingdom.

Robert was among those who returned. But he did so at a leisurely pace. Alexius Comnenus, the Byzantine Emperor, provided him with funds as a reward for his service and allowed him free passage through his territory. Robert stopped in Italy during the winter of 1099-100. There he finally married. His bride was Sibylla of Conversano, whom he had probably met and possibly wooed during his earlier stay in Italy. Orderic described her as "truly good in character, endowed with many virtues and lovable to all who knew her." He tells us that Robert fell in love with her.[12] Her dowry was also a welcome addition to his resources. When the couple returned to Normandy, Sibylla became popular, even beloved, among the barons and general population. She and Robert took a pilgrimage together to the commune of Mont Saint-Michel, where they gave thanks for his safe return from crusading. In 1102, she gave birth to their only child, William of Clito. She died a few months later. The marriage, brief as it was, seems to have been a happy one.

During Robert's dalliance in Italy, startling news reached him from England. By the year 1100, after 13 years of misrule, William Rufus had become despised throughout his realm. On August 2 1100, William died of an arrow shot through his heart while hunting. It might have been an accident. It might have been

---

[11] Jay Rubenstein, *Armies of Heaven: The First Crusade and the Quest for Apocalypse,* Basic Books (2011), p. 309.

[12] *Orderic Vitalis, vol. V,* p. 279.

murder. No one cared and no one investigated. Robert was widely expected to be the king's successor. It was not to be.

Because Robert was in Italy, news of his brother's death did not reach him for quite some time. When he heard the news, he belatedly returned to Normandy. One man, however, acted promptly after the king's death. The youngest brother, Henry, was nearby when his brother was killed and might have been part of the same hunting party. No evidence exists that Henry was complicit in William's death, but he acted decisively to win the throne. He argued that because, unlike Robert, he was "born to the purple," that is, born *after* his father had become king (he was born around 1068, after the Battle of Hastings), he was entitled to succeed to the throne. Far more important than any legalistic argument, however, was the fact that Henry was on the scene and Robert was far away. Henry raced to Winchester and seized the royal treasury. Although some of the nobles espoused Robert's claim, Henry was able to persuade enough of the barons to support him. With the money he had seized and the support he had won, Henry was crowned as King Henry I at Westminster Abbey on August 5, just three days after William Rufus's death.

Henry promptly set about consolidating his hold on the throne, rewarding many of his supporters with positions of power to ensure their loyalty. He issued a Charter of Liberties (or Coronation Charter), promising to undo many of his predecessor's unpopular policies and practices and to guarantee the rights of the Church and nobles. This charter, while not particularly famous today, was, in some of its terms, a forerunner of the Magna Carta a century later. Henry also deposed one of William Rufus's key advisors, the unpopular Ranulf Flambard, Bishop of Durham, and imprisoned him in the Tower of London.

When Robert finally returned from crusading, he administered his duchy and sought to gain what he considered his rightful position as King of England. He did both poorly. If he thought that his reputation as a returning crusader would aid him, he was soon to become sorely disappointed.

To support his claim to the throne, Robert invoked the short-lived agreement he had reached with William Rufus after their father's death that Robert and Rufus would be each other's heir. Some of the nobles supported his claim. Chief among these was Flambard, the deposed Bishop of Durham. Flambard managed a daring escape by climbing down a rope from the Tower of London. He made his way to Normandy, where he met with Robert. They planned an invasion of England to make good Robert's claim to the throne. Robert formed a small army of a few hundred men and organised a fleet of ships. In July 1101, he crossed the English Channel, landing at Portsmouth. There, some, but not many, of the barons joined Robert's forces. The measures Henry had taken since his coronation had proved popular and many of the nobles, including, importantly, Anselm, the powerful Archbishop of Canterbury, continued to support the King. Henry moved swiftly to thwart the invasion, bringing his forces to nearby Pevensey.

With his claim to the throne in the balance, Robert probably should have marched promptly to Winchester, where the royal treasury was located. But he hesitated, giving the king time to react. Henry raised an army and went to meet Robert. According to Orderic, the king "sent messengers ahead to inquire searchingly on his behalf why he [Robert] had presumed to enter English territory with an armed force. Duke Robert answered to this effect through his envoys, 'I have entered the kingdom of my father with my magnates and I demand the right due to me as the eldest son.' " The king and his forces met Robert's army at Alton in Hampshire. There was no battle, however, but instead peace negotiations. Orderic again: "When they met feelings of brotherly love surged up in both…The two brothers conversed alone in the midst of the circle of onlookers and openly and honestly voiced what they had in their hearts. Finally, after a few words, they embraced one another and, exchanging affectionate kisses, were reconciled without a mediator."[13] Diplomacy, probably mixed with Robert's awareness of how weak his position was, prevailed. The brothers agreed to the 1101 Treaty of Alton.

In the treaty, Robert renounced his claim to the English throne. In return, Henry renounced any claim to Robert's territories in Normandy, retaining possession of only one small portion of the duchy. He agreed to provide Robert a pension of 3,000 pounds a year for life. Any baron whose lands had been seized for supporting one brother or the other was to have them returned and there would otherwise be no reprisals against Robert's supporters. Flambard was reinstated as Bishop of Durham. The brothers agreed that if either died without an heir (neither had one at the time; soon both would), the other would inherit that brother's lands. The two agreed to campaign together in Normandy to defend their mutual interests. After signing the treaty, Robert remained in England for a few months with Henry before returning to Normandy.

---

[13] *Orderic Vitalis, vol. V*, pp. 317-9. Other chroniclers said the brothers negotiated through mediators. See *id.* at pp. 318-9, fn. 2.

Peace between the brothers did not last long. Henry soon stopped paying the promised pension. Robert quarrelled with his barons in Normandy and his control over his lands was weak. Orderic wrote that "Robert, a weak duke, fell far below the might of his ancestors: sunk in sloth and voluptuousness he feared the vassals in his own duchy more than they feared him, with the result that terrible disorders appeared and spread throughout his duchy."[14] The situation in Normandy became chaotic. One particularly troublesome baron was Robert of Bellême, Earl of Shrewsbury. This Robert had rebelled against King Henry and quarrelled with Robert of Normandy. But then, with dwindling support among his barons and in an effort to maintain some kind of control over his realm, Robert chose to ally himself with Robert of Bellême.

Henry claimed that doing so violated the terms of the Treaty of Alton. In 1104, he crossed the English Channel to Normandy, where he met with Robert's disaffected barons. Henry then summoned Robert to a conference, where he berated him for breaking the treaty. According to Orderic, the king also charged that "sunk in lethargy, he [Robert] had abandoned all Normandy to thieves and robbers and other evil-doers." Orderic says that at the time, Robert "was both foolish and friendless, because he did not value the company of good men or the counsel of wise ones, but unhappily chose companions of the opposite sort, thereby harming both himself and many others."[15] On this occasion, however, Henry and Robert made peace and Henry returned to England.

Orderic reports an incident during Easter 1105 that reflects on Robert's character and suggests reasons he had such difficulty administering his duchy. Robert was supposed to attend a sermon by a "venerable" bishop but did not appear. In his sermon, given to an audience that included King Henry, the bishop said that Robert "does not truly hold Normandy, nor does he govern the people as a duke should…Sad to relate, he squanders the wealth of a great duchy on trifles and follies, while he, himself, often fasts until noon for lack of bread. Often, he dares not rise from his bed and cannot attend church, because he is naked and has no breeches, socks, or shoes. Indeed, the jesters and harlots who constantly keep company with him steal his clothes at night while he lies snoring in drunken sleep and guffaw as they boast that they have robbed the duke. So, when the head is sick, the whole body is afflicted; when the ruler is foolish, the

---

[14] *Orderic Vitalis, vol. V*, p. 27.

[15] Marjorie Chibnall, ed. and transl., *The Ecclesiastical History of Orderic Vitalis, vol. VI*, Oxford University Press (1978), pp. 57, 59 (hereafter *Orderic Vitalis, vol. VI*).

whole province is in danger and the wretched people suffer utter deprivation."[16] To the extent this account is accurate, it helps explain why Robert did not endear himself to those who should have been his supporters.

Henry invaded Normandy again in 1105. Many of Robert's barons were prepared to side with the king. However, as in the previous year, the campaign ended inconclusively. The king captured and burned the city of Bayeux, after which Caen surrendered to his forces. But the fighting between the opposing forces reached a stalemate and the brothers opened negotiations that resolved nothing. Because of difficulties arising back home, the king returned to England around Christmas time.

The next year came the final confrontation between Henry and Robert. Henry returned to Normandy in July 1106. He laid siege to the castle on the hill above the town of Tinchebray, in the southwest of Normandy. The castle was held by William, Count of Mortain, one of Robert's few remaining allies among the Norman nobility. Within a few days, Robert arrived with a small army to aid his ally. Robert of Bellême and the Count of Mortain remained loyal to Robert. But few, if any, other important barons supported him. Most flocked to Henry's side. The showdown came in September 1106. Henry gave Robert an ultimatum: "Hand over to me all the castles, all judicial and administrative business throughout Normandy and half of the duchy and keep the second half for yourself without toil or responsibility, receiving the equivalent value of the first half annually from my treasure-store in England."[17] Robert refused the ultimatum scornfully. At this point, both Henry and Robert seemed to want to resolve the conflict finally one way or another. The decisive Battle of Tinchebray ensued.

Most of the soldiers on both sides, including dismounted knights, fought on foot, which was unusual given the cavalry tactics the Normans usually employed. The battle lasted only one hour. Robert's forces, which contained veterans of the Crusade but were probably outnumbered, attacked bravely at first. But soon, they were routed and most of his army was captured or killed. Robert of Bellême, who commanded the rear guard, "took to flight and abandoned the duke's shattered army to the victors."[18] He escaped. Not so fortunate were the Count of Mortain and Robert himself. Both were taken prisoner. It is unknown how many

---

[16] *Orderic Vitalis, vol. VI*, pp. 61, 63.

[17] *Orderic Vitalis, vol. VI*, p. 87

[18] *Orderic Vitalis, vol. VI*, p. 91.

causalities the two sides suffered. But it is likely that most of Robert's troops were captured rather than killed.

Robert's status as a glorious warrior for Christ helped him not at all in gathering and maintaining supporters and in fighting his own battles. As a result of his victory, Henry deposed Robert as Duke of Normandy and left Robert no title. Robert's then three-year-old son, William of Clito, was excluded from the inheritance. When this William became older, he made several attempts to win what he believed was his birth right. But all failed and Henry managed to keep the title. Winston Churchill called the Battle of Tinchebray the most important battle since Hastings itself.[19]

Henry released most of the prisoners. But he imprisoned Robert for the rest of Robert's long life, which would last another 28 years. The conditions of imprisonment were gentile. Orderic said that King Henry provided Robert "liberally with every comfort."[20] William of Malmesbury said Robert "had nothing worse to suffer than solitude—if solitude it can be called when he was enjoying the continual attention of his guards and plenty of amusement and good eating." It was unusual for a nobleman to imprison another noble, much less an older brother. But Henry might have felt he had little choice. He wanted to preserve his dynasty and, to the extent possible, achieve peace in his domains. To that end, he could not simply release Robert to fight another day. Given the violent times, he probably could have had Robert executed or simply murdered. He chose not to do that. Instead, he kept Robert a prisoner. William of Malmesbury ascribed Robert's imprisonment, rather than a worse fate, to "his brother's praiseworthy sense of duty."[21]

Robert's life in captivity began in the Tower of London. Later he was moved to Devizes Castle to the west of London. In 1126, he was moved again, this time to Bristol and then to Cardiff Castle in Wales. He undoubtedly learned of the death in July 1128 from a battle wound of his only legitimate son, William of Clito. William was 25 years old when he died. This William was childless and thus Robert's line came to an end. Because William was less than four years old when Robert was imprisoned, Robert never had a chance to see his son grow up.

---

[19] Winston Churchill, *A History of the English-Speaking Peoples*: vol. 1, *The Birth of Britain*, Dodd, Mead and Company (1966), p.183.

[20] *Orderic Vitalis, vol. VI*, p. 99.

[21] *William of Malmesbury, vol. I*, p. 707.

Robert Curthose, the former Duke of Normandy, finally died at Cardiff Castle in February 1134, over 80 years of age, very old age for those times. The fact that he lived so long suggests that he was, in fact, treated well in captivity. He was buried in Gloucester Cathedral. There, "Henry I endowed a light to burn before the high altar for the repose of his soul."[22] His effigy, carved about 100 years after his death, is decorated with the arms of the "Nine Worthies" of medieval lore (with Edward the Confessor's replacing Joshua's). The Nine Worthies included Robert's fellow crusader, Godfrey of Bouillon, who helped found the Christian Kingdom of Jerusalem.[23]

Robert had the good fortune to be born the son of William the Conqueror, King of England and Duke of Normandy and thus he grew up in an exalted and privileged position. But his life was unfortunate in many respects. Much less able in matters of statecraft than his younger brothers, they continually stymied him. He was clearly courageous. But he could be indolent and was a poor strategist. He seemed unable to govern people or win them to his side. When he had to fight his cause, he was generally a failure. Repeated attempts to gain the English crown failed ignominiously. He could not even retain the Duchy of Normandy, which he had inherited from his father.

Richard was at his best during the First Crusade, where his heroism helped to prevent the Crusade from failing at the outset and to preserve its hold on Jerusalem at the conclusion. Robert was not the most romanticised or glamorised of the English crusaders. His great-grandnephew, Richard, called the Lion-Hearted, has that distinction for his efforts in the Third Crusade. In effect, Richard had the medieval equivalent of good press. Robert did not. But Robert was the most *successful* of all the English crusaders. His illustrious descendant failed to recapture Jerusalem, which was his goal. Robert—and his many allies—succeeded where his descendant would fail. No one, not even his brothers, could take that away from him.

---

[22] *Orderic Vitalis, vol. VI*, p. 380, fn. 4.

[23] The Nine Worthies were nine men, all warriors, whom the post-First Crusade medieval world considered particularly great. They were divided into three groups of three: pagans, Jews and Christians. The pagans were Hector of Troy, Alexander the Great and Julius Caesar. The Jews were Joshua, David and Judas Maccabeus. The Christians were King Arthur, Charlemagne and Godfrey of Bouillon. The first eight of these remain famous today. Godfrey's reputation has suffered greatly since medieval times.

An explanation for Robert's success while crusading and failure while fighting his own battles might be that the Crusade was a relatively straightforward affair. You knew who was on your side and who was not. If you were attacked, you courageously held your position as long as it took. If you had to attack, you did so without hesitation. Robert excelled in the world of crusading, where courage and steadfastness were often required but were also, by and large, sufficient. But he could not thrive in the devious world of his brothers, with continual negotiations, often in bad faith, manoeuvring for advantage and shifting allegiances. In this world, where courage and steadfastness were also often required, but were seldom sufficient, Robert's brothers badly overmatched him.

William of Malmesbury summarised Robert's long life and death: "[H]e was held in captivity until he survived all the companions of his journey [i.e., the Crusade] and was never released until the day of his death. He was a good speaker in his native tongue and no one was better company; in the case of other men a wise counsellor, surpassed by none; an experienced soldier if any man ever was; yet for his softheartedness never thought fit to rule a commonwealth."[24]

Robert's long period of captivity in old age must have been bitter. At Cardiff Castle, he learned Welsh and wrote poetry in that language. One of his Welsh poem states, in English translation, "Woe to him who is not old enough to die."[25] The line might serve as his epitaph.

---

[24] *William of Malmesbury, vol. I*, p. 707.

[25] William M. Aird, *Robert 'Curthose', Duke of Normandy (c. 1050-1134)*, Boydell Press (2008), p. 275.

Chapter 2
A Royal Tragedy: William the Atheling

The month of November 1120 began well for King Henry I and his family. Henry was in Normandy, successfully attending to affairs there. He had one legitimate son, William, 17 years old that year and seemingly poised to succeed Henry on the English throne. Henry had long since defeated and imprisoned his brother, Robert Curthose, and acquired Robert's Duchy of Normandy. He had also defeated rebellious Norman barons and squelched a rebellion on behalf of Robert's son, William of Clito. As a result of these events, Henry appeared to have gained full control over England and Normandy and ensured the succession. Henry had recently forced the French King, Louis the VI, known unflatteringly as the Fat, to agree that Henry's son would succeed him as Duke of Normandy. Content with his accomplishments in Normandy, Henry decided to sail to England with his barons and family from the Norman port of Barfleur. He assembled ships for the crossing and the weather was favourable to depart on 25 November.

A man named Thomas Fitz Stephen offered to transport the king in his ship that he proudly called the Blanche-Neff or, in English, the White Ship. Fitz Stephen was the son of the man who had supplied the flagship for William the Conqueror when he crossed the English Channel in 1066 to conquer England. Fitz Stephen wanted the glory of transporting Henry on this occasion. The White Ship was state of the art for 1120, supposedly the most modern, sleekest and fastest of all ships. William of Malmesbury described it as "a splendid ship, provided with new planking and nails."[26] Henry declined Fitz Stephen's offer, explaining that he had already chosen a different ship for the crossing. But he agreed that his son William and other nobles could sail on the White Ship with

---

[26] *William of Malmesbury, vol. I*, p. 761.

Fitz Stephen. So, when Henry set out across the English Channel on 25 November 1120, he left his heir behind. Some of his courtiers, including his daughter-in-law, went with him. The king crossed to England without incident. Not so, his heir.

Henry's son William boarded the White Ship, as did many other young nobles, some seeking to win favour with the heir by sailing with him. Perhaps some also wanted to sail with young revellers enjoying themselves rather than with the strict king. Among those who boarded were William's illegitimate half-brother, Richard of Lincoln and illegitimate half-sister, Matilda, Countess of Perch (not to be confused with his only legitimate sister, also named Matilda, who is the focus of chapter 3). As many as 300 mostly young people, including some 50 oarsmen, crowded onto the ship.

They were in no hurry to leave. They knew their ship was faster than the king's ship and they could easily catch and pass the king on the way to England. William generously provided wine to all and soon everyone, including the crew, was imbibing freely. As Orderic Vitalis put it, "too much drinking made them tipsy." A few, concerned about all the drinking and too many "wild and headstrong young men on board," left the ship in time to sail with the king or make other plans.[27] Critically, these included William's cousin, Stephen of Blois (later King Stephen), who reportedly blamed a case of diarrhoea for his decision to return to shore.

According to Orderic, priests came to the scene with holy water to bless the ship and its passengers, but the passengers "laughed and drove them away with abuse and guffaws. All too soon they were punished for their disrespect."[28]

William and others urged Captain Fitz Stephen to set sail and try to catch the king's ship. The White Ship left port sometime around midnight. It "sped swifter than a feathered arrow."[29] Confident of capturing the king's ship, the inebriated crew raced carelessly through the sea, heedless of what lay ahead. Then suddenly, without warning, a pleasure trip became a nightmare. Orderic describes what happened next. "As the drunken oarsmen were rowing with all their might and the luckless helmsman paid scant attention to steering the ship through the sea, the port side of the *White Ship* struck violently against a huge rock, which was uncovered each day as the tide ebbed and covered once more at

---

[27] *Orderic Vitalis, vol. VI*, p. 297.

[28] *Orderic Vitalis, vol. VI*, p. 297.

[29] *William of Malmesbury, vol. I*, p. 761.

high tide. Two planks were shattered, terrible to relate and the ship capsized without warning. Everyone cried out at once in their great peril, but the water pouring into the boat soon drowned their cries…"[30]

Panic ensued. The night was dark. The water was calm, but it was freezing cold and few, if any, onboard could swim. The passengers and crew screamed and thrashed about in their panic. And then they drowned. Reportedly, in all the tumult, William managed to climb onto a small boat with a few friends and started to pull away. "[H]e might have made his way back to shore and been saved, had not his half-sister, the countess of Perche, wrestling with death in the main ship, implored her brother…to help and not to leave her so heartlessly. Overcome with pity, he ordered them to bring the boat alongside the hull to take his sister off and this soft-hearted kindness cost, the poor prince, his life; for a mob jumped at once into the boat and she was swamped and took them all together to the bottom."[31]

People "standing together on the shore, as well as the king and his companions who were already far out to sea, heard the terrible cries of the doomed men, but not knowing the cause until the next day, marvelled at it and asked one another what it could mean."[32]

All, but one of those who sailed with the White Ship that night, drowned; as many as 300 men and women, including the sole male heir to the throne. One man survived to tell the tale: a butcher from Rouen named Berold. Berold had come on board the White Ship to collect a loan from a nobleman and remained on board when it sailed away. He and a young nobleman named Geoffrey of Laigle managed to grasp part of the White Ship's mast, or possibly the rock the ship had struck. Berold reported that, as the two were clinging for their lives, Captain Fitz Stephen himself surfaced from the water and asked what had happened to the king's son. When told that he had drowned, Fitz Stephen replied, " 'It is vain for me to go on living.' With these words, in utter despair, he chose to rather sink on the spot than to die beneath the wrath of a king enraged by the loss of his sons, or suffer long years of punishment in fetters."[33]

During the long night, the nobleman, Geoffrey, could hold on no longer. "The night was frosty, so that the young man, after enduring the bitter cold for a

---

[30] *Orderic Vitalis, vol. VI*, p. 299.

[31] *William of Malmesbury, vol. I*, p. 761.

[32] *Orderic Vitalis, vol. VI*, p. 301.

[33] *Orderic Vitalis, vol. VI*, p. 299.

long time, finally lost his grip and, commending his companion to God, fell back to perish in the sea and was never seen again."[34] Berold hung on and was rescued the next morning. He lived another 20 years.

William's body was never found. Another contemporary chronicler, Henry of Huntingdon, wrote that "the head which should have worn a crown of gold, was rudely dashed against the rocks; instead of wearing embroidered robes, he floated naked in the waves; and instead of ascending a lofty throne, he found his grave in the bellies of fishes at the bottom of the sea."[35]

Back in England, no one dared tell Henry what had happened. Finally, a young, terrified boy was sent to the king to tell him that his son and only legitimate heir had drowned, along with two of his other children and hundreds of his nobles. Henry fell to the ground and wept bitterly. It was said that he never smiled again. The boy who was forced to be the messenger of bad news was apparently not harmed.

Who was William and what kind of a king would he have made? He was called William the Atheling or, Latinised, the Adelin, an Anglo-Saxon word meaning of royal blood (related to the modern German word "edel", meaning noble). His mother was christened Edith, but later changed her name to Matilda to endear herself to the Normans. Known to history as Matilda of Scotland, William's mother was the daughter of Malcom III, King of Scotland. Her mother, Scotland's queen consort, was named Margaret. In 1250, Pope Innocent IV canonised her as St Margaret for her piety and charitable works. Through his grandmother, the sainted Margaret, William was descended from the Anglo-Saxon royal line, going back to King Alfred the Great.

After the Battle of Hastings in 1066, English society was divided between the conquering Normans and the conquered Saxons. The Saxons naturally resented their new Norman overlords. Henry married Matilda partly for her reputed beauty but partly also because of her Saxon heritage. He hoped this heritage would help reconcile the Saxons to the Norman Conquest and unify his realm. (In fact, the Saxons did support Henry at the 1106 Battle of Tinchebray, where Henry defeated his brother Robert once and for all.)

---

[34] *Orderic Vitalis, vol. VI*, p. 299.

[35] Thomas Forester, ed. and transl., *The Chronicle of Henry of Huntingdon* (also called *Historia Anglorum or History of the English People*), Henry G. Bohn (1853), pp. 306-7 (hereafter *Henry of Huntingdon*). Henry, who lived around 1088 to 1157, was an archdeacon at Huntingdon in the diocese of Lincoln. He is a highly regarded source.

William was born in Winchester, then the capital of Norman England, on 5 August 1103. His bloodline represented the royal lines of both the conquering Normans (through his father) and the conquered Saxons (through his mother). William was described as a pampered child, which, given his privileged position, is highly credible. In 1108, the king left William in the care of Anselm (later canonised as St Anselm), the Archbishop of Canterbury and the leading intellectual of his time. Anselm arranged for William's education until his death in 1109. During his lifetime, Henry made William the Duke of Normandy. The Duke of Normandy was required to give homage to his feudal overlord, the King of France, Louis VI. As a king himself, Henry did not want to pay homage to another king. He made his son the duke in his place to avoid the problem. Thus, in 1115, he offered to have his son give homage to the French King. Louis resisted, insisting that Henry, himself, had to do so.

During medieval times (and beyond), seemingly interminable warfare existed between France and England. So, it was when William was young. Louis invaded Normandy to support a rebellion on behalf of William of Clito (Robert Curthose's son). On 20 August 1119, when he was 16 years old, William fought alongside his father at the Battle of Brémule, a decisive English victory. William acquitted himself well. The rebellion was crushed and Louis was forced to accept William as Duke of Normandy. As duke, William gave homage to King Louis in 1120, just a few weeks before he sailed on the White Ship.

King Henry had to defend his realm not just against the French king, but also often against rebellious barons and hostile neighbours. To try to secure peace with Anjou, a troublesome neighbour to the south of Normandy (whose people are called Angevins), Henry betrothed William to the oldest daughter of Count Fulk V of Anjou. The daughter was yet another Matilda, known as Matilda of Anjou. The betrothal occurred in February 1113, when William was only nine years old and Matilda around seven. The two married in June 1119, in the Norman city of Lisieux. William was not yet 16 years old, Matilda perhaps 14. Understandably, they had no children at the time William died. Because Matilda did not sail on the White Ship, she survived her husband. She lived at King Henry's court for a while, where she was treated like a daughter; then she returned to her family in Anjou. She never remarried but instead became a nun. Eventually, she became the Abbess of Fontevraud Abbey, near the town of Chinon. There she died in 1154, some 34 years after the White Ship sank.

From his birth, William was educated to become king "with affection and hope and every care."[36] He was formally recognised as Henry's heir at a young age. Around Christmas 1114, "all the freemen of England and Normandy, whatever their order and dignity and whoever their lord, were compelled to bind themselves to him by the giving of homage on oath."[37] William's mother, Queen Matilda, acted as Henry's regent when the king was in Normandy, helping to administer his English realm. When William became a teenager, he sometimes assisted his mother as regent when in England, co-signing charters and other documents. In this way, he was learning to become a king. His mother died in 1118, while he was in Normandy. By this time, William was considered old enough to replace her as regent in England. In this role, he acted on his own behalf, although the king's administrators, including Roger, Bishop of Salisbury, provided crucial advice. William seems to have done well as the king's regent.

Given his premature death, it is hard to say what kind of a king William would have made. As a youth, he acquitted himself well in warfare, a necessary attribute for a king in the medieval world. He also had administrative experience and, it appears, he was competent, although he might merely have been following the advice of his advisors. All this showed promise.

Because he was descended from both Saxon and Norman royalty (as well as Scottish), it was hoped William would be a unifier. However, he was also quoted as saying, "When I am king, I will yoke the English like oxen to the plough." This hardly sounds like a unifier. But we need not make too much out of this. Youths often say things they do not mean. William might merely have said that in a moment of braggadocio. He was his mother's only son and lived with her much while growing up. She must have had considerable influence over him. Despite his rash words, he might well have sympathised with the conquered Saxons, his mother's people. His maternal grandmother was declared a saint because of her piety and good deeds, which also seems promising for William's character.

Assuming King Henry's life span would have been the same had his heir not died so young, William would have been a mature 32 years old when he assumed the English throne on his father's death in December 1135. A foolish statement he made as a youth does not mean he would not have made a good, sympathetic, king years later. Few adults would want to be judged by their statements or acts

---

[36] *William of Malmesbury, vol. I*, p. 759.

[37] *William of Malmesbury, vol. I*, p. 759.

when they were teenagers. William of Malmesbury said that "the hope of England, it was thought… was in the person of that young prince again to blossom and bear fruit, so that, one might hope, the evil times were coming to an end."[38] This contemporary comment suggests the people of the time regarded William highly.

What can we draw from the report that William died trying to save his half-sister, Matilda? First, we have to decide how much to believe the report. It is difficult to credit that, in all the tumult and panic, the butcher, Berold (the only possible source for the story), could have observed such detail over a lengthy period. After all, he was desperately trying to save his own life. Berold's story sounds rehearsed, to provide drama to an otherwise dreary recounting of panic, floundering, screaming and dying. Perhaps it was also designed to curry royal favour by depicting the heir apparent as heroic.

If we credit the story, William's attempt to rescue his sister was probably more foolhardy than heroic. He had never been in that situation (few ever are) and he had little chance to think clearly. He probably did not consider that he might be sacrificing himself to rescue her. He wanted both himself and her to survive and it would not have occurred to him that too many others would also scramble on board in their panic, causing the boat to capsize. On the other hand, it was certainly noble of the boy to interrupt his flight to safety to try to save his sister. The attempt speaks well for him and suggests he might have made a noble king.

Thus, William might well have been a successful and capable king, perhaps a unifier, had he lived a normal life span. His kingship could not have been worse than what actually occurred. King Henry never fathered another child and left only a daughter as his heir. A contested succession and civil war ensued after Henry's death. William of Malmesbury wrote of the White Ship: "No ship that ever sailed brought England such disaster, none was so well known the wide world over."[39]

How it brought such disaster to England is a story for the next chapter.

---

[38] *William of Malmesbury, vol. I*, p. 759.
[39] *William of Malmesbury, vol. I*, p. 761.

Chapter 3
The Anarchy: Matilda (Maud) and Eustace

King Henry's agony following the death of his only legitimate son and heir was not merely the personal grief of a father over a lost child. William's death also portended a succession crisis. William the Atheling had been recognised as Henry's successor throughout his realms and all seemed secure for a smooth transition when Henry died. The heir's early death changed all that. Because Henry's first wife, William's mother, had died, he was free to marry again. He did so, soon after Williams's death, clearly hoping to father another son to become the new heir. The new bride was Adeliza of Louvain, whom Henry married in 1121. Although they remained married for the remaining 14 years of Henry's life, the marriage was childless. Interestingly, after Henry died, Adeliza remarried. In her second marriage, she gave birth to seven children. Clearly, she was not the reason her first marriage was childless. In his earlier days, Henry had fathered two legitimate children and an unknown, but large, number of illegitimate children. It appears and Henry himself might have known or suspected, that something had happened to him to cause his second marriage to be childless. He never faulted his second wife for not producing an heir.

As time went by and it became apparent that Henry, growing ever older, would produce no new male heir, the question became increasingly critical: Who would succeed him? Henry eventually chose as his successor his one other legitimate child, a daughter named, like so many prominent women of the period, Matilda. The English called her Maud, as will this book, mainly to distinguish her from the many other Matildas. (As we will see, one of her main adversaries later in life was another woman named Matilda.) Could Maud, a woman, succeed to the English throne and become a queen in her own right (called a queen regnant, to distinguish the position from queen consort, who was merely the king's wife)? Unlike Salic law in France, which prohibited a woman from inheriting—France never had a queen regnant—nothing in English law prohibited a woman from becoming a reigning queen.

In Maud's time, Britain had at least two precedents of female leadership. The fierce Celtic warrior, Boudica (or Boudicca) led a revolt against the Roman Empire in the first century ACE. Aethelfled, the oldest daughter of King Alfred the Great, known as the Lady of the Mercians, ruled the then-independent state of Mercia in what is today the English Midlands from 911 until she died in 918. She was an effective ruler and successful military leader. But it does not appear that Maud or her supporters invoked either of these women as a precedent to establish that a woman could, indeed, become queen regnant. In actual fact, it would be another four centuries before England first had a queen regnant. (Chapter 10.)

Maud was a daunting person in her own right. Some of the chroniclers criticised her as proud, haughty and arrogant. But perhaps, as some modern feminists have argued, they were merely disparaging qualities in a woman they would have admired in a man. The chroniclers described her brother, William, similarly, but meant it as a compliment. Certainly, one born the daughter of the King of England might well become proud and haughty. In any event, it cannot be doubted that Maud was a strong and determined woman. We do not know what she looked like. The chroniclers said she was beautiful, but that may merely have been conventional, as the chroniclers of the time said the same of most noble women.

Maud was born in Oxfordshire around 2 February 1102. Little is known of her early life. She probably lived with her mother and she was taught to read and write (not all, even among the nobility, became literate in those days). As with her brother, her care and education were entrusted to St Anselm. Among those she knew growing up at court were her uncle, the future King David I of Scotland, her cousin and future rival, Stephen of Blois (the son of the Stephen of Blois who was Robert of Normandy's comrade in arms during the First Crusade) and her illegitimate half-brother, Robert, Earl of Gloucester, a redoubtable warrior who was to become her stoutest and most loyal ally.

When Maud was still a small child, the King of Germany (and future Holy Roman Emperor), Henry V (in German, Heinrich), entered into negotiations to marry her. This Henry was the son of Emperor Henry IV, who famously "went to Canossa" in 1077 to be humbled by Pope Gregory VII over the investiture dispute that raged in Europe in the eleventh and twelfth centuries.[40] The investiture dispute centred on the question of who, monarch or pope, had the authority to appoint high church authorities (bishops and the like) for positions within the monarch's domains. Of course, the popes insisted that they, or their designees, had the authority; emperors and kings tried to exercise the authority themselves. The future Emperor Henry V would become embroiled in the controversy himself. At the time of the marriage negotiations concerning Maud, Henry, the son, had forced his father to abdicate his position as Emperor, but the son, although acknowledged King of Germany, had not yet been crowned Holy Roman Emperor.

The English King Henry must have welcomed the marital overtures, as Maud would be marrying into one of the major families of Europe. He could expect to find, in the German king, an ally in his perpetual struggles with the King of France. One reason the German Henry was interested in Maud was that he expected a large dowry, which he needed to finance a dispute he was then having with the Pope over whether and when he should be crowned Holy Roman Emperor. Marriage negotiations concluded successfully at Winchester in June 1109. Maud herself had no say in the matter. Thereafter, she travelled to Germany with a large entourage and a dowry of some 10,000 marks, a very large sum in those days. To raise the 10,000 marks, Henry had to impose a special tax, which made the marriage less than popular in England.

Maud met her future husband in Liège. The Germans, nobles and commoners alike and probably Henry himself, came to love her. Around Easter 1110, the two were formally betrothed at Utrecht. Maud was eight years old, Henry 24. That July, she was crowned Queen of the Romans in Mainz. Church authorities were entrusted with her education in the ancient city of Trier, on the Mosel River. There she learned the German language and German customs to prepare her for her life as the Holy Roman Emperor's wife. She became fluent in German.

In January 1114, when Maud was not yet 12 years old, she and Henry, now Holy Roman Emperor, were married in a lavish ceremony at Worms Cathedral. During this period, the investiture controversy was again raging between pope

---

[40] The emperor and papacy warred incessantly, with excommunication the popes' primary weapon. In the winter of 1077, Henry IV journeyed to see Pope Gregory at the castle at Canossa, in the mountains of northern Italy. He intended to do penance to try to lift the latest order of excommunication. The pope did see him, but only after forcing him to wait in the snow for three days, reportedly without shoes and wearing a hairshirt.

and emperor. Pope Paschal II employed the papacy's favourite weapon, which was quite effective in those days. He excommunicated Henry. Henry and his wife travelled to Italy to confront the Pope. The couple stayed for a while at the same castle of Canossa where Henry's father had awaited humiliation. In 1117, they entered Rome, causing the Pope to flee. Maurice Bourdin, a high church official who was later elected (with Henry's support) Antipope Gregory VIII, crowned Henry and Maud as Holy Roman Emperor and Empress. This crowning's validity and significance were to be disputed, as Bourdin was later excommunicated and imprisoned. But Maud was to call herself an empress for the rest of her life.

In most regards, Maud faithfully fulfilled her duties as Empress. In one regard, however, she (or Henry) failed to perform a critical duty—the duty to provide an heir. A contemporary source stated that she gave birth to one child, who died soon after birth. Because other chroniclers are silent on the matter, the truth of this is uncertain. In any event, the marriage was otherwise childless. In Germany, hostile chroniclers viewed Henry's lack of an heir as divine retribution for his quarrels with the Church. But the chroniclers generally praised Maud's virtues.

In 1118, Henry returned to Germany to confront rebellions there, leaving Maud to govern the imperial territories in Italy. Despite her youth, she played a personal role in governing the realm. In this role, she presided over court sessions and other formal matters, although she probably relied on advisors for major decisions. She gained valuable experience in government that would aid her later in life. In 1119, she re-joined her husband in Germany. In 1122, Maud wanted to visit her father in England. But she was prevented from doing so because the Count of Flanders, who was hostile to her husband, refused to permit her to travel through his lands. Such were the times. Later that year, at the Council of Worms, a peace, called the Concordant of Worms, was negotiated between Pope and Emperor, in which the Emperor largely yielded the power of investiture to the Pope. Maud was probably present during the negotiations.

Sometime after her return to Germany, Maud would have learned of her brother's death in the White Ship disaster. Being human and continually reminded of her exalted position and as an astute woman, she must have thought about whether she might become her father's heir. But she was the wife of the Holy Roman Emperor. It was far from clear whether or how an empress consort could simultaneously become a queen regnant of England, not to mention

Duchess of Normandy. Moreover, the still vigorous King Henry (he was in his early fifties) was soon to remarry. It seemed likely he would still father one or more male heirs, which would moot the question entirely. In twelfth-century England, it was conceivable a daughter could inherit her father's kingdom. But it was inconceivable a daughter, even an older, capable daughter, could inherit when a male heir was available. Under the circumstances, for the time being, Maud was probably content with her position as Empress of the Holy Roman Empire.

Is it possible that, in addition to practical considerations, Maud grieved as a sister who lost her brother? From today's perspective, several centuries later, it sometimes appears that medieval princes and princesses were mere pawns in the great game of statecraft chess. Human emotions were irrelevant and, accordingly, seemed non-existent. It is unclear how well Maud knew her brother. They were separated much of her life. But she probably grieved for her brother, so near her in age and removed from this life so young, on a personal level as well as a pragmatic one. The news of his death must have affected her in several ways.

Whatever she felt about her brother's death and its potential consequences, Maud continued to help Henry administer the Empire. Throughout this period and often with his wife at his side, Henry was forced to deal with unrest and outright rebellion in the empire. Unfortunately for him and the succession, Henry developed cancer. He died without an acknowledged heir in Utrecht in May 1125, when Maud was 23 years old. The absence of an heir caused the Empire's own succession crisis, a crisis that is, however, beyond the scope of his book.[41]

The death of her husband left Maud in an uncertain position. Because she had no children, she could not remain at court as a regent to the heir or act as some kind of empress-mother. Especially given the uncertainty over who would succeed her husband, she no longer had an acknowledged court role. When her father heard of her husband's death, he summoned her to Normandy, possibly with the English succession in mind. Despite her love of Germany and her widespread popularity among the German people, she reluctantly decided to obey the summons. Expecting never to return, she left Germany in December 1125, joining her father for Christmas. She took with her some precious jewellery, her imperial regalia, two crowns and a venerated relic—what was

---

[41] After some eight years of uncertainty, one of Henry's previous enemies eventually succeeded him as Emperor Lothair II.

believed to be the hand of St James the Apostle. She donated the relic to Reading Abbey.

Until Maud's return, King Henry had not decided whom to declare as his heir. For the first years of his second marriage, he probably expected, or at least hoped, to obtain another male heir. So, the matter did not seem urgent. As long as she remained empress in Germany, Maud was not a likely candidate. Henry might have considered candidates within his family, perhaps Stephen of Blois, the son of his older sister Adela (who had left the White Ship before the disaster, citing a case of diarrhoea). This Stephen had two older brothers. One, William, called the Simple, was said to be mentally disabled (to use a modern term that seems to fit) and was never considered a candidate. The other, Theobald, a capable man, was also a logical candidate. But he was primarily concerned with continental affairs. He played an insignificant role in England and the events surrounding the succession. He never urged his position as Stephen's older brother.

Another possibility that must have tempted Henry was one of his illegitimate sons, Robert of Gloucester, an extraordinarily capable and vigorous man. This Robert, a scholar and a warrior (he was a patron of the chronicler William of Malmesbury), would have made a good king. However and despite the fact that William the Conqueror himself had been illegitimate, the circumstance of his birth was too much of a stigma for him to be seriously considered for the succession. Another possible candidate with an impeccable bloodline was Henry's nephew, William of Clito, the son of Henry's brother Robert. Unlike other legitimate candidates, this William was directly descended through the male line from William the Conqueror, the dynasty's founder. But Henry had quarrelled with Robert too often and this William had rebelled against him too often, for Henry ever to consider him.

In 1125, Maud suddenly became available when her husband died. This circumstance, combined with the increasing likelihood that Henry's marriage would remain childless, brought him to a decision. He chose Maud. Although a woman, she was also descended from William the Conqueror through the male line. Like Henry and unlike any other possible candidate, she had been born to the purple, that is, born to a reigning king. Henry had used that circumstance to argue that he, not Robert, should succeed to the English crown. The same argument could be used now and it supported Maud. Henry decided to make Maud his heir, or at least try to do so.

Over Christmas 1126, many of the major barons and high church officials, bishops and archbishops, gathered at Westminster, where they swore an oath to recognise Maud and any legitimate heir she might produce as Henry's heirs. Among those who took the oath were Maud's half-brother, Robert of Gloucester and her cousin, Stephen of Blois. Some of the proud barons did so only reluctantly, under compulsion, they later claimed. Some, at least, might not have wished to be governed by a woman, although there is no recorded objection to her on that basis. A major concern among the barons was the likelihood that Maud would remarry. Her future husband might demand greater influence in England than the barons were willing to grant, especially if he were a foreigner. They conditioned their oath of allegiance on Maud's not marrying someone outside England without their consent. The French king, Louis VI, strongly opposed the idea of Maud's succession. He backed William of Clito, whom he was supporting in his claim to the Duchy of Normandy.

King Henry did intend for Maud to remarry. And, just as he had negotiated Maud's first marriage, he negotiated her second. Several years earlier, Henry had attempted to ensure the friendship of the County of Anjou, Normandy's traditional enemy to the south, by negotiating with the Count of Anjou, Fulk V, to have his son William marry the Count's daughter, Matilda of Anjou. The plan succeeded for a while, as the marriage did take place and the alliance was cemented. But this alliance by marriage ended with William's death and Matilda's subsequent entry into a nunnery. (Chapter 2.) Now Henry turned to the same source for marriage and the same reason—to ensure good relations with Anjou. He negotiated with Fulk to have his son, Geoffrey of Anjou (Matilda of Anjou's younger brother), marry Maud. With possibly a few exceptions, Henry did not consult with, or obtain the consent of, his barons and high church officials, including those who had earlier sworn allegiance to Maud.

As with her first marriage, Maud had no say in the matter. Aside from the fact that she did not know this Geoffrey, she had two reasons to be reluctant to agree to this second marriage. Given her status as former Empress of the Holy Roman Empire, she considered it demeaning to marry someone who was merely destined to become a count. Second, was the age difference. Whereas Maud had been much younger than her first husband, now she was to be much older. She was 25 years old when the marriage was negotiated, Geoffrey a mere 13. At first, Maud refused to go along with her father's plans. But, partly due to the intervention of Hildebert, Archbishop of Tours, she finally consented, although reluctantly.

In May 1127, Maud travelled to Rouen, accompanied by Robert of Gloucester and others, where she met Geoffrey and the two became formally betrothed. The marriage ceremony was performed in a magnificent ceremony in Le Mans on 17 June 1128. As a dowry, King Henry promised the couple certain castles in Normandy, but he never stated when they could take possession. The promised castles were never delivered, a situation that created tension in later years. After seeing his son marry the English king's daughter, Count Fulk departed for the Holy Land, never to return. There he married Melisandre, the heiress of the Frankish Kingdom of Jerusalem. After the death of her father, they became the joint King and Queen of Jerusalem.

Fulk left his European possessions for Geoffrey, who became Geoffrey V, Count of Anjou. Maud's marriage to Geoffrey created grave difficulties for the magnates who had sworn to recognise her as Henry's successor, that is, as the future Queen of England. They had not been consulted and had not consented to the marriage. Geoffrey was mostly unknown in England, except that he was known to be the Count of Anjou, a traditional enemy of England and, especially, Normandy. There was no precedent for the role the husband of a queen regnant would have. The role a queen consort played in governmental and other matters, was essentially whatever the king, her husband, granted her, which was often significant but always at the king's discretion. But the situation might be different for a male consort of a queen regnant. Given the general dominance of men over women in medieval times, a man might demand and obtain a major part in governance, perhaps even the kingship itself. The barons were undoubtedly concerned that, if Maud became queen, Geoffrey might bring to England a large number of his own nobility from Anjou to help govern the kingdom, which would threaten their position. What role Henry himself intended for Geoffrey after his death is unknown, perhaps to Henry himself. He never made his plans clear regarding Geoffrey.

The marriage was not always amicable, to say the least. Maud left Geoffrey in 1129 to return to her father. The reasons were unclear, but probably personal animosity played a large role. They seemed simply not to like each other. But Geoffrey sought her return. Henry called a meeting of a royal council in 1131. The council determined that Maud should return to Geoffrey and she did later that year. Possibly aware that Maud's marriage to Geoffrey without the barons' consent violated a condition of their previous oath of allegiance to Maud, the king also forced the council members to take or renew the oath. All present did so, but again reluctantly.

After Maud returned to Geoffrey, the couple apparently decided to try to make their marriage succeed, at least enough to produce heirs. Despite the disparity in their ages and their apparent dislike of each other, Maud and Geoffrey performed their marital duties at least often enough for Matilda to give birth to three sons. The first, a healthy boy named Henry after the king, was born in March 1133. This Henry would, in time, become King Henry II. He would be the first of the Plantagenet line of kings. Geoffrey unwittingly provided the name. His nickname was Plantagenet, probably because of a flower, the planta genesta, he customarily wore in his hat. The name stuck and is what the ruling line was called for more than three centuries, beginning with Maud's son, Henry and continuing (although later divided into the Lancaster and York branches) until the end of the Wars of the Roses in 1485, when the Tudors displaced the Plantagenets.

King Henry was overjoyed to hear the news of the baby Henry's birth. He travelled to Normandy—as it turned out, for the last time—where he proudly visited the grandson he had long desired. One source states that the king elicited yet another oath of allegiance to Maud from his barons in Normandy during this visit, but this is uncertain. By this time, Maud was pregnant again. A second son, named Geoffrey after his father, was born in May 1134, with the king present. The second birth was difficult and almost killed Maud. She was so ill that she made her will, which included numerous charitable bequests. She also quarrelled with her father about where she should be buried. She wanted to be buried in the abbey at Bec-Hellouin, an important monastery near Rouen; the king preferred the more sumptuous Cathedral of Rouen. But she was not to be buried anywhere just yet. She recovered. She was to give birth to a third son, William, her last child, in July 1136.

During this time, Henry learned of the February 1134 death of his long time fraternal adversary, Robert, formerly Duke of Normandy, in lonely old age at Cardiff Castle. Coming on the heels of the death from a battle wound of Robert's son, William of Clito, several years earlier, it must have been a relief for him to know that his brothers' bloodlines had come to an end. (William Rufus had never married.) He might have felt a twinge of remorse, for he ordered a light to burn for the repose of Robert's soul. (Chapter 1.)

King Henry I himself died of a sudden illness at the age of 67 on 1 December 1135, caused, according to one account, by eating, against his doctor's advice, too many lampreys, a kind of jawless fish. Considerable tension existed between father and daughter the last year of his life. Henry never delivered the castles in Normandy he had promised as a dowry and he granted her little independent authority. Maud, and perhaps Henry himself, suspected her support in England was weak. Henry's refusal to strengthen her hand in Normandy did not help. When her father died, Maud was in Angers, the capital of Geoffrey's County of Anjou. Neither Maud nor Geoffrey moved quickly to enforce her right to the throne. Maud was pregnant with her third and last son. To what extent her pregnancy affected her limited response is unclear.

Maud's cousin, Stephen, however, moved promptly and decisively, but on his own behalf. One of King Henry's noblemen told Stephen, probably falsely, that on his deathbed, Henry had changed his mind and named Stephen his rightful heir. The Archbishop of Canterbury, hearing the same report, declared all previous oaths of allegiance to Maud invalid. What really happened on Henry's deathbed is uncertain. The chroniclers give conflicting accounts. Those later sympathetic with Maud's claim to the throne generally asserted that Henry reaffirmed that she was to be his heir; those who supported Stephen asserted that Henry changed his mind. It seems unlikely that, after all of his effort to make Maud his recognised heir, Henry would simply tell someone on his death bed that Stephen was to be his heir after all. However, being ambitious, Stephen wanted to believe the report. Perhaps, he actually did believe it. In any event, even though he had sworn an oath of allegiance to recognise Maud as Henry's rightful heir, he took immediate steps to obtain the throne for himself.

This Stephen was the son of Henry's older sister Adela. As such, he was directly descended from William the Conqueror, but through the female line. Accordingly, his claim to the throne was inferior to Maud's, the daughter of a reigning king. But he was a man and, perhaps more important, he was far better known and liked in England than Maud. Maud had merely visited England on occasion. She lived most of her life on the European continent. Stephen was considered capable and had long been involved in English affairs. As future events were to prove, he had another important asset—his wife. He was married to another Matilda, called Matilda of Boulogne. This Matilda was the daughter of a sister of Matilda of Scotland, Henry's queen, and thus was also a cousin of both her husband and Maud. Matilda of Boulogne and Maud were to become each other's primary adversary on many occasions in future years. Both were strong and determined women, one asserting her own claim to the English throne, the other defending her husband's claim to the same throne.

Stephen, in his wife's county of Boulogne when Henry died, immediately crossed the English Channel and moved to the capital of Winchester, where the treasury was kept. The powerful and wealthy Bishop of Winchester happened to be Stephen's younger brother, Henry of Blois. With Henry's assistance, Stephen seized the treasury, which he used to obtain additional support. From there, he moved on to London, where he promised the populace the right to self-government. Enthusiastically supported by the Londoners, Stephen was crowned King of England at Westminster Abbey on 22 December 1135, three weeks after Henry's death. As one chronicler stated, the Archbishop of Canterbury, "who had been the first to swear allegiance to the king's daughter [Maud], alas! Crowned Stephen King."[42] Other nobles who had sworn allegiance to Maud also sided with Stephen. At that time, Stephen's oldest son, Eustace of Boulogne, became his heir and could expect to succeed to the throne on the king's death. He never did and thus is also among the ranks of heirs who never reigned.

Having seized the throne, Stephen could not keep it peacefully. Matters began well for him. Pope Innocent II recognised him as king, providing essential support. But soon his troubles began. David, the King of Scotland, Maud's uncle, invaded northern England, forcing Stephen to move north and blunt the threat. Revolts flared in various parts of his realm. For the first three years, Matilda contented herself with attempting to consolidate her position in Normandy.

The situation changed beginning in 1138. In that year, Robert of Gloucester, Maud's illegitimate but powerful half-brother, rebelled against Stephen and declared his support for Maud. Robert, perhaps the most capable of the magnates and a son of King Henry himself, must have been tempted to put himself forward as a candidate. But he was shrewd enough to know that his illegitimacy made any such attempt unlikely to succeed. Instead, he contented himself with fighting his sister's cause. He would be her most stalwart supporter for the rest of his life, one of the few who never switched sides. His support was critical, as he could raise an army and he controlled considerable territory in the west of England.

---

[42] Henry of Huntingdon, complied in David C. Douglas, ed., *English Historical Documents, vol. II, 1042-1189*, Oxford University Press (1953), p. 305 (hereafter *EHD, vol. II*).

Another ardent supporter was King David. The Scottish king repeatedly invaded from the north to support her and gain territory at England's expense. His support was a mixed blessing. To the extent Stephen had to move against him in the north, Stephen had fewer resources to oppose Maud directly. But people came to associate David's depredations in the north with Maud's cause, which harmed her efforts to win the hearts of the English people.

When Robert declared his support, Maud and Geoffrey themselves moved to assert her right to be queen. In early 1139, they began preparing for a cross-channel invasion. The invasion came that summer. In late September, Matilda and Robert landed with an army of about 3,000 men near Arundel Castle, in Sussex. Geoffrey stayed behind in Normandy with the couple's sons. He concentrated on bringing that Duchy under his control. He and Maud probably realised that Geoffrey's presence in England would be counterproductive. He was an Angevin, England's traditional foe and was unlikely to win friends for Maud in England. Maud's step-mother, Adeliza (King Henry's second queen), announced her support for Maud and invited her to reside at Arundel Castle. While Maud remained at the castle, Robert drove north, seeking support.

Stephen responded to the initial invasion by moving south and besieging Arundel Castle, trapping Maud inside. Stephen might have been able to capture the Empress, ending the war before it effectively began. But instead, he agreed to a truce, the exact terms of which are unknown. He eventually lifted the siege and permitted Maud to travel safely to Bristol. The reasons Stephen treated Maud so generously are unclear today. It may have been feelings of chivalry (he was reluctant to make war on a woman), poor judgment, bad advice, or a belief that Arundel Castle was too strong for him to capture. He may have been reluctant to invest resources in a lengthy siege, resources needed elsewhere. His actions were probably due to a combination of these factors. Whatever the reasons for Stephen's actions, Maud was reunited with Robert and continued her quest to become queen.

Soon Robert captured Gloucester Castle and Maud moved her base of operations there. From this point on, it was a civil war, with Stephen seeking to defeat the rebellion and Maud and her supporters seeking to gain what they thought was her birth right—the English throne. At first, it was a dreary war of attrition, with shifting alliances and changing fortunes, but no clear winner. Stephen was unable to quell the rebellion, but Maud and her supporters were equally unable to defeat him and get her crowned. Many skirmishes, but no pitched battles, were fought. Castles were besieged and captured and then besieged and recaptured in succession. Nobles changed allegiances regularly, depending on their views of what was best for them at a particular time.

Maud and her supporters controlled areas in southwest England including Bristol, Robert's lands in Gloucester, and areas as far east as Oxford. The Scottish king, also supporting Maud, held parts of the disputed north. Stephen held, at least nominally, most of the rest of England, although many areas were effectively beyond his control. His real power base was the southeast, largely due to the lands and efforts of his Queen Matilda. The key city of London also supported Stephen.

A break in the stalemate came in 1141. Stephen proved to be an ineffective ruler and many of his original adherents became disillusioned with him. Ranulf, Earl of Chester, a powerful baron of the north, switched sides (common in those days) and threw his considerable resources in Maud's favour. In response, Stephen rushed to Ranulf's castle at Lincoln and laid siege to it. Ranulf was not there at the time. Soon Ranulf and Robert approached the castle with combined forces larger than the besiegers, including a substantial Welsh contingent. Rather than flee, Stephen chose to fight. The Battle of Lincoln, which should have been decisive but turned out not to be, was fought on 2 February 1141. At first, the battle went well for the king and his forces largely destroyed the Welsh contingent. But ultimately, Stephen was beaten, largely due to Robert's superiority in cavalry. Stephen, who commanded the centre, was surrounded and captured. At long last, just as her father had captured his adversary Robert of Normandy, Maud's forces had captured her adversary. The time had seemingly come for Maud finally make good her claim and be crowned Queen of England. It was not to be.

Matilda met with Stephen personally at her base in Gloucester. What was said between them is unknown. Maud then ordered Stephen to be transferred as a captive to Bristol Castle. It was assumed that Stephen would be kept perpetually a prisoner, just as King Henry's brother, Robert of Normandy, had been. Apparently, the king was placed in chains at Maud's order. This harsh treatment later helped to undermine her support.

With Stephen a prisoner, many barons, bishops and others flocked to Maud's side. She was able to make a deal with Stephen's brother, Henry, Bishop of Winchester, to gain even his support. Henry made the treasury at Winchester available to her, although it was greatly depleted after years of warfare. She was acclaimed "Lady of the English," a precursor to her intended coronation as Queen of England. Maud moved on to London where she hoped to be crowned that June at Westminster. Geoffrey de Mandeville, who possessed the Tower of London, assessed the changed political situation with Stephen's imprisonment. He too switched sides and declared his allegiance to Maud. All seemed secure for her to be crowned.

At this time, the high point of her career, Maud should have drawn a lesson from her father. When Henry seized the throne, he made many promises to grant greater liberties to the barons. He never honoured many of the promises and possibly never intended to honour them. But the promises made him popular and garnered him enough support to consolidate his position. Maud should have done something similar. She needed to win over the people of London. This would not be easy. The Londoners were independent-minded and valued their liberties and their limited right to self-government. Stephen had promised them privileges, which made him popular in the city. Maud should have acted like her father did when he seized a contested throne. She could have, and should have, wooed the Londoners with promises of greater self-government, more liberties and less taxation. She should also have nurtured her support within the Church.

Instead, she did the opposite. As one chronicler summarised it, "she was swollen with insufferable pride by her success in war and alienated the affections of nearly everyone."[43] She raised taxes and threatened to restrict, not expand, the privileges of the proud people of London. She issued decrees confiscating the property of those who still supported the king. According to some of the chroniclers, she even acted haughtily to her new-found supporters.

She also managed to alienate the Church. With Bishop Henry as a new ally and the king a prisoner, Maud had gained considerable support from the Church, previously a strong adherent of King Stephen. But she wasted it with injudicious policy decisions. In an egregious blunder, she attempted to appoint a bishop against the wishes of the Church. Doing this unnecessarily revived the same investiture controversy that had haunted her first husband, the Emperor Henry V. It also violated her agreement with Bishop Henry that she would consult with him in all church matters. She made other ecclesiastical decisions that angered the Church. Maud lost critical support within the Church, the support she would never regain.

---

[43] Henry of Huntingdon, compiled in *EHD, vol. II*, p. 308.

In the meantime, one of Maud's key adversaries fought on. Even though her husband was a prisoner, the intrepid Queen Matilda raised an army in southeast England and moved towards London. This Matilda did nothing to alienate the good citizens of London. With her army nearby, the Londoners summoned up the courage to act against the now-hated Maud. As William of Malmesbury described it, "But behold, at the very moment when [Maud] imagined she should get possession of all England, everything was changed. The Londoners, ever suspicious and murmuring among themselves, now burst out into open expressions of hatred."[44]

On 24 June 1141, the people of London rose up against Maud and an armed mob advanced on her residence near Westminster. Maud and her entourage, including Robert of Gloucester and Bishop Henry, were taken by surprise and forced to flee the city ignominiously on horseback. Their flight was chaotic and Maud had to leave behind much of her personal property. After their flight, the Londoners plundered everything she had left behind. Maud and the others arrived in Oxford, safe for the time being. But her hope of being crowned at Westminster was shattered. As it turned out, this had been her best and last chance to become Queen of England.

Matters turned worse for the empress. Largely because of her high-handed ecclesiastical actions, her alliance with Bishop Henry proved short-lived. After the flight from Oxford, Henry deserted her and returned to his brother's side. In July, Maud and Robert laid siege to Henry's castle at Winchester. But Queen Matilda came to Henry's rescue. She marched to Winchester with the army she had raised, bolstered by Londoners. Her son, Eustace, accompanied her. There, Matilda's army surrounded Maud's forces and the besiegers became the besieged. After a siege and counter siege lasting some two months, the supply situation became untenable for Maud's forces. She and Robert decided to break out and flee.

On 14 September 1141, in an action later called the "Rout of Winchester," Maud and a small entourage succeeded in getting away to safety at the castle at Devizes. Robert was not so fortunate. He remained behind with the bulk of their army to protect Maud's flight and ensure that she got away safely. In the battle that ensued, he was surrounded by hostile forces and was forced to surrender. Like Stephen, Robert was now himself a prisoner. He had sacrificed himself so

---

[44] Emilie Amt, ed., *Medieval England, 1000-1500: A Reader*, Broadview Press (2001), p. 109 (hereafter Amt, *Medieval England*).

Maud could escape. His loss was a devastating blow to her cause. He had been her key support and she could do little without him.

Negotiations between Maud and Queen Matilda followed the rout. The queen also attempted to convince Robert to switch sides, as many had done for many reasons. She and her supporters made many and sundry promises to Robert to entice him to abandon his sister, including granting him his freedom and, with it, considerable power to govern England in the king's name. To his credit, Robert resisted all such offers. "[H]e always deemed his fraternal affection of greater importance than any promise which could be made him."[45]

Efforts to reach a comprehensive settlement failed, as the queen refused to compromise with her cousin Maud. In November, however, the parties agreed to a prisoner exchange. Robert was released and re-joined Maud at Oxford. Stephen was released from his captivity in Bristol Castle and allowed to re-join his wife. Soon the Church, led by Bishop Henry, once again declared Stephen the rightful King of England. He and Queen Matilda were crowned anew that Christmas season. Maud remained at Oxford.

In 1142, Robert travelled to Normandy briefly to join Geoffrey's struggle against King Stephen's adherents there. Robert returned to England that autumn with fresh forces, as well as Maud's son Henry, now nine years old. But Stephen's cause was rejuvenated. That September, he suddenly appeared at Oxford with a large army and began to besiege the city. Oxford was nearly impregnable, protected by the rivers Thames and Isis on one side and a castle and fortress on the other. Maud was confident the city would never be taken. But on September 26, in a brazen move, Stephen himself, with his men following, swam across the river. Once across, he led a sudden attack and stormed into the city. Maud and her forces were forced to abandon the city and seek refuge within the castle walls. Stephen held the city of Oxford. Maud was trapped inside the castle.

This time, Stephen was determined to capture Maud, which he hoped would finally end the war and permit him to rule his country in peace. He was not going to let her go peacefully, as he had when she was trapped at Arundel Castle three years earlier. The castle at Oxford was too strong to take by storm, so Stephen patiently settled in for a siege. Queen Matilda arrived with reinforcements for the king. Robert and Maud's other supporters gathered troops but could not hope to capture the city. Although Stephen could not take the castle by storm, his

---

[45] William of Malmesbury, quoted in Amt, *Medieval England*, p. 111

defensive position, within the city, was so strong that Maud's forces could not effectively attack it. These must have been desperate times for the Empress.

The siege of the castle of Oxford lasted some two months, until December 1142. While Robert and his forces were considering how to rescue the Empress, she took matters into her own hands. She made a daring escape from the castle, accompanied by only three or four knights. At night, shortly before Christmas, dressed all in white to serve as camouflage against the snow and ice, she climbed down one of the castle towers by rope and passed through a gate. Evading nearby troops and sentries, who seemed to be everywhere, she and her entourage walked across the frozen Thames. On the other side, she continued to walk through the snow several miles to a station where she found horses. From there she rode to safety at Wallingford, arriving that same night. The next day, the garrison of the castle at Oxford surrendered to the king's forces.

This was Maud's fourth narrow escape since her first arrival in England three years earlier. She had been granted safe passage after being trapped at Arundel Castle. She had fled from the London mob. She had escaped during the Rout of Winchester. And she had made a night-time escape from Oxford through the snow. Some of the chroniclers commented on her good fortune, which seemed miraculous.

Maud's escapes might have been miraculous, but her position remained precarious. The war of attrition resumed, with minor skirmishing and manoeuvring for advantage, but with neither side able to decisively defeat the other. In the areas affected by the warfare, law and order had long since broken down, as no strong authority existed to keep the peace.

The Anglo-Saxon Chronicle describes the sufferings in the southwest of England. "[E]very powerful man built his castles and held them against him [the king]… They oppressed the wretched people of the country severely with castle-building. When the castles were built, they filled them with devils and wicked men. Then, both by night and day they took those people that they thought had any goods—men and women—and put them in prison and tortured them with indescribable torture to extort gold and silver… Many thousands they killed by starvation. I have neither the ability nor the power to tell all the horrors nor all the torments they inflicted upon wretched people in this country: and that lasted the nineteen years while Stephen was king and it was always going from bad to worse. They levied taxes on the villages every so often and called it 'protection money.' When the wretched people had no more to give, they robbed and burned all the villages, so that you could easily go a whole day's journey and never find anyone occupying a village, nor land tilled. Then the corn was dear and meat and butter and cheese, because there was none in the country… [S]ome lived by begging for alms, who had once been rich men; some fled the country." It seemed that "Christ and his saints were asleep."[46]

This description might have been exaggerated; certainly, it did not describe the situation in all of England. But it gives a flavour of what went on during the long civil war. The period would later be bitterly remembered, with justification, as the "Anarchy."

During these years, despite the anarchy in many places, Maud presided, as well as she could, over a court that was parallel to that of King Stephen, with a royal household and a chancellor. She divided her residence among Gloucester, Bristol and Devizes. She collected revenues from those districts loyal to her, appointed sheriffs and other officials, granted charters and minted coins. But, given the overall chaos, her ability to administer her domains was limited. She was unable to establish effective law courts.

Matters dragged on this way for year after dreary year, with skirmishing but no major battles. At times, Maud seemed to be in the ascendency. At other times, it was Stephen who gained the upper hand. Gradually, attitudes changed. Maud began to realise that she would never become queen. Stephen took steps to have his son, Eustace, recognised as his heir, but he must have realised that a smooth transition of power in favour of his son was unlikely. He might have begun to consider a compromise. The common citizens of England and many of the nobles became less concerned with who would win the struggle and more concerned that it simply end, one way or another. People desperately wanted the Anarchy, a time with no effective central authority, to end and to have it replaced by a strong leader, any strong leader.

Some of the main combatants left the scene. In October 1147, Robert of Gloucester, Maud's mainstay, died at Bristol Castle. Rather surprisingly for a warrior, he died of natural causes, a fever. Queen Matilda, Stephen's mainstay, died in May 1152 in the presence of her son, Eustace, and the king. Before her death she had attempted, in vain, to have her son Eustace crowned as the young king, to ensure he would succeed to the throne on Stephen's death.

In the meantime, Geoffrey managed to secure Normandy for himself and his family. In 1144, he became the Duke of Normandy by conquest. In 1147, he sent

---

[46] *EHD, vol. II,* pp. 199-200.

his and Maud's son Henry with a small mercenary force to aid Maud. At the age of 14, Henry was rapidly becoming a man. On this occasion, Henry accomplished nothing. He ran short of funds to pay his mercenaries. He turned to his mother for help, but she was financially hard-pressed herself and was unable to come to his aid. Eventually, for reasons that remain unclear—perhaps simply a wish to be rid of him—Stephen himself helped pay for Henry's return to Normandy.

After the death of Robert of Gloucester, it became increasingly difficult for Maud to maintain a court in England and continue the struggle. Although not formally renouncing her claim to be the legitimate Queen of England, she decided to move back to Normandy, which she did in 1148. In Normandy, she received a warm welcome and reunited with her husband, whom she had not seen for nine years. She established a court at Rouen and began to administer the duchy. She lived primarily in Rouen for the rest of her life. It must have been somewhat of a relief for her to be safely away from the perpetual skirmishing and struggling in England. She became more and more involved in matters in Normandy and less and less with the war in England. Her plans for the future now centred on her son, Henry. In September 1151, her husband, Geoffrey, died unexpectedly, leaving Henry to inherit the title of Duke of Normandy.

People began to turn their attention more and more towards Henry and away from Maud. He was raised almost from birth to be a future king. At a young age, Geoffrey began involving him in the government in Anjou and Normandy. As he became older, he promised to become, to borrow from Shakespeare, "every inch a king."[47] Henry spent some time in England, where he impressed people with his good looks, winning personality and apparent ability.

Henry also gained a rather surprising prize. We now meet, for the first time, but far from the last time, the greatest, richest, and, if the commentaries are to be believed, most glamourous and beautiful of medieval heiresses, the formidable Eleanor of Aquitaine. Eleanor was not herself an heir who never reigned. But she was to become the daughter-in-law of one (Maud), the mother of two more (chapter 4) and the grandmother of yet another (chapter 5). Almost all of the significant events in their stories occurred during her long lifetime. She was personally involved in many of those events.

When she was very young, Eleanor inherited the fabulously rich Duchy of Aquitaine, in southern France, as well as other lands. In 1137, when she was

---

[47] *King Lear*, act IV, scene vi, line 110.

around 13 years old, she married the soon-to-become French King Louis VII. As queen consort of France, she gave birth to two daughters. She and Louis left in 1147 on the Second Crusade, which became an abject failure. At first, at least for the couple, the trip resembled a pleasure trip to exotic locales more than a serious military expedition. They were feted in Constantinople. Then came horror, hardship, and, partly due to her husband's incompetence, defeat. They returned to France, having accomplished nothing the Crusaders set out to accomplish. Back in France, a disillusioned Eleanor demanded that Louis give her an annulment (or a divorce—the terms have been used interchangeably in this context). He eventually agreed, possibly because she had borne him only daughters and no sons. The Church went along and she received her annulment on the grounds of consanguinity—that she and Louis were too closely related to be married lawfully. Custody of her daughters, still considered to be legitimate, went to Louis.

Eleanor had her eye on Henry, now the Duke of Normandy. She believed he was destined for great things and she wanted to be part of it. He was dazzled by her possessions and reputation and was probably flattered that the older and more experienced Eleanor—she was around 30 years old at the time, Henry 19 (i.e., roughly the same age difference as between Maud and Geoffrey)—was interested in him. When they met and despite their age difference, they fell in love with each other—or at least with each other's prospects. It is not clear to what extent their relationship was based on love and to what extent on pragmatism. Even though Eleanor and Henry were more closely related to each other than had been Eleanor and Louis, they were married in May 1152, eight weeks after Eleanor obtained her annulment. Maud met her new daughter-in-law the following January, when Henry brought her to Rouen. What they thought of each other has not been recorded. There is no reason to believe they were antagonistic.

Now that he was married to the great Eleanor and given his direct descent from William the Conqueror and King Henry I, this Henry had a strong claim to the throne. Additionally, he was male, which his mother decidedly was not. In 1153, Henry, now a mature 20 years old, invaded England again with a small army, determined to assert his right to the throne, if not his mother's.

That August, his army confronted Stephen's larger forces at the town of Wallingford on the Thames south of Oxford. All was set for the biggest pitched battle of the long civil war. Many would inevitably die. But something unexpected happened. After so many years of war, of stalemate, of suffering, few were willing to fight and die for either side. Neither army wanted a battle. Stephen was a broken man; his wife and chief strength was no longer there to support him. Henry's men preferred compromise to battle. In these circumstances, "the king and the duke conferred together alone on an island in the river concerning the conclusion of a permanent peace between them…"[48] They arranged a provisional truce. They tentatively agreed that Stephen would remain king as long as he lived, but Henry, not Maud and not Eustace, would succeed to the throne on Stephen's death. Peace prevailed over war, a rare event in those times.

Had she been alive, Queen Matilda, the intrepid fighter that she was, would certainly not have agreed to her son's being disinherited in this way. She would have opposed the agreement with every fibre of her body and every strand of her strong spirit. But she was dead. Eustace, naturally, was livid. Eustace had been born around 1127 and was, thus, around 26 years old at this time. He was married to Constance of France, a sister of the French King Louis VII (Eleanor's first husband). According to the *Anglo-Saxon Chronicle*, Constance was a "good woman…but she had little happiness with him." In 1151, Eustace allied himself with the French king, now his brother-in-law and they invaded Henry's territory in Normandy. Louis had always supported Eustace, both as a possible future Duke of Normandy and as Stephen's successor in England. The two accomplished little and Louis soon made a separate peace with Henry. These and other actions, as well as Eustace's character, alienated many. He gained a reputation in some quarters as vicious and vindictive.

Given the nature of the sources, it is difficult to gauge Eustace's character. The *Anglo-Saxon Chronicle* wrote that "he did not prosper much and by good right for he was a bad man—for wherever he went he did more harm than good. He robbed the lands and levied heavy taxes."[49] Henry of Huntingdon said he was "a good soldier, but an ungodly man, who dealt harshly with the rulers of the church, being their determined persecutor."[50] On the other hand, the anonymous, but contemporary, chronicler of the Acts of King Stephen, a source generally favourable to Stephen and his family, described Eustace as "a young man of high

---

[48] Henry of Huntingdon, compiled in *EHD, vol. II*, p. 310.

[49] The two quotations in this and the previous paragraph from the *Anglo-Saxon Chronicle* are found in *EHD, vol. II*, pp. 202-3.

[50] *Henry of Huntingdon*, p. 293.

character... Young as Eustace was, his manners were grave; he excelled in warlike exercises, had great natural courage and stood high in military fame; above all, he was courteous and affable, scattering his gifts with generous munificence."[51]

Eustace did what he could to oppose the truce Henry and Stephen had negotiated. He plundered church lands near Bury St Edmunds in Suffolk. But he died suddenly on August 17 while eating. He was buried at Faversham Abbey in Kent, a monastery that his mother and father had founded a few years previously. Contemporaries ascribed his death either to a fit of madness or to divine retribution for his depredations. In those days, the chroniclers often invoked divine intervention to try to explain what they could not otherwise explain. Whatever the reason for Eustace's sudden death at such a young age, most people welcomed it as removing the last obstacle to permanent peace. That Eustace never reigned was probably a good thing. It is hard to imagine he could have become a successful king, certainly not the king Henry turned out to be.

After avoiding battle near Wallingford, Stephen and Henry travelled peacefully together towards London to everyone's joy. Henry of Huntingdon reported, "What boundless joy! What a happy day! when in the city of Winchester, in the midst of a splendid procession of prelates and nobles and with the acclamations of a countless host of spectators the illustrious young prince was conducted by the king himself and received with all honour." In London, the truce provisionally arranged at Wallingford was formalised and signed in November as the Treaty of Westminster. Henry did homage to Stephen as king as long as he lived. In return, Stephen formally recognised Henry as his adopted son and heir. Stephen's surviving son, another William, did homage to Henry and renounced any claim he may have had to the crown. (Although this William nominally became Stephen's heir on Eustace's death, by that time it was obvious that Henry, not a son of Stephen, would succeed the king. Accordingly, William cannot reasonably be considered an heir who never reigned.) Henry of Huntingdon again: "Thus, by God's mercy, he [Henry] contrived to bring to a close the gloomy night, that had darkened the ruined realm of England and to herald the dawn of peace." [52]

---

[51] Thomas Forester, ed. and transl., *Acts of King Stephen* (also called *Gesta Regis Stephani*), Henry G. Bohn (1853), p. 427.

[52] Both quotations in this paragraph are found in *EHD, vol. II,* p. 311.

Maud was in Normandy and had no control over affairs in England at that time, although she never formally renounced her claim to the throne. What she felt when she heard that she had been passed over in favour of her son is not recorded. She probably had mixed feelings and recognised that it had become inevitable. As one of Maud's biographers put it, "She had lost her battles, but her son had won the war and the crown was to return to the rightful royal line."[53]

The following March, Henry returned in triumph to Normandy, where his mother received him and he was reunited with Eleanor. Their first child, a son named William (who was fated to die at the age of three), was with them. Henry was in Normandy when he heard the news that Stephen died on 25 October 1154, less than a year after the Treaty of Westminster. Henry was now king. Before he left for his new realm and the formal crowning, he travelled to Rouen, where he again met with, and probably received advice from, his mother. He and his new queen were crowned at Westminster Abbey on 19 December 1154. Henry was crowned with the larger of the two crowns his mother had brought from Germany all those years ago after the death of her first husband, the Emperor Henry V. When she was crowned, Eleanor became the only woman ever to be queen consort of both France and England. Maud did not travel to England for the coronation, possibly due to her ambivalence in seeing her son crowned rather than herself.

With her son safely on the English throne and peace and prosperity finally returning to England and Normandy, Maud settled into the role of an elder stateswoman. She spent most of her remaining years at Rouen, living in the priory of Notre Dame du Pre, just south of the city. There she administered Normandy in her son's absence and acted as a valued advisor to him during the first part of his reign. She issued charters in her name and the king's. In 1155, Henry considered invading Ireland to conquer lands for Maud's youngest son, William. Pope Adrian IV, formerly Nicholas Breakspear (the only Englishman ever to become Pope), had granted Henry overlordship over Ireland. The Pope wanted Henry to invade Ireland to bring a measure of order to the island. Maud went to England for the last time and advised against the invasion. Henry wisely heeded her advice and decided to stay home and conserve his resources. Maud returned to Normandy, where she remained for the rest of her life. In 1156, King Henry and Queen Eleanor named their first daughter Matilda, after his mother.

---

[53] Alison Weir, *Queens of the Conquest: England's Medieval Queens*, book one, Ballantyne Books (2017), p. 383 (hereafter Weir, *Queens of the Conquest*).

Fittingly, this Matilda would later marry Henry the Lion (in German, Heinrich der Löwe), Duke of Saxony and Bavaria, a powerful German prince. This Matilda moved to Germany, just as her grandmother had done so many years earlier.

A quarrel broke out between Henry and his younger brother, Geoffrey, over Geoffrey's demands to receive lands on the continent. Maud presided over a family conference in Rouen in February 1156 to try to arrange peace between the brothers. No firm agreement was reached. The quarrel would only end with Geoffrey's sudden death two years later. But Maud undoubtedly exercised a moderating influence on both of her sons.

Maud also became involved in international affairs. She sometimes mediated between Henry and the French King Louis VII, her daughter-in-law's first husband. She especially helped her son in affairs concerning the Holy Roman Empire, where she had been Empress. Her knowledge of German no doubt helped. On one occasion, the Emperor Frederick Barbarossa demanded the return of the hand of St James, the relic Maud had brought to England from Germany and donated to Reading Abbey. The Emperor considered the relic to be German property. Maud and, at this point, more importantly, Henry considered it English property. Probably assisted by Maud's diplomacy, Henry managed to satisfy the Emperor by giving him expensive gifts, including a lavish tent the Emperor later used while travelling. The relic remained at Reading.

Maud advised Henry in the escalating, soon to become historic, clash between the king and Thomas Becket. Becket and the king had once been great friends; indeed, Becket had been the king's chancellor. But then Henry made Becket Archbishop of Canterbury in the hope and expectation that Becket would help the king in his quarrels with the Church. Soon friendship changed to enmity. Becket took his new position seriously. He pursued the Church's interests even when they conflicted with Henry's. Maud had advised Henry against making his chancellor the archbishop. She astutely foresaw that Becket, as archbishop, might not remain loyal to the king but would faithfully pursue his new duty to the Church. In later years, she attempted to mediate the quarrel. Ultimately, she failed. Years after her death, Becket was famously murdered in Canterbury Cathedral by four of Henry's knights acting, they believed, on Henry's behalf and possibly at his instigation.

Increasingly, Maud became a benefactress of the Church. In her later years, she took a special interest in the Cistercian Order. In 1157, she re-founded a

Cistercian abbey near Cherbourg. She was also a leading patron of the abbey of Bec-Hellouin, the monastery near Rouen where she had wished to be buried when she nearly died in 1134, after the birth of her second son.

In Maud's final years, as her health declined, so too did her influence, although she participated in public affairs to the end. Her two younger sons died before she did, Geoffrey in 1158 and William in 1164. The Empress herself died in Rouen on 10 September 1167, aged around 65, an advanced age for the times. She prevailed in her earlier disagreement with her father about where she should be buried. She was buried in front of the altar of the abbey of Bec-Hellouin. The Archbishop of Rouen presided over the service. Most of her personal property was given to the Church.

What can we say about Maud's character? The English chroniclers were generally antagonistic towards her. Indeed, she did appear to be proud and haughty in her years in England, when she was seeking the throne; the people of London did rise up against her and drive her out of town. She might have succeeded in becoming queen had she been just a bit more diplomatic, especially after King Stephen was captured at the Battle of Lincoln. Her largely negative reputation today is primarily based on those times. Yet, in her younger days, she was beloved in Germany. The chroniclers there universally praised her virtues and her abilities. In her later years at Rouen, she was generally seen as a wise and moderating advisor to the king and a good administrator over Normandy. What happened and why was she so proud and haughty in between?

A recent biographer suggests one explanation for Maud's mood swings and emotional reactions might have been the early onset of menopause.[54] The theory is plausible and might help explain her erratic behaviour when it mattered most. But other explanations exist. Maud did have reason to be aggrieved by her treatment in England. She had been present during the Christmas season of 1126 when, one by one, the great magnates of England, including the future King Stephen himself, swore solemn oaths of allegiance to her as King Henry's successor. Many of them broke their oaths, which understandably infuriated her. The people of London had especially favoured Stephen over Maud. She had little reason, other than pragmatic self-interest, to treat the Londoners gently.

Moreover, after receiving only adulation in Germany, Maud must have come to expect it. The largely negative treatment she received in England would have surprised and saddened her. And those who opposed her, especially the oath-

---

[54] Weir, *Queens of the Conquest*, p. 402.

breakers, sought any excuse for their actions. They would have needed to view her negatively and so probably exaggerated her faults. Maud also continually operated under the handicap of being a woman in a male-dominated society. Maybe she felt she had to act as she did to overcome perceptions of feminine frailty. Finally, Maud was under tremendous pressure much of the time she was seeking the throne in England, especially between the Battle of Lincoln and her final flight from Oxford. All this might explain her behaviour that was so detrimental to her cause.

Given the passage of centuries and the sparse and occasionally partisan, nature of the sources, it is impossible today to judge her character with certainty. But this author prefers to think that the wise and virtuous Maud in imperial Germany and her mature years in Rouen when she gave good advice to the king and administered Normandy well, reflect her true character more than her tempestuous behaviour while seeking the throne in England.

Was Maud denied the throne because she was a woman? Certainly, in the sense that, had she been a man, she would surely have succeeded her father without opposition, just as her brother, William the Atheling, would have done had he lived. But being a woman did not automatically disqualify her, even in twelfth-century England. It just meant she had to compete with a male opponent who was better known in England than she, who took immediate steps to claim the crown while she was pregnant and who had only a slightly inferior dynastic claim than hers. Had things gone a bit differently, she might have won and become Queen of England in her own right, four centuries before any woman did so. That she failed was due to some extent to fate, to some extent to her failings at critical times, and, probably, to some extent to inherent reluctance among the proud English lords to be ruled by a woman. But the fact that she almost succeeded despite her handicaps says much about her abilities, her determination and her good qualities.

It is a shame that Maud's story is not better known today. The image of the former empress, dressed all in white, desperately descending by rope down a castle wall in the middle of the night, then making her lonely way to safety in the snow and ice of midwinter, first on foot and then on horseback, through a besieging army determined to capture her, all in quest of becoming the first woman to rule England, should be etched on the public consciousness far more than it is. A partial explanation for this relative lack of awareness might be that the Tudors—with all their cruelties, vices, and propaganda (chapters 8, 9, 10)—

have dominated the public imagination, to the exclusion of other stories at least as compelling. Truly, the victors write the history.

Maud was the mother and daughter of a king and the wife of an emperor, all named Henry. Her epitaph summarises her: "Great by birth, greater by marriage, greatest in her offspring, here lies Matilda, the daughter, wife and mother of Henry."

Chapter 4
The Sons of Henry II: Henry and Geoffrey

Queen Eleanor gave birth to eight children for King Henry II. Seven, including four sons, survived into adulthood, although only one son, her youngest, would outlive her. The four surviving sons were Henry, born in 1155, Richard, born in 1157, Geoffrey, born in 1158 and John, born in 1166, when Eleanor was around 43 years old. Thus, Henry, Richard and Geoffrey were within three years of age, while John was eight years younger than Geoffrey. Given that a daughter, Matilda, was born between Henry and Richard, Eleanor was pregnant almost continuously between 1155 and 1158. The family turned out to be dysfunctional—very dysfunctional.

The three daughters were not part of the dysfunction. They did what medieval princesses were told to do—marry well to whomever the parents arranged and, often, move far away to live with their new husbands. Matilda, the oldest daughter, married Henry the Lion and moved to Saxony to become the Duchess of Saxony. The second daughter, Eleanor, married King Alfonso VIII of Castile and moved to that country to become its queen. The youngest daughter, Joan, went the farthest. She married King William II of Sicily and became Queen of Sicily. As will be seen, the sons, unlike the daughters, did not do as they were told.

Richard, well known today as Richard Coeur de Lion (the Lion-Hearted) and John became kings of England. Henry, known during his lifetime as the Young Henry or the Young King, was crowned king during Henry II's lifetime as a co-regent, but he never reigned on his own. He died too soon. Geoffrey, the heir presumptive during Richard's reign, would have become king when Richard died childless. But he also died too soon to become king. Accordingly, Young Henry and Geoffrey were also heirs who never reigned.

The Young Henry became his father's heir apparent as a toddler when his older brother died at the age of three. The barons of the realm swore homage to him at that time. His father, King Henry, wanted to establish some form of friendship with the French King, Louis VII (Queen Eleanor's first husband). So, at the ripe age of five years, the Young Henry was betrothed in a solemn ceremony to the two-year-old Margaret of France, Louis's daughter by his second wife. As a dowry, Henry was to receive possession of two castles. In 1162, when the boy was six years old, he was sent to the home of Thomas Becket—not yet Archbishop of Canterbury—to be educated. Two years later, when the rift between the king and Becket, now the Archbishop of Canterbury, began, the king removed the boy from Becket's household. The action aggravated the hard feelings between the two.

The king also had marriage plans for his third son, Geoffrey. His plans involved the Duchy of Brittany. In July 1166, in order to secure control over Brittany, the king deposed his vassal, Conan IV, Duke of Brittany and took possession of the region himself. He betrothed the eight-year-old Geoffrey to Conan's five-year-old daughter and sole heiress, Constance of Brittany (of whom we will hear more in chapter 5). The idea was that Geoffrey would become the Duke of Brittany in due course.

Although the Young Henry was betrothed to be married to the daughter of the King of France, true peace had not been established between the two kingdoms. In January 1169, after careful negotiations, King Henry and the King of France met at a castle in the province of Maine, just south of Normandy. The thirteen-year-old Young Henry and Richard were present with their father and attended the ceremonies. There the kings entered into the Treaty of Montmirail with the hope of achieving an enduring peace. The treaty had major implications for King Henry's sons. After the king's death, his possessions were to be divided among his three oldest sons. Richard, Eleanor of Aquitaine's favourite son, would receive Aquitaine as a vassal of the French king. As was fitting given his betrothal to Constance of Brittany, Geoffrey would receive Brittany. The Young Henry would receive England and the rest of Henry's possessions in what is today France. John, only two years old at the time, would receive no territories.

In 1170, when the Young Henry was coming of age, the king wanted to make him his co-regent in order to formalise his position as heir apparent. A problem existed, however. The Archbishop of Canterbury traditionally crowned the English kings. But Becket, the current Archbishop, was in exile as a result of his quarrel with the king. Determined to have his son crowned, the king arranged for the Archbishop of York to preside in Becket's absence, another insult that rankled Becket, as well as the Pope and much of the English Church. Despite substantial opposition to bypassing the Archbishop of Canterbury, the Young Henry, fifteen years old at the time, was crowned in June of that year in a ceremony presided over by the Archbishop of York. A contemporary account described the prince as tall, good looking, well proportioned, with bright blue eyes and reddish-gold hair.

Around the time of the coronation, William the Marshall, one of the most gallant and famous knights medieval chivalry ever produced, was appointed Henry's tutor. The Marshall taught the boy all about chivalry and jousting and tournaments. The boy was an eager student. Two years later, in August 1172, he and Margaret of France were married in another lavish ceremony at Winchester Cathedral. He was also crowned king a second time, with Margaret crowned alongside him. The two were to have only one child, a boy named William, who was born in 1177 and died soon thereafter. Their failure to produce an heir had major repercussions for the future succession.

The Young King, as the Young Henry was now called, was not particularly interested in governmental affairs. He seemed irresponsible and interested only in himself and living as glamorously and expensively as he could. His passion was jousting, the sport in which the great Marshall had tutored him. This was the heyday of chivalry. Large tournaments were held throughout Europe, attended by knights, great and less great, from all over. Hundreds, even thousands, of knights participated in some of the tournaments. Great anticipation accompanied them, with large stands built for spectators and patrons sponsoring banquets to open the events. After meticulous ceremonies, usually including a parade of the participants in full battle regalia, the contests would begin. Heralds would announce the participants and the contests, much as stadium and broadcast announcers do today. Often there would be a melee, either a free-for-all mock battle or, slightly more regimented, two teams of knights fighting each other. Individual jousting might consist of two knights, in full armour, racing at each other on horseback with a lance, trying to knock the opponent off his horse. Generally accompanied by the Marshall and a large entourage of his own knights, Henry was a familiar figure at the major tournaments in France. He spent enormous sums of money to present a front worthy of a king. He had courage and, if jousting were involved, could be energetic. An enthusiastic competitor, he was reputed to be among the best at the sport.

Henry's younger brother, Geoffrey, was also an enthusiastic participant in these tournaments. As Geoffrey would experience, the contests were dangerous. When a knight, suited in full armour—which could provide protection but also could be a hindrance when one is trying to get up after being knocked down—tilts at full speed against an opponent determined to unhorse him and with horses stomping around everywhere, serious injuries, maiming and even death were an all-too-common occurrence at the tournaments.

Possibly because he did not consider his son ready to rule, or possibly because he did not want to yield power, his father gave the Young King no actual authority even after he had been crowned as co-regent. Henry, the son, wanted some part of his patrimony to govern now, ideally England but, if not that, at least one or more of the lands in France that were supposed to become his. The king refused all requests. Between tournaments, when he had a chance to contemplate matters, Henry became more and more unsatisfied with his lack of actual authority or lands to rule over. What was the use of being crowned king if he could not act as one? The Young King also felt that his father was too stingy with funds. The son lived expensively, which, he felt, was entirely appropriate, given his exalted status. Jousting at tournaments all over France cost money. He could not be expected to appear without all the necessary accoutrements and a large retinue of his own knights, all themselves appropriately fitted out. The king had unlimited funds, or so it seemed to the son, and the son chafed at what he considered too small an allowance. He became heavily in debt, the fault—from his perspective—of his father's parsimony.

So, in 1173, at the age of eighteen, he did what noble sons often did in those days. He rebelled against his father, a rebellion that led to the Great Revolt of 1173-4. He was joined in rebellion by the two brothers closest to him in age, Richard (age fifteen) and Geoffrey (age fourteen). The youngest brother, John, was six years old at the time, which provides an explanation, and perhaps the only explanation, of why he did not join the rebellion.

The immediate cause of the revolt was King Henry's decision to grant the young John, landless at that point, three important castles, including Chinon Castle, as part of marriage arrangements for the young boy. Young Henry considered the castles his own and refused to give them up. Soon after he heard about the grant, the Young King rode to France and the residence of his father-in-law, the French King Louis VII. Richard and Geoffrey joined him there. Louis was always ready to stir up trouble for King Henry, partly due to the traditional rivalry between the French and English monarchies, but also for personal reasons. When he granted his first wife, Eleanor, an annulment on the grounds of consanguinity, Louis had not expected her to immediately marry the future King of England, to whom she was even closer related than Louis and Eleanor had been. Many disaffected barons, both on the continent and in England, joined in the rebellion. The new King of Scotland, William the Lion, also always seeking to discomfit England, also joined.

Another who joined, perhaps helped instigate, the rebellion was King Henry's own wife, Queen Eleanor. Why she did so has been the subject of much speculation. One reason might have been that the king was increasingly flaunting his mistresses, more recently one in particular: Rosamund Clifford, known as the Fair Rosamund (Rose of the World). Rosamund was a historical figure, but she became the subject of many legends in later centuries. She might have been the true love of the king's life, especially at this precise time, and she might have caused Eleanor much pain and resentment. But there might have been more prosaic reasons for Eleanor joining her sons in revolt. After many years of dutiful and continuous childbearing, she was ready to move on. She especially wanted to resume her rule over her own domain of Aquitaine. But just as the king would not cede power to his sons, he refused power to his wife. Another factor might be that Eleanor, like much of Europe, had been repulsed by the murder of Thomas Becket in Canterbury Cathedral less than three years previously and, like much of Europe, she blamed her husband. For these and, no doubt, other reasons, Queen Eleanor joined her sons in revolt against her husband. Joining her sons also meant, at least tacitly, allying with her first husband against her second and current husband.

So, Eleanor set out to join her sons in France. But King Henry's forces intercepted her and took her prisoner at Chinon Castle. The rebellion's loss of the queen early in the campaign was a substantial blow, as she was among the most capable of the rebels that, as a whole, consisted of mediocrities at best. But the rebellion hit the king hard and on many fronts. The counts of Flanders and Boulogne invaded Normandy from one direction, the Duke of Brittany from another and King Louis, with the Young Henry, Richard and Geoffrey at his side, from another. The King of Scotland invaded from the north and rebels attacked various castles in England. Their strategy, if it could be called that, was simple—attack as many places from as many directions as possible.

At a superficial glance, the rebels should have won. The difference largely came down to King Henry himself. He was a leader of men. After nearly two decades of strong kingship, Henry had developed an administration and military base that were both capable—the king's appointments were largely based on merit and not mere friendship—and fiercely loyal to the king. The king's support was deep; the Young King's support appeared widespread, but it was shallow. The Young King attempted to buy support by promises of money and titles that he might or might not ever be able to deliver. As he would learn, buying loyalty is different than developing personal relationships over the years. Ultimately, every rebel was loyal only to himself and not to the Young King personally, or even to the cause, whatever it was. When things went badly, each rebel did what he considered best for himself, which might include negotiating a separate settlement with the king.

During the revolt, the king's three sons were essentially pawns of the French King, merely doing his bidding. They and especially the Young King, did very little on their own initiative. During their entire lifetimes, the Young King and Geoffrey never displayed much military ability; they certainly did not do so during the revolt. At fifteen, Richard was not yet the great military leader he would become later—at least in legend and, to some extent, in reality. This circumstance led to another great advantage King Henry had over his enemies. To the extent King Louis was in charge, he exhibited the same limited military acumen that had contributed so heavily to the complete failure of the Second Crusade. King Henry out-led, out-hustled and out-manoeuvred his opponents on all fronts.

With seemingly inexhaustible energy, the king rode from place to place as needed to relieve a castle under siege or blunt a threat, most of the time on the continent. In July 1173, King Louis, with the Young King in tow, laid siege to the castle at Verneuil, in Normandy. But they did so in a leisurely fashion, which allowed King Henry to race to the castle with crack troops and lift the siege. Shortly after that, the king made a quick trip to England, where he scored numerous demoralising victories over the rebels. He could also count on his forces to act capably and courageously on their own initiative when he was not present. It took the king 18 months of hard campaigning, but he was able to put the revolt down in the end. Henry's supporters captured the Scottish king, thus neutralising the threat in the north. After a few more reversals, the sons grew discouraged. When the king offered peace overtures, they accepted and the father and sons were reconciled, at least outwardly.

In victory, the king was generous with his wayward sons. He forced the Young King to accept the grant of the three castles to John, but in return, the king gave him two castles in Normandy and thousands of pounds a year of additional revenue. Geoffrey received substantial revenues in Brittany, the home of his intended future bride Constance. The king was less generous with his wife. He kept her a prisoner, albeit in comfortable circumstances, for the rest of his life—another 15 years—in various castles, generally in southern England. She was sometimes let out for special occasions, but always under strict guard. The king never trusted her again and they never again lived as husband and wife.

The Young King Henry maintained a low profile for the next several years. With his increased income, he spent most of his time at tournaments. In November 1179, Louis VII's son and heir, Philip, was crowned king during his father's life, just as the Young Henry had earlier. The Young King represented his family at the coronation, carrying the crown during the ceremony. Geoffrey also attended the coronation and initiated a friendship with the future French King. After the ceremony, Henry and a retinue of some 500 knights played a starring role in the great tournament to commemorate the occasion. A year later, Philip became King Philip II, called Augustus, on his own when Louis died at the age of 60. Philip became a close friend of both the Young King and Geoffrey.

In the summer of 1182, the Young Henry, still frustrated by his lack of power or lands to call his own, again demanded of his father possession of Normandy or some other territory. Again, Henry refused. Again, the Young King, in a rage, flew into the arms of the French King, this time Louis's son. Later, reluctantly, he returned to the family at his father's bidding. During the Christmas season that year, a family conference was held at Le Mans—today the site of the famous 24 Hours of Le Mans automobile race, then an important administrative centre. King Henry was present with his three oldest sons. The King wanted to reconcile his heirs to having his dominions divided among all three. The conference was a failure, possibly because the mother, Queen Eleanor, perhaps the only one who could have negotiated peace among the men in her family, languished a prisoner somewhere, probably in a castle in southern England. Rather than establishing peace, the conference aggravated tension between the Young King and Richard.[55]

Henry resented the obvious fact that his mother had always favoured Richard. Richard resented Henry's predominance as the older brother. The upshot was that Richard left the conference, returned to Aquitaine and fortified his castles, readying for war. The king supported Richard. The Young King allied himself with his brother, Geoffrey, also ready for war, against his father and Richard. Another intra-family war threatened. The Young Henry attempted, with little success, to convince the local barons in Aquitaine to rise in rebellion against Richard. He and Geoffrey plundered monasteries to raise money to pay for a mercenary army. He sent his wife, King Philip's sister, to safekeeping in Paris. Richard and the king raised their own army. It appeared that, just as in 1173, a large war would erupt. But other than local violence (meaningless to all but the victims) and the plundering of those unfortunate enough to get in the way, events intervened to limit the conflict.

In June 1183, the Young King contracted dysentery. He weakened fast and it soon became apparent that the illness would be fatal. Dying, he asked William the Marshall, his former tutor and fellow jouster, to take his cloak containing a crusader's cross to the Holy Sepulchre in Jerusalem. His conscience was bothering him because he had sworn to go on a pilgrimage to Jerusalem but never did. He also sent word to his father to come to him to reconcile before he died. King Henry suspected a trick (unfortunately, not without reason) and refused to come. Thus, the two were never reunited. "Instead, he [the king] dispatched to his son a familiar ring as a token of mercy and forgiveness and a pledge of his paternal affection. On receiving the ring, the son kissed it and immediately expired while the archbishop of Bordeaux stood by."[56] Henry, the Young King, died without an heir on 11 June 1183, at the age of 28, in the city of Martel. His body was transported to Rouen for burial. Today his remains are in Rouen Cathedral, not far from the heart (but not the rest) of his brother Richard.

---

[55] The 1968 film, *The Lion in Winter*, based on the play of the same name, starring Peter O'Toole as King Henry II and Katharine Hepburn as Eleanor of Aquitaine, portrays the tensions within the royal family during a fictitious family gathering over Christmas 1183, after the Young King's death.

[56] William of Newburgh, compiled in *EHD, vol. II,* p. 360. William, who lived from 1136-98, wrote a history of England that is considered reasonably reliable and quite readable even today.

The Young Henry was tall and good looking, but he had never really grown up. Never allowed to rule, he spent most of his adult life participating in tournaments and other shallow amusements. He never learned how to lead men or act independently, which helps explain why he had so little success in his attempts to rebel and make something of himself. The king reportedly was grief-stricken when he heard of his death, saying, "He cost me much, but I wish he had lived to cost me more." But the world at large lost little and mourned little, when the Young King died. The contemporary chronicler, William of Newburgh, wrote of him that he "met an untimely death, untimely, that is to say, in respect of his age, but too late by consideration of his acts. For he had sullied his early years by an indelible stain… On his coming to manhood, he would not change his youthful conduct and, as at first, he violated nature, so now he also violated his solemn compacts and rebelled against his father a second time."[57]

Henry's death without an heir, however, had consequences. Richard was now the heir apparent. Brother number three, Geoffrey, was next in line to the throne as the heir presumptive, seemingly destined to succeed when, as he did, Richard died childless. Some considered Geoffrey the most intelligent of King Henry's sons. But he was also shallow, concerned only with himself. A contemporary chronicler, Gerald of Wales, described him as "having within 'more of aloes than of honey', soft of face, pouring out words smoother than oil with sweet and persuasive eloquence, able to unknit whatever has been joined together and with a tongue powerful enough to ruin two kingdoms; of wonderful energy, an unreliable hypocrite and dissembler in all things."[58] Another chronicler, Roger of Hoveden, wrote that "Geoffrey, utterly forgetful of God and of respect for his father and unmindful of his commands, did not bring peace, but the sword, and, slighting his oath, his homage and the fealty which he had so often sworn to his father, entered into a compact with the enemies of his father, for the purpose of harassing him, and induced a sacrilegious race and one detested by the Church

[57] William of Newburgh, compiled in *EHD, vol. II,* p. 360.

[58] Robert Bartlett, ed. and transl., *Gerald of Wales: Instruction for a Ruler,* Oxford University Press (2018), p. 481 (hereafter *Gerald of Wales*), quoting Juvenal, *Satires,* vi., 181. Gerald, who lived around 1146 to 1223, was an archdeacon of Brecon, in Wales.

of Rome, to ravage the territories of the father." The same chronicler also referred to Geoffrey as "that son of iniquity."[59]

Geoffrey finally married Constance of Brittany in July 1181, when he was 22 years old and she around 20, and he became the Duke of Brittany. He also nurtured his friendship with King Philip II of France. Philip even made him his seneschal, a position overseeing the entire country. The two seemed to get along well personally, which helped explain the friendship. Undoubtedly, Philip also solicited Geoffrey's friendship as a way to cause trouble for his adversary, King Henry. He skilfully played son against father for his own ends. Geoffrey, in turn, probably solicited Philip's friendship to gain a potential ally when and as needed against his father or brothers. But whether the friendship was personal or merely practical, Geoffrey spent much time at Philip's court in Paris, where he often participated in tournaments and schemed with his friend.

Geoffrey was in Paris during the summer of 1186, probably scheming once again with the French King against his own family. Gerald of Wales wrote that "he had stirred up the King of the French and the whole of France against his father and brother with persuasive words, for he was very eloquent and agreeable, to such an extent that he would, without a doubt, have prepared for them trouble such as they had never seen before, had not he been forestalled by death." He died suddenly in the middle of August at the age of 27. Gerald said he died of the same "hot fever" that killed his brother, Henry.[60] But other accounts, which historians today generally consider more credible, say he died of wounds suffered during a tournament. It appears that Geoffrey was knocked off his horse during a melee and, although wearing his armour, he was trampled underfoot by other horses.

Geoffrey was widely mourned by the French, not so much by the English. At King Philip's orders, he was buried with much ceremony in the choir of Notre Dame Cathedral, "as a mark of honour and love." Gerald of Wales reported that Philip was so distraught by the loss of his friend that "he would have been ready to throw himself with him into the gaping tomb, had not his men pulled him back by force."[61]

---

[59] Henry T. Riley, ed. and transl., *The Annals of Roger de Hoveden*, H.G. Bohn (1853), pp. 22, 25. Roger was active around 1174 to 1201. Little is known of him, but he probably lived in Yorkshire.

[60] *Gerald of Wales*, p. 479.

[61] *Gerald of Wales*, p. 479.

Geoffrey's death did not end the rebellions of King Henry's sons against their father. In 1189, Richard, this time joined by the now-adult John (the only son who had previously remained loyal to his father) and supported by King Philip, again rebelled, but with greater success than before. King Henry became ill during his vain efforts to put down the rebellion. He died a defeated and broken king on 6 July 1189. In his final delirium, he was heard to mutter, "Shame, shame on a conquered king!"

Richard succeeded King Henry as King Richard I. He died childless in 1199 of an arrow wound suffered while fighting a minor skirmish in the south of France. Had Geoffrey not been killed in the jousting tournament, he would have succeeded Richard as King Geoffrey, becoming the only English King of that name. As it was, the succession would be disputed.

When he died, Geoffrey left behind a two-year-old daughter, named Eleanor after her grandmother, and, fatefully, a pregnant wife. The son Constance of Brittany later bore, named Arthur, was destined to become another heir who never reigned.

Chapter 5
The First Non-King Arthur

In some respects, Geoffrey's only son, Arthur, was fortunate in his birth. He was born into royalty and thus lived a pampered life when growing up. Except for King Richard the Lion-Hearted, his father was the oldest remaining son of King Henry II. This gave him a strong claim to the English throne when Richard died without an heir. But in one crucial respect, Arthur was quite unfortunate in his birth. He was his father's *posthumous* son. His mother, Constance of Brittany, gave birth to him on Easter Day, 29 March 1187, several months after his father was killed during a melee at a jousting tournament in Paris. Thus, Arthur had no father to guide him and, more importantly, no father to protect him and ensure his inheritance.

Arthur was not raised in England but instead in his mother's Duchy of Brittany. His name was not happenstance. Brittany is a region in the far west of France. It was and still is distinct from the rest of France. It has its own Celtic language, called Breton and its own Celtic culture and customs. Its inhabitants identified themselves with their fellow Celts in Wales more closely than they did with their neighbours on the continent. When the child was born, the king wanted him named Henry, after himself. But his mother wanted to give him his own name, one that resonated with her people. The Bretons had long dreamed of a second coming of the legendary King Arthur, who had brought glory to all Celts several hundred years earlier. Because Constance was beyond King Henry's effective control, she did as she wanted. She named the boy Arthur, intending to evoke the legendary king's memory and hoping that her son would reflect his namesake's glory later in life. He became a patriotic symbol and rallying cry for the Bretons.

In 1190, when Arthur was three years old, his uncle, King Richard, named him as his heir before the king embarked on the expedition to become known as the Third Crusade. Later, the king tried to become Arthur's guardian in England, but the Bretons kept him in Brittany. In ♠196, his mother named him Duke of Brittany and made him her co-ruler in the Duchy. When King Richard demanded that she bring the boy to his own court, she refused. Instead, she sent him to the French court, where he spent several months living with the French King Philip II. The French King was thrilled to have Arthur as a possible pawn to use against Richard. In France, Arthur became friends with Philip's son, the future King Louis VIII, who was very close to him in age. Arthur then returned to Brittany, where his mother began to involve him in the government.

King Richard died childless in April 1199, when Arthur was 12 years old, leaving an uncertain succession. There were two candidates, Richard's brother John and his nephew Arthur. Although he had earlier named Arthur his heir, he reportedly changed his mind and named John his heir on his deathbed. John was a still-living brother, but he had been younger than Arthur's father, Geoffrey. Under medieval law, it was not clear who had the better claim to the throne when a king died without an heir: a living brother (in this case, John), or the son of an older brother who had died (Arthur). Pragmatic considerations would play an important role. In this situation, Arthur had a double disadvantage. No one in England wanted a 12-year-old king. And he was Breton, not English. On the other hand, few liked or trusted John.

When news arrived of Richard's death, John was, by chance, visiting Arthur and Constance in Brittany. He quickly left them and moved decisively to claim the throne. A majority of the English magnates, led by William the Marshall, the great knight who had been the Young Henry's tutor, wary of having a young Breton as king, reluctantly declared for John. The French King, of course, always looking for a chance to weaken the English monarchy, supported Arthur, as did some of the magnates on the continent, including the rulers of Anjou, Maine and Touraine, three important regions in France. Brittany naturally supported its native son. Constance was also determined that her son should win the English throne. The contest was on.

John promptly seized the royal treasury at the castle of Chinon. Constance raised an army of Bretons and seized the city of Angers. At Le Mans, French and Breton forces led by Arthur and Philip nearly captured John. But he escaped to Normandy and, eventually, made his way to England. His mother, Eleanor, still active in her mid-seventies, declared for her son over her grandson and secured support for him in Aquitaine. In England, John was accepted as king, but with a remarkable lack of enthusiasm. At the urging of William the Marshall, the Archbishop of Canterbury also declared in favour of John. This and other support in England proved decisive. John was crowned king at Westminster Abbey on 27 May 1199. However, like his predecessor, Stephen, he could seize the throne, but he could not rule his realm peacefully.

After his coronation, John returned to Normandy, where he fought to defend his crown against mainly French and Breton troops. A powerful magnate, William des Roches, who had been a strong supporter of Arthur, suddenly switched sides. He met with John at Le Mans. With him, either voluntarily or as his prisoners, came none other than Constance and Arthur, prepared to make peace. Arthur submitted to John, recognising him as king, in September 1199. Peace appeared to have prevailed. But Arthur and his mother did not trust John. Soon, they fled the kingdom and returned to France, where they re-joined Philip.

With Arthur's submission, the main reason for Philip to continue to make war on John disappeared. But the war continued between the two kings nonetheless, now focused largely on who would control Normandy. Neither side was enthusiastic about fighting and the Pope declared a truce. Many of the barons were leaving the area to join the upcoming Fourth Crusade. To end the conflict, the two kings met face to face in January 1200. In May, they signed the Treaty of Le Goulet. Philip recognised John as rightful king of England and heir to King Richard's possessions in France. Thus, Philip abandoned his support for Arthur's claim to the throne, although, as it turned out, only for the time being. John, in turn, recognised Philip as his overlord with respect to his French lands. Arthur remained Duke of Brittany. In this role, he was one of John's vassals. John also made substantial territorial concessions to Philip. The Treaty of Le Goulet was considered a victory for Philip and gained for John the derogatory nickname of John Softsword.

Thus, matters stood for a while. Friendship reigned, at least nominally, between King John and Arthur and his mother and peace existed between the two kings. Constance died in September 1201, of causes variously ascribed as either leprosy or complications arising from childbirth (she had remarried after Geoffrey's death). When she died, she was, apparently, still on friendly terms with the king and reconciled to her son's position as the king's vassal. However, peace did not last long.

In August 1200, John married Isabella of Angouleme, supposedly partly for love, but probably for more practical reasons. To do so, he had to get an annulment of his existing marriage, which he got based on consanguinity, similar to Eleanor of Aquitaine's annulment of her marriage to Louis VII. But another problem existed. This Isabella was already engaged to Hugh de Lusignan, the scion of a powerful family in Poitou. Rather than negotiate a settlement, John treated the Lusignans with contempt (from their perspective) and simply married Isabella. The Lusignans rebelled against John in favour of Arthur and appealed to Philip for assistance. Philip was John's feudal overlord in John's capacity as Count of Poitou.

Philip, always ready to make trouble for the English kings, responded to the appeal eagerly. Relying on the terms of the Treaty of Le Goulet, Philip ordered John to come to court in Paris as the Count of Poitou to answer the Lusignan's' complaints. John naturally refused, and, in the summer of 1202, war broke out anew between Philip and John. Claiming that John had violated the Treaty of Le Goulet, Philip reasserted Arthur's right to John's French possessions, if not to the English throne itself. He knighted the now fifteen-year-old Arthur.

At this point, Arthur began to take a more active part in his own affairs. He became betrothed to marry Philip's daughter, Marie, although the marriage never occurred. In the summer of 1202, Arthur, supported by Hugh de Lusignan, led an army against John into Anjou. In the meantime, his grandmother, Eleanor, now approaching 80 years of age, had retired to the monastery at Fontevraud Abbey, near Chinon in Anjou. She was in the path of Arthur's forces and was about to become embroiled in politics and warfare for the last time. She was informed that Arthur's army was approaching and believed, correctly, that Arthur wanted to capture her, probably to use as a bartering chip. Eleanor fled the convent and raced north towards Normandy and safety. During her flight, she managed to send a frantic message to John pleading for help. Arthur's army caught up to her at the town of Mirebeau and trapped her inside the castle. Arthur moved into the town and began to besiege the castle. It was a mistake—for him, a fatal mistake.

John was 80 miles away when he received his mother's plea for help. Reacting, for once, with a speed that even his father, King Henry II, would have found difficult to match, John and his troops travelled the 80 miles in less than 48 hours. In the meantime, Eleanor met with Arthur and stalled for time. John arrived at Mirebeau on 31 July to find Arthur and his forces inside the town itself, preparing to storm the castle. William des Roches, who knew the castle well, had joined John. He agreed to lead an attack on Arthur and his men, but only on the conditions that John would not execute them and would consult with him regarding Arthur's treatment.

A historian has described what happened the next morning. "At dawn Hugh de Lusignan's brother Geoffrey was enjoying a breakfast of roasted pigeons when a vicious assault on the one working gate to the city took him by surprise. John's men surrounded the town and before long, they had battered down the gate. Heavy street fighting ensued, led by the indomitable des Roches, who lost three horses from under him as he led charge after charge against the town gates. Seeing the strength and unusual vigour of their opponents, the rebels fled for the safety of the castle. But they were unable to hold out. Under des Roches ferocious leadership John's men completed a stunning rout and Eleanor was freed from the castle and told that Arthur, Hugh and Geoffrey Lusignan, 'and 252 of the worthiest knights' had been captured."[62]

Arthur was now John's prisoner. Eleanor pleaded with John not to harm Arthur. Both she and William des Roches advised John to make peace with his nephew. But he did not do so. John sent Arthur in chains to the castle at Falaise, in Normandy. He treated other prisoners, many of them kin of some of his own supporters, so wretchedly that 22 of them died. His treatment of these highborn captives caused many to abandon their support of him.

Arthur spent the rest of his life as John's captive and was never seen in public again. Exactly what transpired after his capture is uncertain. As might be expected given the secrecy involved, reports are conflicting and generally unreliable.

At Falaise, Hubert de Burgh guarded Arthur. At first, Arthur confronted his captors courageously. But then, according to one account (not certain to be true), John ordered two of his minions to blind and castrate Arthur, believing that a boy so maimed could not be a serious rival. To do this to a person of royal blood, and his own nephew, would have been considered an atrocity even in those violent days. When he learned of his intended fate, Arthur broke down and pleaded for mercy. Defying John, de Burgh refused to allow his charge to be treated this way and he spared Arthur. To protect the boy from further attempts to harm him and possibly fearing the King's displeasure, de Burgh declared that Arthur had died of natural causes. Unfortunately, this led to demands for revenge in Brittany and de Burgh had to admit that Arthur was alive after all.

---

[62] Dan Jones, *The Plantagenets: The Warrior Kings and Queens Who Made England*, Viking (2012) p. 142 (hereafter Dan Jones, *The Plantagenets*).

At some point, probably in early 1203, Arthur was moved to the castle at Rouen, where he disappears from history. He was almost certainly murdered, either by John personally or at his command, but exactly how and when is unknown. One account, which might or might not be credible, is that the Thursday night before Easter 1203, at Rouen, John went to the boy's dungeon cell and killed the boy in a drunken fury. He then tied the body to a heavy stone and went outside to dispose of it in the Seine. A fisherman discovered the body and, fearing the King, buried it secretly. Another story, far from credible, is that John drove a sword through Arthur while riding with him on a boat on the Seine.

It seems more likely that John ordered Arthur's death but did not personally commit the murder. One William de Braose was rumoured to have killed Arthur. Years later, de Braose's wife publicly accused John of murdering the boy. But whatever Arthur's exact fate, most historians today believe Arthur died sometime during the year 1203 or soon thereafter, probably by murder, possibly of natural causes exacerbated by his harsh imprisonment. Arthur thus died young and never could become Richard's heir despite Richard's designation of him as such when he was three years old. But after his death, he got a measure of revenge.

Although John managed to dispose of his rival, it came at a high cost to him. If we do not know today what happened to Arthur, at the time, most of Europe, including king Philip, the Bretons and William des Roches, did not know either. Rumours abounded about his fate, but no one knew for sure. Most people assumed then, as they do now, that John had him murdered and they were outraged. The presumed murder was long considered the most dastardly of John's many acts of cruelty during his reign. Arthur's fate became a cause célèbre. Unhappy that John had not consulted with him regarding Arthur, William des Roches withdrew his support. The Bretons demanded that John produce a live Arthur. When he failed or, more likely, was unable to do so, they rebelled. So did others, abetted by Philip. Philip, correctly judging that this was his great chance to weaken the English monarchy, invaded John's territories. John's cause suffered a further blow on 1 April 1204, when his mother, the intrepid Eleanor of Aquitaine, finally died at Fontevraud Abbey, at the ancient age of over 80 years. Whatever moral support for his cause she may have generated died with her. People would not support or even negotiate with John unless and until he produced a live Arthur, which he could not do.

By the end of 1204, John had lost most of the English possession in what is today France, possessions the English monarchy had held (sometimes more and sometimes less) since the Battle of Hastings in 1066. This loss was almost directly attributable to John's treatment of Arthur and, to a lesser degree, to his treatment of the other prisoners taken in the action at Mirabeau Castle. It gave him another derogatory nickname—John Lackland.

John also had another royal captive, Eleanor, Arthur's older sister, known as the Fair Maid of Brittany or the Pearl of Brittany. Exactly how she came into his clutches is unknown, possibly during the Battle of Mirabeau, but certainly around that time. As another potential rival, John kept her a prisoner for the rest of his reign. His successor, King Henry III, continued to keep her captive, albeit in comfortable circumstances, for the rest of her life. She finally died on 10 August 1241, in her late fifties, after some 39 years as a prisoner. She was thus the longest-held prisoner of any member of the royal family in English history.

Given his short life and the nature of the records, it is difficult to discern what Arthur was like personally. He seemed energetic, capable and determined. He was said to have confronted his capturers courageously at first, although he broke down and pleaded for mercy when informed that he would be blinded and castrated, as would anyone. It is unknown what kind of a king he would have become. He had helped his mother rule over Brittany for a while, so he had some administrative experience. Whatever kind of a king he might have become, it is hard to imagine he would have been worse than King John.

John continued to rule England, although never peacefully. In 1215, after years of tyranny and discord with his barons, he had a rendezvous with history at Runnymede, where he was forced to submit to the terms of the Magna Carta. The Magna Carta was partly a reaffirmation and strengthening of the Charter of Liberties that King Henry I had issued at the outset of his reign a century earlier but that had rarely been given effect. When John died the next year, his son peacefully succeeded him.

Chapter 6
Edward, the Black Prince

After King John's death, the son followed the father regularly for over a century. John was followed by his son, Henry III, who was followed by his son, Edward I, who was followed by his son, Edward II, who was followed by his son Edward III.

Edward III did not follow his father peacefully. Edward II's reign had been a disaster in many respects. Militarily, he lost wars against the Scots, especially the 1314 Battle of Bannockburn, and did poorly against the French. He also had despised favourites, who effectively ruled the country in his name. In 1326, the favourite was one Hugh Despenser. In addition to enriching himself at the expense of the established nobility, it appears that Despenser stole the king's affections from his queen. This queen, Isabella, known as the She-Wolf of France, was (fatefully) the daughter of the French King, Philip IV. In 1326, Edward II sent her as an ambassador to the court of her brother, the then-reigning French King, Charles IV. Later he sent his thirteen-year-old son, Edward, to join her. Doing so was a mistake. Isabella very much resented Despenser and had given up on her marriage. In France, she took a paramour, a leading English lord, Roger Mortimer. With covert assistance from the French King and overt assistance from William, Count of Hainault, she and Mortimer led an invasion of England. Supported by disaffected nobles in that country, they managed, in 1327, to depose Edward II in favour of Isabella's now fourteen-year-old son, who became King Edward III. Edward II was probably murdered a short time later, although his precise fate is uncertain.

For three years, Isabella and Mortimer effectively ruled England in Edward III's name. But in 1330, with the help of friends, Edward managed to overthrow the two. Mortimer was executed for treason and Isabella was banished from the court. Edward now ruled on his own behalf. In 1328, while still under his mother's domination, he had married Philippa, the daughter of the Count of Hainault. Philippa later claimed that she and Edward had fallen in love during a visit a few years earlier. That may be so, but the marriage was purely an example of cynical realpolitik. Isabella negotiated the marriage in 1326 with Philippa's father, Count William. The father gained by having his daughter married to a future King of England. Isabella gained critical military assistance for her intended invasion of England. In accordance with the marriage agreement, the Count provided her with ships and 1,500 soldiers. However, despite its negotiated nature, the marriage appears to have been a success. Philippa was devoted to her husband and he to her; she often accompanied him on his many military campaigns. She became a loving mother to her many children until she died in 1369.

Philippa gave birth to her first child, also named Edward, at Woodstock in Oxfordshire on 15 June 1330. In honour of his birthplace, he was known during his lifetime as Edward of Woodstock. Later he was to enter historical legend as the Black Prince, the name by which he is universally known today. The prince's father was 17 years old when he was born. The relatively small age difference between father and son meant that the son would have a long wait before he could succeed to the throne. The wait turned out to be too long. The Black Prince died a year too soon to follow his father and was thus destined to become another heir who never reigned. Another century would elapse before there would be King Edward IV.

Edward was never called the Black Prince during his lifetime. The appellation first appears in histories of the sixteenth century. What the name refers to is uncertain. It might refer to black armour or a black shield the prince supposedly wore or wielded at the Battle of Crecy, although no contemporary record exists suggesting that his armour or shield was black. It might also refer to his alleged cruelty, primarily towards the common people. In any event, the Black Prince he became and the Black Prince he remains.

As a young boy, Edward grew up with some of his sisters and a young girl two years older than he, his reputedly beautiful cousin Joan, later known as the Fair Maid of Kent. Joan's father had been a younger half-brother of King Edward II, the Black Prince's grandfather. This father was executed during the time of Roger Mortimer's ascendency when Joan was two years old. When King Edward III began to rule in his own right, he took the orphaned Joan under his wing and raised her with his own family. The prince might have become smitten with his older cousin during this time.

From his early childhood, Edward was raised to be a king and appreciate the values of chivalry. He was trained to abide by its rules and was expected to be pious, courageous, courteous and honourable. In early 1337, his father gave the six-year-old boy the title of Duke of Cornwall. It was the first time the French title "Duc" was translated into English as "duke" and became a title in England. Around the same time, the king also gave his son the title of "guardian of the realm" during his frequent absences. Clearly, the young boy acted only nominally in this role; a council advised him and wielded the real authority. But the prince occasionally presided over formal occasions and, in this way, he was schooled early in the art of governance. In 1339, the boy formally opened a session of Parliament in his father's absence. He was also prepared early for a military career. At the age of seven, he received his first suit of armour, his own size but otherwise genuine. He became the prince of Wales in 1343, although he never visited that country.

Edward began his rise to legendary status in the early stages of what later was called the Hundred Years' War. In 1328, the French King Charles IV died without an heir. There were two viable candidates to succeed him: King Edward III himself, through his mother, the daughter of the French King Philip IV and sister of Charles IV; and Edward's cousin, Philip of Valois, whose connection to the French crown was not as close as Edward's but was through the male line. The French chose Philip, who became King Philip VI, the first King of the Valois dynasty. The choice was not surprising. Salic law prohibited inheriting through the female line in France (although not, as we have seen, in England). Additionally, the French were understandably reluctant to have the King of England become the King of France. In 1328, King Edward was still under his mother's domination and was in no position to assert his claim. However, after he began to rule on his own behalf, Edward asserted his claim and styled himself King of England and France. He determined to enforce his claim by conquest. In a nutshell, that was what the Hundred Years' War was about, at least in the early stages.

Fighting began in 1337. In July 1346, Edward invaded France, accompanied by the sixteen-year-old Prince Edward, now tall and handsome and well on this way to manhood. The king knighted his son as soon as they landed on French soil. Knighting someone was symbolic, but a very formal and, to the participants, meaningful ceremony that signifies the person knighted is now a fully-fledged warrior.

After the army landed, the king and prince engaged in a form of medieval warfare they often employed called *chevauchee*. Literally translated as a horse charge, it meant raiding through enemy territory inflicting as much destruction as possible, to weaken the enemy or perhaps force it to come out of its defensive shell and fight. The goal was to humiliate and eventually defeat, the nobleman who ruled that territory. But the ordinary people, peasants and townspeople, bore the brunt of *chevauchee*, as crops and homes were destroyed and humans were maimed, mutilated and killed. It seems unspeakably cruel today, but it was a fully accepted form of warfare in the fourteenth century. With the prince often taking the lead, the English armies ravished the French countryside in Normandy, inflicting a wide swath of death and destruction.

Nominally led by the prince himself, but with seasoned commanders, a wing of the army captured the city of Caen in intense fighting. One of the heroes of the day was a knight named Sir Thomas Holland, who will play another role later in this story. Many French, mostly ordinary citizens, were killed during and after the fighting, the usual fate of a city that resisted attack rather than surrender. The prince was exhilarated. His first taste of serious combat was a success and whetted an unquenchable appetite for ever more.

The French King did what he believed he had to do to stop the destruction. He brought out his large army, containing the flower of French chivalry, to fight. The English and French armies met on 26 August 1346, near the town of Crecy in northeast France. Despite being outnumbered some two to one, the English scored a decisive and (from their perspective) glorious victory. Welsh bowmen, wielding the devastating weapon called the longbow, played a crucial role in the victory.

Wanting to give his son the chance to prove his mettle, a chance the prince eagerly embraced, the king put him in charge of the vanguard. During the heaviest fighting, French troops pressed hard against Prince Edward and his men at arms. This was, it appears, the only time the French army at Crecy presented a serious threat to any part of the English army. The contemporary chronicler, Jean Froissart, tells a story that has become part of the legend of the warrior prince but that might not be entirely true. The prince's battalion sent a messenger to tell the king that he was hard-pressed and needed assistance. The king asked the messenger whether his son was dead or wounded. When told he was neither, the king ordered the messenger to "go back to him and to those that sent you and tell them not to ask for any help from me while my son is still alive. Say that I want them to let the boy win his spurs."[63]

Win his spurs the young prince did. As another contemporary chronicler described it, he "showed his valour to the French, piercing horses, laying low the riders, shattering helmets and breaking spears, skilfully parrying blows aimed against him, helping his men, defending himself, helping to their feet friends who had fallen and showing to all an example in well-doing."[64] At one point, according to reports, he was slightly wounded and thrown to the ground. With his life hanging in the balance, his standard-bearer threw his standard over him to protect him until he could regain his feet. He did and managed to fight his way out of danger.

The French lost thousands of men that day, including much of the nobility. When the battle was over, Prince Edward was adjudged the hero of the day. After the battle, in front of his men, the king told him he had acquitted himself well. In response, the prince bowed low to his father, as chivalry demanded. The day after the battle, the king and prince surveyed the battlefield together. They found the body of Jean of Luxembourg, the blind King of Bohemia, renowned throughout Europe as a champion of chivalry. A warrior to the end despite his blindness, Jean had died in a reckless charge with several of his men at arms. Impressed by the courage Jean had displayed, the prince noted Jean's emblem, an ostrich plume and made it part of his own emblem from that time on.

Later that same summer, the king, again with his son at his side, began to besiege the city of Calais on the French coast. After a brutal siege lasting over a

---

[63] John Jolliffe, ed. and transl., *Froissart's Chronicles*, The Modern Library (1968), p. 147. Froissart, a French speaking author who lived around 1337 to 1405, is an important source of information about the first half of the Hundred Years' War, but his accuracy on certain points has been questioned.

Geoffrey le Baker (or Geoffrey the Baker), a contemporary English chronicler, wrote about the Battle of Crecy that one of the prince's men "ran or rode to the King" and asked for help and that the messenger "was sent with twenty knights to help the prince." Le Baker said nothing about the King wanting his son to win his spurs. A.R. Myers, ed., *English Historical Documents, vol. IV, 1327-485*, Oxford University Press (1969), p. 81 (hereafter *EHD, vol. IV*). Le Baker's version seems more credible (i.e., more consistent with what a father would likely do) and makes one wonder whether Froissart was merely telling a good story rather than what actually occurred.

[64] Geoffrey le Baker, compiled in *EHD, vol. IV,* p. 81.

year, the city surrendered. Several leading citizens of the city, near starvation, prostrated themselves in subjection to the king. In a well-publicised scene, Queen Philippa pleaded for the king to spare their lives. The king put on a show of reluctance, but finally, he acquiesced and spared them. He had, however, conquered Calais. The city would remain in English hands for two more centuries; eventually, it became the last English stronghold on the continent.

In November 1347, the king and prince returned to England, where they were feted as glorious victors. It was not certain who—king or prince—was the more celebrated of the two. The next year (or perhaps sooner; the true founding date is a bit murky), King Edward established the Order of the Garter, the highest order of chivalry in England still today. The prince was a charter member. The order was dedicated to St George, England's patron saint. Membership was limited to no more than 26 living persons at any given time, including the monarch and the heir. The monarch chooses the membership in his or her sole discretion. The Order's emblem is, naturally enough, a garter. The emblem contains the Order's motto in gold lettering: "Honi soit qui mal y pense" (middle French, meaning, "shame on him who thinks evil of it").

A story that first surfaced two centuries later attributed the name of the order and the motto to events involving Prince Edward's cousin, Joan of Kent. According to the story, King Edward, struck by the then 20-year-old Joan's beauty, danced with her at a ball. During the dance, Joan somehow lost her garter. The king picked it up and, looking at the other revellers, muttered the famous words that became the order's motto. The story is charming but is almost certainly only a story. It is dubious for at least two reasons: there is no contemporary evidence to support it; and in the fourteenth century, men wore garters, not women. It was not until well into the following century that women wore garters.

The months following the prince's return to England were spent celebrating their victories in grand style, with jousting tournaments (no royal fatalities), plays and other events throughout southern England. The king and the prince and most of the rest of the English, thought the war was largely won. In fact, it had only begun.

Over the next few years, the prince returned to France and helped his father in various campaigns. France proved very difficult to subdue. In late 1349, hearing that Calais, captured at great cost, was to be betrayed to the French, King Edward and his son hastened to the city and secretly entered it with a small group of trusted warriors. A traitor was supposed to open the city to French invaders at midnight, 31 December to 1 January. The king and prince, hiding inside the city, made it appear the betrayal was proceeding according to plan. Then they sprung a trap and charged the intruders, who were astonished to meet resistance. In desperate fighting that added to the prince's growing reputation as a warrior, they defeated the invaders and preserved Calais as an English possession. When they returned to England, the king told his wife that their son had personally saved him from being captured.

In August 1350, the prince fought in the naval Battle of Winchelsea, off the English coast, against a Castilian fleet allied to France. It became another English victory, but not before the prince found himself in the midst of hot combat. A Castilian ship grappled his own ship and its crew scrambled on board. Desperate fighting followed. Henry of Grosmont, the Duke of Lancaster and one of the prince's greatest friends, as well as a charter member of the Order of the Garter, came to the rescue. He and his men boarded the ship from the opposite side. With these reinforcements, the English were able to defeat the enemy and throw them into the water. But Edward's ship was badly damaged and foundering fast. The prince and his men were able to board the Castilian ship shortly before his own sank. The king's ship also sank, although he, too, was able to transfer to another. Although victorious, both father and son were fortunate to have survived. Good fortune in combat seemed to smile on the prince.

During these years, fighting became sporadic. Beginning in 1348, the plague, then called the Great Mortality, today called the Black Death, made its appearance. It ravished the population of both England and France, making campaigning difficult and, to some at least, pointless. As much as one-third of the entire population of Europe, perhaps more, died of the plague within a year. In its early stages, before anyone fully appreciated the danger, the plague killed Edward's own sister, Joan (not to be confused with his cousin of the same name). Joan was in Bordeaux while travelling to Castile to be married to Pedro, the son of Alfonso XI, King of Castile, when she was struck down in July 1348 at the age of 15. Pedro will reappear later in this story.

The Black Death attacked the labouring class with special ferocity, causing severe labour shortages and social disruption. Landlords suffered a substantial reduction in revenues from the far fewer surviving tenants. Major landowners, such as Prince Edward, suffered proportionally larger reductions in revenues. During a period of unrest in Cheshire, in which one of the prince's bailiffs was murdered, the prince, as Earl of Chester, travelled to the area to see what the problem was and what he could do about it. Showing a different side of his character, the prince appeared sincere in his efforts to understand the local circumstances and to improve them. He largely succeeded in winning the locals over to his side. In return for commencing public works projects and granting the city a charter of liberties, the people of Cheshire agreed to pay a fine of 5,000 pounds over four years, with all of the citizenry except the poorest contributing. Cheshire was to provide many of the archers in the prince's armies.

In 1355, King Edward renewed the war. This time, he gave his now 25-year-old son his own independent command. The king ordered him to invade Aquitaine. The king and his younger son, John of Gaunt, were to campaign in Normandy and Brittany. After spending time in Bordeaux, the prince and his small army marched east, plundering as they went. It was more warfare by *chevauchee*. This time the local enemy was the Count of Armagnac, a region in Gascony. In an impressive display of military leadership, the prince led his army from Bordeaux near the Atlantic Ocean to the Mediterranean coast, destroying as he went and sacking wealthy cities such as Carcassonne and Narbonne. After seizing huge amounts of booty, the prince returned to Bordeaux for the winter. In the meantime, the new French King John (or Jean) II, anxious to avenge the defeat at Crecy and stop the devastation of the countryside, began to raise a large army against the prince.

The following year, Edward continued his depredations in Aquitaine, reducing castles, capturing towns and plundering everywhere. He had a small army, perhaps 2,000 longbowmen, 4,000 infantry and some cavalry. King John crossed the Loire and stalked the prince with an army at least twice that size. Many in the French army were Scottish allies, anxious to fight and defeat their traditional enemy. Henry Grossmont, who had rescued the prince during the Battle of Winchelsea, tried to aid the prince once again with another small army. However, this time he was unable to cross the Loire and join with the prince's forces. King Edward remained in England. The prince was on his own, hemmed in by a much larger army.

The two armies confronted each other near Poitiers, one of the major cities in Aquitaine. Knowing the danger he was in, the prince was willing to negotiate—or perhaps just stall for time while he strengthened his defences. With Cardinal Talleyrand de Périgord, an envoy of Pope Innocent VI, acting as a mediator, he offered King John major concessions to avoid battle, including giving up the booty he had seized and not fighting against the French for seven years. But the French King, believing he could easily defeat an outnumbered foe, wanted more. He demanded that the prince himself surrender to him, along with 100 of his best knights. Edward scorned that proposition and prepared to fight.

Although he seemed trapped in a desperate situation, the Black Prince had some advantages. Many of his troops were battle-hardened veterans of the Crecy campaign. He had excellent commanders, who cooperated and coordinated well. He also had the longbow, a most effective weapon, as it had proven at Crecy and would again in 1415 at Agincourt. The French army was inexperienced. Its commanders were generally mediocre and they did not always cooperate or coordinate well. Additionally, during the protracted negotiations, Edward was able to improve the defences around his army.

Edward chose the ground and placed his army in a fortified defensive position. In a typical fashion, he placed his troops in three divisions, with himself commanding the middle division. Critically, he placed his archers in a protected position behind a thick hedge. The French army was divided into four divisions. But they were placed one behind the other, so they could not all attack at once. Thus, the advantage of numbers was diminished. Moreover, a retreating division could cause havoc with the division behind it. The French did not seem to have considered using some troops in the rear to outflank a badly outnumbered enemy.

On the morning of 19 September 1356, Edward addressed his troops. Then the fighting began. As is often the case with medieval battles, exactly how it played out is uncertain. The sources are conflicting. Because the longbow was so effective in disabling or killing horses, most of the French army dismounted and fought on foot, something many were not accustomed to doing. It appears the fighting began with an attack by three hundred elite men-at-arms from the French army down a lane. But the archers decimated them. A well-timed English cavalry charge broke one flank of the French army, causing it to flee. It ran into the division behind it, creating great confusion. The English counterattacked and the carnage commenced. Fighting lasted until mid-afternoon. It ended in a devastating French defeat. One of the heroes of the day was William Montagu, Earl of Salisbury, whom we will also meet later in this story. English losses were minimal. The French lost thousands killed (how many is not known precisely). Many of the dead were members of the high nobility. Thousands more were captured. Importantly, in an age when victors would ransom their prisoners for as high a price as the market would bear, more than a thousand of the prisoners would be ransomed, including 14 counts and other high lords. Their ransoms would fill many English purses.

Among the prisoners was King John II himself, along with his son, Philip the Bold. By all accounts, John had fought courageously, until he was surrounded and captured. In the tradition of chivalry, the prince held a banquet to honour his highborn captives the night of the battle. According to the chronicler Jean Froissart, he showed John great deference as a king, humbling himself in his presence as a mere prince. In the highest tradition of chivalry (or perhaps the oddest from today's perspective), the prince personally served the captive French King at his meal. He also praised John's courage, telling him, "methinks you ought to rejoice, though the day did not go as you would have had it, for this day you have won the high renown of prowess and you have surpassed this day in valour all others of your party."[65]

The French gave Edward great credit for his chivalrous conduct. But chivalry did not prevent the prince from transporting his royal prisoners into captivity in England, although it was a comfortable, even regal, captivity. When they arrived in London in May 1357 and the prince triumphantly presented his royal captive to the populace, King John rode a much finer horse than the prince.

Back in England, the prince once again enjoyed life as a returning hero, this time a hero under his own command. The Battle of Poitiers and its aftermath cemented, in England at least, the legend of the Black Prince as exemplifying the finest dual traditions of chivalry—valour in battle, courtesy in victory. During this time, the prince established a relationship with his paternal grandmother, Isabella, still vibrant in exile, although only a shadow of her former "She-Wolf of France" persona. He visited her several times at her home at Castle Rising in Norfolk. He impressed his grandmother so much that when she died in August 1358, she left most of her property to him, including the castle itself.

Unfortunately, peace did not last long after the Battle of Poitiers. In November 1359, the king, Prince Edward and the prince's younger brother, John of Gaunt, led an army out of Calais towards Reims, in whose soaring cathedral all French kings had been crowned since the ninth century. King Edward hoped

---

[65] Jean Froissart, compiled in *EHD, vol. IV*, p. 100. Geoffrey le Baker has a slightly different account. According to him, the prince left the dinner early to attend to a wounded comrade, apologizing to the French King for doing so. Richard Barber, *Oxford Dictionary of National Biography, Edward, the Black Prince*, Oxford University Press (2008).

to be crowned King of France himself in the same cathedral. But he failed to reach his target. The campaign bogged down. Some of the king's advisors urged him to compromise and he reluctantly agreed. With Prince Edward the primary negotiator on the English side, the parties negotiated the Treaty of Brétigny. Edward renounced his claim to the French throne, but France ceded Aquitaine and other territories to England.

King John's ransom was set at three million francs, to be paid in instalments. Modern historians assure us that, when the Black Death was rampant, France was in political disarray and enemy armies ravished the countryside, this was an almost impossible sum for the French people to raise. King John was released and allowed to return to France to raise the ransom, leaving behind one of his sons as a hostage. Later, when John learned that this son had escaped from captivity before the ransom was paid, he returned voluntarily to captivity in London, to the great dismay of his people. (This was yet another example of chivalry that seems astounding today.) He died, still a prisoner but in comfortable circumstances, in the Savoy Palace in 1364. His 26-year-old son succeeded him as Charles V.

The Black Prince returned once again to England in late 1360. Now it was time for the 30-year-old prince to marry. Edward had fathered at least two illegitimate sons. There had been considerations of marriage in the past, leading to preliminary negotiations seeking the usual dynastic advantages royal marriages were supposed to provide. But nothing ever came of the negotiations, as the prince was preoccupied with his martial career. It is also possible that his true love was not available and he did not want to marry anyone else. But eventually, he had to think about producing an heir. When he did choose, he did not look very far. And, to all appearances, he chose for a reason rare among medieval royalty. He married for love, not political advantage. He chose his cousin, Joan, Countess of Kent, the maiden who had supposedly danced with the king and lost her garter many years earlier. She was two years older than the prince, but they had lived together as children. The king originally opposed the marriage. Joan, although heiress to Kent, did not bring to the marriage the political or dynastic gain normally expected of royal marriages.

Joan also came with substantial baggage. She had been married twice before, for a while, it appeared, to both husbands simultaneously. The second of her former husbands was still alive when Prince Edward decided to marry her. Her first two husbands were heroes of the early stages of the Hundred Years' War. Her third and final husband would be the greatest hero of them all.

When Joan was 12 years old, she secretly married the then 26-year-old Sir Thomas Holland (later, the hero of the battle for Caen). At least that is what he and she later claimed. A short time after this alleged marriage, while Holland was campaigning in France, Joan's family arranged for her to marry William Montagu, future Earl of Salisbury, the son of one of King Edward's major allies (and himself later a hero of the Battle of Poitiers). Joan said nothing at the time about her earlier marriage, possibly out of fear, possibly because she believed the marriage was invalid or Holland was dead—but possibly because that marriage never actually occurred. Holland returned in 1348 and claimed that he was Joan's husband. Montagu disputed the claim. The matter was referred to Pope Clement VI in Avignon for arbitration. Joan preferred Holland and supported his testimony that they had married. The Pope gratified her by ruling that she and Holland had, indeed, been married and that the marriage remained valid. The Pope nullified her marriage to William. It seems likely that during the period of litigation, Joan and Prince Edward renewed their acquaintance.

After the Pope's ruling, Joan, who had been living with Montagu, returned to Holland. Over the next 11 years, as Holland's wife, Joan gave birth five times. Holland died in 1360, possibly of the Black Death, leaving behind a widow with four surviving children, two of them sons who would later be invited to join the Order of the Garter. If Edward married Joan, he would have the dubious distinction of being the first royal prince to marry a divorced woman since the future King Henry II married Eleanor of Aquitaine two centuries previously.

On the other hand, Joan was reputed to be the most beautiful woman in England. Most medieval chroniclers conventionally described royal princesses as beautiful. But it appears true in this case that Joan had been remarkably beautiful when young and that, even at the relatively advanced age (for medieval times) of 32 years, she still was. And it seems Edward and Joan truly loved each other. Holland's death gave Edward his chance. He took it and proposed to Joan. She accepted. Because the two were so closely related, they had to obtain a special dispensation from the Pope to marry, which Pope Innocent VI promptly granted. Faced with his son's insistence on marrying for love rather than dynastic gain, King Edward graciously relented and consented to the marriage. His son had done well for him and the king was not about to stand in the way of his happiness.

On 10 October 1361, Edward and Joan were married at Windsor Castle in one of the major social events of the decade. The celebrated prince was 31 years old, his almost-as-celebrated bride 33. The Archbishop of Canterbury presided over the ceremonies. The king, the queen, two of Edward's brothers and many of the English elite were present. Judging from the guest list, William Montagu, husband number two, although still alive, was not invited. Like that of Edward's own parents, this marriage turned out to be happy for both. As far as the records show, the two were truly devoted to one another. There has never been even a hint that either of them was anything but faithful to the other as long as they both lived.

At first, the newly married couple lived in a palace in Kennington, in Kent. But King Edward had other ideas for his oldest son. In 1362, he granted the prince the Duchy of Aquitaine and Gascony to rule over. The prince had already proved himself as a warrior. Now would be his chance to further prepare for his future kingship by administering a large fiefdom. He would not be as successful at this as he was at fighting. Neither administration nor living within a budget was among his strengths. Nevertheless, Edward accepted the new assignment gratefully, as he always loved the south and especially Bordeaux. After considerable preparation and some delays, the couple left for their new lives in 1363.

Edward's time as prince of Aquitaine began auspiciously. His fame went before him. When he and Joan arrived in Aquitaine in the summer of 1363, Edward met and received homage from the local nobles. He travelled around his new realm and his new subjects generally received him enthusiastically. After that, he and Joan kept a brilliant court, living mainly at Bordeaux and Angouleme. However, although their court was one of the most splendid in Europe, it gradually became unpopular with the locals. Edward and Joan continually lived beyond their means. Part of the reason was the prince's extravagant generosity in rewarding those who served him well. To stay solvent, Edward imposed a series of taxes, called a "*fouage*," a tax on each hearth kept in family homes. A *fouage* was a tax on each family unit. As it became more and more apparent that the prince primarily imposed the taxes to pay for his extravagant lifestyle and not to benefit the Duchy, the taxes became ever more unpopular. He was also increasingly viewed as just another foreign conqueror. The new French King Charles V sought to take advantage of the dissatisfaction to foment trouble.

During this time, Queen Joan bore the couple's first child, a boy named Edward after his father. This boy was destined to live for only five years.

After a few years of living graciously and regally—and peacefully—with a loving wife and the beginning of a family, Edward decided to undertake another military adventure, one that would prove successful militarily but disastrous for him personally. In 1366, the King of Castile, then its own country in the north of what is today Spain, was Pedro, the only legitimate son of King Alfonso XI. This was the same Pedro whom the Black Prince's sister, Joan, was travelling to marry when she died of the Black Death back in 1348. But he had since acquired the name Pedro the Cruel, a sobriquet well-earned and deserved. When he finally did marry in 1353, he abandoned his wife, Blanche of Bourbon, within days of the marriage, imprisoned her and probably ordered her death in 1361 at the age of 22. (Had Joan not died on the way to marrying Pedro, she might have suffered a similar fate.)

Early in his reign, Pedro shifted his allegiance from France to England. But his despotic and cruel behaviour generated opposition to his reign within Castile. When Charles V became King of France in 1364, he punished Pedro for abandoning the French alliance (and hoped to cause trouble for Edward) by championing a rival claimant to the Castilian throne, Pedro's illegitimate half-brother, Henry (or Enrique) of Trastámara. In 1366, with Charles's encouragement and assisted by French knights including Bertrand du Guesclin, perhaps the most celebrated French knight of medieval times, Pedro's opponents managed to drive him from the country and install Henry in his place.

Pedro naturally fled to his new ally, Prince Edward, and pleaded for help to regain his crown. No logical reason existed for the prince to aid Pedro. The English had no stake in Castile. And a mountain range, the Pyrenees, posed a barrier to any military intervention in Castile. Many of the prince's top advisors urged him to ignore Pedro's pleas. But Pedro was persuasive and Edward's sense of chivalry came to the fore. Whatever the respective merits of Pedro and Henry of Trastámara (as persons, Henry appeared vastly preferable), Pedro was, in Edward's eyes, the rightful King of Castile. No monarch's illegitimate son should ever sit on a throne. Additionally, had his sister Joan not died of the Black Death while travelling to Castile many years earlier, he and Pedro would have been brothers-in-law. Edward might also have been itching to lead another military campaign after several years of peace.

It is, however, possible that the prince had grave doubts about the wisdom of aiding Pedro. The prince sent a delegation to his father seeking his instructions in the matter. Wishing to maintain and strengthen the Castilian-English alliance, the king strongly supported Pedro. A recent biographer blames the king, not the prince, for the decision to intervene. Based on documentary evidence, he argues that the king ordered his son to help Pedro regain his crown and that the son, ever obedient to his father, reluctantly obeyed.[66]

A military expedition, especially one into Iberia, was extraordinarily expensive and the prince had little money to spare. But Pedro promised to reimburse Edward for the expenses of a military expedition that would replace him on the throne. It appears Edward never considered how and when a small country like Castile could raise enough revenue to pay his expenses. Pedro also offered to leave two daughters in Aquitaine as hostages until the debt was repaid. (The daughters later married two of the prince's younger brothers, including John of Gaunt.) Whatever the reasons for the decision, Edward agreed to help Pedro regain the throne. He even agreed to bear the entire cost, subject to Pedro's later reimbursing him for those costs. When King Charles learned of this, he was thrilled, anticipating that the venture would end badly for the prince. But the king also cautiously advised Henry of Trastámara to avoid a pitched battle, as the prince could draw on veterans of his earlier campaigns, the best knights on the continent. The prince, he warned, was invincible in battle.

Once the decision to help Pedro was made, Edward acted decisively. He assembled an army and, bolstered by troops under John of Gaunt, prepared to invade Castile with Pedro at his side. In January 1367, while preparations were ongoing, Joan gave birth to the couple's second son, named Richard, after the Lion-Hearted son of King Henry II and Eleanor of Aquitaine. This second son was destined to succeed Edward III as King Richard II. Edward now had two seemingly healthy sons and was well on the way to securing the succession after his own expected time as king. Edward did not pause long to celebrate the birth, however. He had a war to fight.

Edward negotiated with the local nobility to obtain safe passage over the Pyrenees into Castile. In February 1367, he led his troops over the pass at Roncesvalles, where, as recounted in the Song of Roland, the legendary Roland died heroically protecting Charlemagne's retreat from Moorish Spain some six

---

[66] Michael Jones, *The Black Prince: England's Greatest Medieval Warrior*, Pegasus Books (2018), pp. 294-97 (hereafter Michael Jones, *The Black Prince*).

centuries previously. A winter crossing of the Pyrenees was always perilous, but the army met no opposition and managed to arrive in Castile intact. There, they had to deal with Henry's army. Bolstered by French troops, it was probably substantially larger than Edward's, perhaps twice its size, although this is not certain today. Estimates by contemporary chroniclers varied widely. Whatever the relative size of the armies, the prince remained confident. He had prevailed in the past against long odds and with a veteran army, he believed he could do so again.

But once they were down from the mountains, the campaign began badly. The troops suffered seriously from lack of provisions and the wet and windy weather. Henry's army made a surprise night attack against a portion of the prince's army that, according to widespread contemporary opinion, the prince had not properly prepared for. A close friend of the prince was killed along with many of the friend's comrades-in-arms. This night attack had a dual effect. It made Edward more determined than ever to prevail and avenge his friend's death. It also gave Henry misplaced confidence. Edward advanced towards the river Najerilla, where Henry waited defiantly. Attempts at negotiating a settlement failed and the armies prepared for battle. Confident of victory, Henry ignored King Charles's advice to avoid a pitched battle.

On 3 April 1367, near the town of Najera, the armies clashed. The battle was a reprise of Crecy and Poitiers, a complete tactical victory for the prince. After a night march, Edward's forces surprised and attacked the enemy's flank instead of its prepared defensive position. Rapid volleys from the longbows began the action and a determined attack by dismounted warriors followed. A cavalry charge against Henry's retreating army completed the rout. Thousands of the enemy died that day. Henry managed to flee from the wreckage of his army and lived to fight another day. Not so fortunate was Bertrand du Guesclin, the great French knight. Fighting where the fighting was thickest, as he usually did, the knight was taken prisoner. Later he was forced to pay a large ransom to regain his freedom. The prince's army suffered far fewer casualties.

The victory at Najera allowed Pedro the Cruel to regain his throne. But Edward benefited not in the slightest from his victory. Despite his promise to do so, Pedro never paid Edward a single coin for any of his expenses. He probably never intended to do so. The ransom money Edward received from his noble captives did not come close to paying for the heavy cost of the war. The debts he incurred effectively bankrupted him. Edward's army remained in Spain for months in hot and miserable weather while waiting to receive the expected payments. When the army finally retreated back over the pass at Roncesvalles, disease and malnutrition had greatly weakened it. One contemporary chronicler stated that after the battle, "so many of the English died in Spain of dysentery and other diseases that scarce one man in five returned to England."[67] The statement is probably exaggerated, but the army, clearly, suffered greatly.

The utter futility of the Najera campaign became clear over the next two years. Henry of Trustmark managed to return to Castile, where he overthrew, captured and murdered Pedro. Henry remained King of Castile the remaining ten years of his life. Once again, Castile became an ally of the French, not the English. Edward made no effort to aid Pedro a second time.

Sometime during the Castilian campaign, Edward became ill with a debilitating disease that he never fully recovered from and that eventually killed him. No one knows exactly what it was. It might have been dysentery, or malaria, or dropsy (or more modern, oedema). It might have been some slow form of cancer. It might have been something entirely different. What is known for certain is that it was beyond the ken of doctors in those days. There was no known cure or even effective treatment. Sometimes Edward would be better, sometimes worse. In his bad days, he often could not walk or ride a horse and had to remain in bed or be carried on a stretcher.

Somehow Edward had to raise money to pay the debts incurred in the Castilian campaign. Once again, in January 1368, he imposed a *fouage* tax on the people of Aquitaine. The local barons protested. Some appealed for relief to the King of France, as Edward's overlord in his role as the lord in Aquitaine. Always seeking to cause trouble for the English, the king sent envoys to the prince in early 1369 demanding that he appear in person before the *parlement* in Paris to answer to charges of mismanagement. The prince famously responded that he would willingly come to Paris at the appointed time, but he would only do so wearing a helmet and with 60,000 men at his back.

Such defiance was insufficient. The prince was sick and bankrupt. Many of the local nobles and towns rose against him and declared their allegiance to the King of France. Another round of warfare ensued, but the prince could not stem the tide. Because of his poor health, the prince's brother, John of Gaunt, replaced

---

[67] G.H. Martin, ed. and transl., *Knighton's Chronicle, 1337-96*, Clarendon Press (1995), p. 195. Henry Knighton was a canon at St Mary of the Meadows abbey near Leicester. He died around 1396 and is considered reasonably reliable.

him as lord in Aquitaine. But the prince did have one more battle left to fight. The Bishop of Limoges, a trusted friend of the prince, treacherously surrendered the city to the French. The prince swore he would regain it. And he did.

Edward led a small army to Limoges and laid siege to it. A month later, on the fourteenth anniversary of the Battle of Poitiers, 19 September 1370, the besiegers broke into the city. The ailing Edward followed, carried on a stretcher. True to his chivalric ideals, he spared the bishop who had betrayed the city. But, according to the chronicler Froissart, he took vengeance on the ordinary inhabitants, who were mostly innocent in the affair: "The prince, the Duke of Lancaster [i.e., John of Gaunt; Henry of Grosmont had died in 1361], the Earl of Cambridge, the Earl of Pembroke, Sir Guichard d'Angle and the rest entered the city on foot with their companies and their hordes of hangers-on. All of them were equipped for evil... It was heart-rending to see the inhabitants throwing themselves to the ground as he passed, crying out 'Mercy, noble lord, Mercy!' He was so enraged that he heard them not. No one listened to their appeals as the invaders ran through with their swords everyone, they found in their way... Three thousand people, men, women and children died on that day... And the looting did not stop until the whole city was stripped and left in flames."[68] (As discussed below, today many doubt the truth of this description.)

The recapture and alleged sack of Limoges did the prince no good. Due largely to Froissart's eloquent words, its main effect was to sully his reputation for centuries. It may have contributed to later historians calling him the Black Prince. A few days after the battle, he learned that his namesake son, Edward, had died, news that devastated him. In January 1371, he returned to England after an absence of nearly eight years, an ill and defeated man. The prince managed to cling to life another five years, but he was never again the dynamic leader he had been. In October 1372, he formally relinquished his principality of Aquitaine and Gascony, claiming it no longer provided sufficient revenues to cover his expenses.

The last few years of Edward's life were relatively uneventful. The war in France was going poorly, but the prince was unable to help. Never again would he lead soldiers into battle. His health sometimes improved, sometimes got worse. The end came in the spring of 1376. By that time, the king himself had become old and feeble. The prince's brother, John of Gaunt, the Duke of Lancaster, had become the leader of a government that was increasingly

---

[68] Dan Jones, *The Plantagenets*, p. 436.

perceived as ineffective and corrupt. A Parliament, later known as the "Good Parliament," sat from April 28 to July 10 of that year, making it the longest-running parliament in England to that time. It received its name because of reforming steps it took on behalf of the populace and against official corruption.

During the early stages of the Good Parliament, Edward was as active as his weakening health permitted. He was considered a leader of the reforming party that opposed John of Gaunt. At one point, a royal official, who was charged with major financial fraud, sent the prince a bribe of one thousand pounds to gain his support, a huge sum in those days. To his credit, the prince refused the bribe and the official was later convicted and punished.

But it soon became apparent that the prince was dying. In his last days, he threw open the doors of his house to receive visitors. Because of his own impending death and the king's weakening condition, it became increasingly apparent that his nine-year-old son, Richard, would soon inherit the throne. The prince did what he could to protect his son's inheritance. The king and John of Gaunt came to his home. Fearful that John might desire the throne for himself, Edward begged both his father and brother to protect Richard's inheritance. They promised to support the boy and John swore an oath to that effect, possibly with some misgivings. (When the time came, John took no steps to oppose Richard's coronation.) Edward also met with his wife, Joan and Richard himself. Many members of the nobility also came by; each swore to support Richard's accession.

On 8 June 1376, one week before what would have been his 46th birthday, while the Good Parliament was still in session, Edward of Woodstock, later called the Black Prince, the greatest military hero of his age, died, not gloriously in battle, but slowly and agonisingly of a debilitating illness. The English, if not the French, mourned his death as they have mourned very few. The people overlooked his faults because of his overarching virtues. He made England great in battle and served as a symbol of hope and defiance in the face of the Black Death, one of the worst scourges humanity has ever encountered, a catastrophe no one could understand. He had also served as an object of hope when the war with France was going badly.

The prince's funeral was held on 29 September 1376, with great pomp and considerable circumspection at Canterbury Cathedral. He was buried in the cathedral beside Thomas Becket, as his will had directed. His tomb is still there, along with many items commemorating his life. The prince died with many debts still outstanding. The king did what he could to ensure that the debts would be repaid and, it appears, most were.

King Edward III followed his son in death in 1377, which meant that the Black Prince died a single year too soon to become king himself. The prince's surviving son, Richard, did inherit the throne at the age of ten years as Richard II, although he was destined to be overthrown in 1399 by the son of John of Gaunt, the Lancastrian Duke who became King Henry IV. (These events laid the seeds of the Wars of the Roses a few generations later.) The prince's wife, Joan, never married again. She died in 1385, still beloved although probably no longer as beautiful as in her earlier years.

The Black Prince was perhaps the finest exemplar of chivalry the Age of Chivalry ever produced in England. He was religious—at least superficially in ways similar to others of his class, but possibly sincerely—literate and well-read, especially enjoying tales of chivalry and books on conducting oneself chivalrously. He enjoyed music and art and, when not on campaign, the good life. He also pursued typical avocations of his class such as jousting, falconry and hunting. He was generous to a fault with his supporters and those who served him well, one reason he could never seem to live within his means. He lived by two mottoes that represented his own view of himself. One, spelt variously as "houmout" or "houmont," is a French word generally translated as "courage." The second, variously given as "ich dene" or "ich dien," is essentially the modern German words, "ich diene," meaning, "I serve."

Most historians agree that the Black Prince exemplified chivalry at its best. Did he also exemplify it at its worst? Generations of historians have believed so, taking their cue largely from Jean Froissart's description of the dreadful massacre following the sack of Limoges in 1370. More recent scholarship has generally concluded that Froissart greatly exaggerated the actual events and that only around 300, not 3,000, inhabitants were slain. But even reducing the numbers to 300 would suggest the prince had total disdain for commoners, at least those of the enemy. A recent historian, while acknowledging that Froissart "may have embroidered his account and exaggerated the number of deaths by some tenfold," states: "It was a pathetic sight: The Black Prince carried around on a litter, commanding the deaths of innocent people in a fruitless, spiteful revenge."[69]

---

[69] Dan Jones, *The Plantagenets*, p. 436.

On the other hand, the author of a very recent biography of the prince consulted other sources, including a recently discovered letter the prince himself wrote a few days after the siege and records of a lawsuit between two merchants that was litigated in France years after the battle. He concluded that Froissart's account, which he described as the "the greatest slur on his [the Black Prince's] reputation," was merely "black propaganda." He argued that a portion of the city of Limoges had remained loyal to the English, that the *French* garrison was responsible for massacring citizens of that part of the city and that the Black Prince, rather than perpetrating the massacre of citizens, had tried to prevent it. The author "think[s] it is time to dismiss this slur by Froissart..."[70]

Whatever one thinks exactly happened after the sack of Limoges, the fact remains that Edward, and, indeed, chivalry itself had little regard for the common people. The kind of warfare called *chevauchee*, which chivalry accepted and even considered glorious, was intended to harm ordinary people as much as possible. Edward excelled in such tactics. The practise of ransoming prisoners also contributed to the tribulations the common people suffered. Noble prisoners could generally provide a ransom that exceeded the cost of capturing and incarcerating them. Commoners could not. Thus, commoners were often mowed down when nobles would have been taken prisoner. Because the prince was so effective in this kind of warfare, arguably he does exemplify chivalry at its worst, as well as at its best. The Black Prince might not have been crueller than chivalry permitted, but chivalry itself permitted great cruelty. (Of course, something similar could be said of warfare in general, especially during modern times.)

During his earlier days, the prince seemed to have had a positive outlook on life. Years of slowly wasting away of a disease no one could understand undoubtedly changed his outlook. His will contained detailed instructions for his funeral and burial, which were followed precisely. At his direction, a French poem (translated here into modern English) was inscribed on his tomb to serve both as his epitaph and as an admonition to those who read it:

"Such as thou art, sometime was I.
Such as I am, such shalt thou be.
I thought little on th'our of Death
So long as I enjoyed breath.
But now a wretched captive am I,
Deep in the ground, lo here I lie.

---

[70] Michael Jones, *The Black Prince*, pp. 366-7, 372-3, 405-8.

My beauty great, is all quite gone,

My flesh is wasted to the bone."[71]

These words are especially poignant coming from a man who came agonisingly close and, thus, agonisingly far, from achieving his ultimate goal in life, a goal he had been trained for since his early childhood—to become not just a prince but the King of England. His death with this goal unrealised must have been every bit as bitter as that of his imprisoned forebear Robert, Duke of Normandy.

---

[71] Dan Jones, *The Plantagenets*, p. 441.

Chapter 7
The Wars of the Roses, Part I: Richard, Duke of York and Edward of Lancaster

The death of Edward, the Black Prince, set in motion the series of events that led to the convulsions in the second half of the fifteenth century called the Wars of the Roses. As is well known, the wars pitted two branches of the Plantagenet family—Lancaster and York. The name given to the wars refers to the emblems of the respective branches—the red rose of Lancaster and the white rose of York. The early stages of the wars resulted in two heirs to the throne becoming heirs who never reigned, one on each side. One was King Henry VI's only son, Edward, known as Edward of Westminster, after his birthplace, or Edward of Lancaster, after his lineage. The other was Richard, the third Duke of York, who was descended from King Edward III through both his father and his mother.

When King Edward III died in 1377, he was succeeded by his grandson (the Black Prince's son), who became King Richard II. But in 1399, Richard's cousin, John of Gaunt's son, Henry, the Duke of Lancaster, overthrew him and became King Henry IV, the first Lancastrian king. Henry's prevailing over Richard set the precedent that the strength of dynastic claim alone was not always enough to become or remain king. Richard, not Henry, had the valid dynastic claim, but his misrule gave Henry his chance to obtain the crown. This proved that, at least with the consent of Parliament, someone with a lesser claim, but more ability, might become king.

Henry IV was succeeded by his son, Henry V, a strong and popular king and the victor of the 1415 Battle of Agincourt, the last great English victory in the Hundred Years' War. But Henry V died prematurely of dysentery in 1422 at the age of 35, leaving behind an infant son, who became King Henry VI, the third King of the Lancastrian branch. Due to his father's victories that led to the 1420 Treaty of Troyes, Henry also became—for a while—the King of France as an infant, when the French King Charles VI died shortly after Henry V's death. Henry was the only Englishman to be King of both countries. A long and difficult regency ensued until Henry came of age. During these years, partly due to the inspired leadership of Joan of Arc, England slowly lost its grip on France. Ultimately, although it won the major battles (Crecy, Poitiers and Agincourt), it lost the war. The war ended in 1453 with the port city of Calais remaining as the only English possession in France. Calais was all the English had to show for over 100 years of fighting.

Matters did not improve greatly when Henry came of age and assumed kingship on his own. He was a weak and ineffectual king and suffered recurrent periods of insanity. Exceptionally pious, Henry might have made an excellent monk, but he was a failure as a king. The Yorkists, led by Richard, rose to challenge him. When Henry VI proved to be weak and especially as the war in France was being lost, Richard sought more influence over the government and, eventually, the throne itself. To support his claim to the throne, he, backed by his Yorkist allies, contended that his dynastic claim was superior to that of the Lancastrians.

It all went back to the sons of Edward III. When Richard II died without an heir (probably by murder), the line of the Black Prince, the oldest son, came to an end. John of Gaunt, the father of Henry IV and thus the progenitor of the Lancastrian line, was the third son of those who survived infancy. The Yorkist leader, Richard, Duke of York, was descended on his father's side from Edmund of Langley, another son of King Edward III, the first Duke of York. Edmund was the *fourth* son. So, any claim based on this line was inferior to the Lancastrian claim. But through his mother, Richard was descended from Lionel of Antwerp, Duke of Clarence, who was the *second* son. Based on this descent (not, interestingly enough, the Yorkist descent), the Yorkists asserted that Richard had a superior claim to the throne. If one disregards the fact that Henry VI was the son and grandson of recognised kings of England and focuses solely on the sons of Edward III, then, under English law, arguably Richard did have a better claim to the throne than Henry.

Apart from any dynastic claim to the throne, Richard, as a direct descendant of Edward III, became one of the leading and wealthiest noblemen in the country. Born in September 1411, he acquired great wealth and titles from both sides of his family at an early age. His mother died when he was born. His father was beheaded in 1415 for his alleged involvement in a plot against Henry V, making

Richard an orphan at four. Around the same time, his uncle, the second Duke of York, was killed in the Battle of Agincourt. As the uncle was childless, Richard assumed the title and became the third Duke of York. On his mother's side, he became the Earl of March, a fabulously wealthy inheritance. He was also the Earl of Cambridge and Earl of Ulster. He owned property in many areas of England and Ireland and, especially, in the Welsh marches, the territory on the border of England and Wales.

Richard did not assert any claim to the throne until late in his life, but from an early age, he played an active role in government, as his position warranted. While an orphan, he became the ward of Ralph Neville, Earl of Westmoreland, one of England's major magnates. Ralph had several daughters, one of whom was Cecily, who became known as the Rose of Raby, after the castle in which she was born. Ralph betrothed Cecily to Richard at an early age and they married at an uncertain date, possibly around October 1429. They were to have several children, including four sons who survived infancy, two of whom became kings of England. The Neville family would become a critical ally to Richard in years to come. In May 1426, John, Duke of Bedford, a younger brother of Henry V, knighted Richard. Richard was present at the formal coronations of Henry as King of England (in November 1429 at Westminster Abbey) and King of France (in December 1431 at the Cathedral of Notre Dame in Paris). (In the meantime, the son of Charles VI had been crowned as King Charles VII at Reims as a rival French King.) In April 1433, Richard was admitted to the Order of the Garter.

During these times, Richard did not appear to be anything but a loyal subject of the king. In his early years of service, while the Hundred Years' War was raging, he contented himself with working within the government. Two of the king's uncles (younger brothers of Henry V), John, Duke of Bedford, and Humphrey, Duke of Gloucester, led the regency government during the king's minority. Bedford led the English military forces in France during Joan of Arc (active 1429-30) and later. Despite Bedford's substantial ability and determination to prosecute the war, the English position deteriorated. The 1435 Treaty of Arras, in which the Duchy of Burgundy switched alliances from England to France, was a diplomatic fiasco. Bedford died without an heir in September 1435. A few months later, Richard, the only remaining magnate descended from Edward III other than Humphrey, was named to succeed Bedford as the English commander in France. His term, however, was scheduled to last only one year, which limited what he could accomplish.

In France during the years 1436-7, Richard played an administrative role primarily, largely leaving military matters to his generals. The English scored some temporary military successes during his time in France. Nevertheless, in 1437, Richard yielded his position and returned to England, where he continued to act as a major figure supporting the increasingly burdensome and unpopular war. In November of that year, King Henry, now nearly 16 years old, was deemed to be able to rule on his own behalf and he assumed full powers. Over time, English leaders divided into two camps, one determined to prosecute the war to a victorious conclusion, the other seeking diplomatic ways to get out. Richard and Humphrey were leaders of the pro-war faction. The king himself increasingly favoured the peace party. As a result, Richard found himself largely an outsider in the king's government.

However, as the situation in France continued to deteriorate, the king once again appointed Richard his lieutenant in France, a duty he performed from 1440-5. Richard was based mainly in Normandy during these years. His wife Cecily joined him. Their first three children, including sons Edward (later King Edward IV) and Edmund, were born in Rouen. One of Richard's major military efforts was to raise the French siege of Pontoise, a critical English outpost on the Seine near Paris. He attempted, but failed, to force the French to fight a major battle. Ultimately, his manoeuvring failed and his army was forced to retreat to Normandy. Pontoise fell to the French in September 1441. This was a serious blow to the English and was the last military campaign Richard led personally in France. Increasing difficulty in receiving sufficient funding from England hampered his war efforts more and more over time.

While maintaining a largely defensive posture in Normandy, Richard turned to diplomacy. He was able to negotiate a truce with Burgundy in 1443. But the same year his position was undercut (or at least he so perceived it) when the king gave John Beaufort, the newly created Duke of Somerset, command of an army of some 8,000 men to operate in Gascony, far from the centre of Richard's war effort in Normandy. The division of authority in France between Richard and Somerset was never made clear; Richard viewed Somerset's role as reducing his own. This John Beaufort was a grandson of John of Gaunt and his long time mistress (later wife) Katherine Swynford. John and Katherine's children were illegitimate when born, but they were retroactively made legitimate when they finally married late in life. By law, however, their progeny were not supposed to be included in any line of inheritance to the throne (a rule that would later be disregarded; chapter 9).

The Duke of Somerset accomplished little in Gascony and he soon returned to England a failure, where he died in 1444. But his presence in Gascony and the resources diverted to him and away from Richard, made it impossible for Richard to accomplish much against the French in Normandy. After the Duke's death, another Beaufort, his brother Edmund, replaced him as Duke of Somerset. These early experiences with the Beauforts probably initiated Richard's dislike for the family. Richard and the Beauforts, especially Edmund, the new Duke of Somerset, were to become implacable opponents in the upcoming political struggles.

In the meantime, a wife had to be found for King Henry. After various possibilities were considered, Henry and his advisors settled on Margaret of Anjou, a niece of the current French King, Charles VII. This Charles was the Dauphin who was crowned king as a rival king to Henry due to Joan of Arc's heroics. Henry hoped, vainly, as it turned out, that the marriage might lead to peace between the countries. Around this time, Richard and Margaret met under relatively friendly circumstances. They were to become bitter and ultimately deadly enemies. The king and Margaret were married on 23 April 1445, when the king was 23 years old and she 15. In sharp contrast to her husband, Margaret proved to be a strong and determined woman. At times, because the king himself was weak and vacillating, she became the power behind the throne. Somewhat like the role Queen Matilda played in aiding her husband, King Stephen, in his protracted struggle with Empress Maud (chapter 3), Margaret would become, increasingly over time, her husband's strongest supporter and most important personal advisor.

Richard left France and returned to England and English politics in 1445. Edmund Beaufort, the new Duke of Somerset, replaced him as a lieutenant in France. In English governmental circles, despite his lofty noble status, Richard remained largely an outsider. Along with Humphrey, Duke of Gloucester, he was considered a member of the pro-war party when Henry and his chosen advisors wanted to end the war. Richard attended Parliament and the king's council meetings but spent most of his time administering his large estates. Humphrey died, also without an heir, in February 1447, which meant that there was at yet no heir to the throne descended from Henry V. Richard was now unquestionably the leading nobleman of the realm. Should Henry VI remain childless, he was the logical person to succeed him, a possibility the Lancastrians dreaded.

Possibly to get him out of the way, but also because he was the Earl of Ulster, Richard was named the crown's lieutenant in Ireland in 1447. After some delays, he and his family moved to Ireland in 1449, where he remained for about a year. During that year, Richard solicited the friendship of various important families and magnates, with considerable success. The Irish supported him in his later endeavours and Ireland always offered a safe haven when Richard needed one. However, at this point of his career, Richard appeared to be, and probably was, a loyal subject of the Lancastrian King Henry.

Richard returned, again, to England in late 1450 to find a changed political situation. Loss of public confidence in the government caused by military failures in France and official corruption, as well as the king's personal weakness, led to civic unrest, culminating in 1450 in what was called Jack Cade's Rebellion. For a while, the rebels obtained control of London, where they executed two of the leading citizens. The unpopular Duke of Somerset, the most powerful official in Henry's government, was placed in the Tower of London for his own protection. Richard did not instigate or participate in the rebellion—he was still in Ireland—but he might have sympathised with it, at least until it became too violent. He definitely benefited from it. Although the rebellion was put down quickly and Cade himself was killed, the events exposed the weakness of the Lancastrian government.

Richard now made his first play for personal power, although it does not appear he sought at this time to replace Henry as King. After the collapse of Cade's Rebellion, he landed in England from Ireland accompanied by troops. Gaining forces as he went, he entered London on 27 September 1450, with some 3,000 to 5,000 troops. He met briefly with the king, a meeting that resolved nothing. Richard insisted, probably sincerely, that his intentions were peaceful and that he was loyal to the king; he merely wanted to remove some of his corrupt and evil advisors and improve the government. His main target was Edmund Beaufort, the Duke of Somerset, whom he blamed for the military failures in France. Richard positioned himself as a popular reformer, trying to eliminate incompetence and corruption in the government. Some of the grievances Cade's rebels had presented were reflected in Richard's demands for reform. Richard was popular with the Commons in Parliament—indeed, the Commons elected Richard's own chamberlain as its speaker that December—but not so much with the lords. The king, or at least his key advisors and certainly the queen, viewed Richard as a threat to the king himself and did all they could to stymie him. Somerset was released from the Tower of London and restored to his position of power.

In 1452, Richard again tried to increase his influence in the government at the expense of the Duke of Somerset. He sought to be recognised as Henry's heir presumptive, as the king had produced no heir of his own. Because the royal marriage had been childless for several years and the king seemed incapable of doing much of anything, many believed he would never produce an heir. However, once again, Richard received little support from the great magnates. In a confrontation with the king and Somerset at Dartford in Kent, he was forced to back down. He was allowed to present his grievances against Somerset (without effect), but he was effectively arrested and taken a virtual prisoner to London. Two weeks later, he was released, but only after he was humiliated by being forced to swear an oath of loyalty to the king at St Paul's Cathedral. His cause was waning. But that would soon change.

1453 was an eventful year for Richard and all of England. The Hundred Years' War finally came to an end with a crushing English defeat at the July 17 Battle of Castillon in Gascony. All English possessions on the continent were lost except for Calais. But this bad news was tempered by good news for the Lancastrians on the dynastic front. Early in 1453, to the consternation of the Yorkists and delight of the Lancastrians, the queen announced that, after almost eight years of marriage, she had become pregnant. On October 13, she gave birth at Westminster to a son, named Edward, a boy destined to become the king and queen's only child. Now Richard could no longer credibly claim to be Henry's heir. Because the king's marriage had been childless for so long and the king had seemed sexually incompetent, rumours abounded that Edward was not really the king's son. The Duke of Somerset was one of those suspected of being the real father. However, no evidence existed then or now that anyone other than Henry fathered Edward and the king never doubted (at least publicly) that Edward was his son. In 1454, Edward was invested as Prince of Wales at Windsor Castle, official recognition of his status as the king's son and heir. His mother was the one mostly entrusted with raising him when he was young.

During the same year of 1453, Henry, who had mental problems off and on his entire life, suffered a mental breakdown. In August, two months before his son was born, he became hopelessly insane. For a long time, he was catatonic.

He could not even recognise his son. Because the king was incapacitated, a regency government needed to be formed. Over the strong opposition of the queen, who favoured the Duke of Somerset, Richard, supported by the Neville family, managed to have himself named Protector of the Realm. He appointed as chancellor his brother-in-law, Richard Neville, the Earl of Salisbury. He ordered the Duke of Somerset again incarcerated in the Tower of London. Otherwise, Richard tried to exercise his authority even-handedly. One chronicler wrote that "for a whole year, he governed the whole realm of England most nobly and in the best way."[72] He gave no indication of seeking the throne for himself.

During these years, the rivalry between the two opposing sides—Lancaster and York—gradually developed into enmity. Somerset and the powerful Percy family of the north, headed by the Earl of Northumberland, supported the Lancaster side. The Percys had long feuded with the Nevilles. The queen, of course, strongly supported her husband. The Neville family was Richard's main ally. While Henry's insanity lasted, Richard was in the ascendant and the queen's influence was insignificant.

Unfortunately for the Yorkist cause, Henry regained his sanity during the Christmas season of 1454. He now recognised his son for the first time. According to one source, "the queen came to him and brought my Lord Prince with her. And then he asked what the prince's name was, and the queen told him Edward, and then he held up his hands and thanked God thereof. And he said he never knew till that time."[73] Now able to act again, the king removed Richard and the Earl of Salisbury from their positions as Protector of the Realm and chancellor. He released Somerset from the Tower and restored him to power, naming him the Captain of Calais, England's sole possession in France and the site of a major naval force. The queen regained her influence over the king. She had come to believe that Richard was a serious threat to her husband's crown. It is uncertain exactly when she developed a great hatred for Richard, but they became increasingly bitter enemies over time, especially on her part.

The king and his advisors, including Margaret, called for a Great Council that would consist primarily of their supporters and Richard's enemies, a Council

---

[72] John Watts, *Oxford Dictionary of National Biography, Richard of York, Third Duke of York*, Oxford University Press (2011).

[73] R.A. Griffiths, *Oxford Dictionary of National Biography, Edward of Westminster, Prince of Wales*, Oxford University Press (2004) (hereafter *ODNB, Edward of Westminster*), spelling modernized by the author.

that greatly threatened Richard and the Neville family. With justification, Richard and the Nevilles feared that Margaret and the Duke of Somerset intended their destruction. The Council was to meet in Leicester, far from Richard's power base. To meet the threat, Richard prepared for war. His likely aim at this stage was still not to become king but only to remove what he viewed as the king's evil counsellors and to eliminate the queen's ability to threaten his own position.

Richard and the Earl of Salisbury recruited an army, aided by Salisbury's son, another Richard Neville who had become the powerful Earl of Warwick by marriage. This Earl of Warwick would go down in history as the "Kingmaker" for reasons that will become apparent. (He could also have been called the Kingbreaker.) Richard and the two Nevilles moved to block the route from London to Leicester. Somerset attempted to raise troops, but he acted too late to raise an army to match Richard's. He had around 2,000 poorly trained troops, Richard and the Nevilles perhaps twice that number. The opposing forces met at St Albans, north of London.

On 22 May 1455, the First Battle of St Albans was fought. It is generally considered the beginning of the Wars of the Roses. As battles go (and especially compared with later battles in these wars), it was small, over within an hour with few casualties among the common soldiers. Partly due to the heroics of the Earl of Warwick, the Yorkists won a resounding victory. The Duke of Somerset was killed, as were Henry Percy, Earl of Northumberland and another prominent Lancastrian leader, Lord Thomas Clifford, an in-law of the Percy family. The Yorkists also took many prisoners, among them the king himself, who had been slightly wounded by an arrow and may again have lost his sanity. Richard and his allies assured the king that they remained his faithful servants and treated him well. They took the king to London, parading him before the people and showing him great honour.

The battle sent shockwaves throughout England, as it signified that what had been political rivalry had escalated into warfare. The Yorkists had managed to kill three of their most prominent enemies (or perhaps, until then, merely opponents), but they had acquired implacable, determined enemies in the sons of those killed. The nature of the struggle between Lancaster and York would never be the same.

But, for a while, peace seemed to return to England. The parties appeared to want to return to the time of peaceful rivalry, limited to political manoeuvring, rather than open warfare. Richard had Henry his effective prisoner, but he had to keep him safe. As long as he had Henry prisoner, Richard was in control. But Henry's death would lead to the king's son, the not-quite two-year-old Edward of Westminster, becoming king. In that event and during the new king's minority, Queen Margaret and her faction would undoubtedly dominate the regency government that would have to be formed. Richard was not yet strong enough to assert any claim of his own. With Henry still nominally king, Parliament appointed Richard Protector of the Realm, the same position he had held a few years previously when Henry was insane. In this role, Richard appointed the Earl of Warwick the Captain of Calais to replace the dead Duke of Somerset. Eventually, Henry was released from captivity on the understanding that Richard and the Nevilles would play prominent roles in his government. Margaret strongly opposed any such notion.

Everyone coexisted for a while. The ultimate symbol of apparent peace and accord occurred in 1458 when the king organised what was called a "Love Day." This was one of the few times the king himself took the initiative to try to end the dispute and resolve his problems. On 25 March of that year, after much negotiation and persuasion, aided by the Archbishop of Canterbury, the feuding parties marched together in a procession in London from Westminster to St Paul's Cathedral. The queen walked hand in hand with Richard and others acted similarly. The sons of the nobles killed at St Albans represented their fathers in a show of peace. The king followed behind, presumably thrilled with what he had accomplished that day. The Love Day must have been an astounding spectacle for the London onlookers—the queen and Richard, known to be bitter enemies, acting as friends.

The public display of friendship was impressive and, to those who hoped it was real, inspiring. But it was all for show, to make the king happy and, for some at least, in the hope that appearance might become a reality. Little was actually accomplished, as is usually the case with artificial shows of friendship among enemies when the underlying causes of the enmity are unresolved. The queen still controlled the king and was determined that her son would succeed him. The Yorkists still distrusted the queen and, increasingly, believed that Richard should replace Henry or, at a minimum, become his heir in place of the king's son.

Fighting resumed in 1459. The Earl of Warwick, in his position as Captain of Calais, attacked neutral shipping in the English Channel. He was summoned to London to explain himself, but he refused to attend. A meeting of the royal council was scheduled to be held in June at Coventry. Fearing arrest on charges of treason, Richard and the Earls of Salisbury and Warwick refused to attend. The Lancastrians, led by Margaret, raised an army. The Yorkists raised their own army and, under the command of the Earl of Salisbury, achieved an initial victory at the Battle of Blore Heath in September.

Richard wrote to the king asserting his continued loyalty; all he wanted, he claimed, was his right to be involved in the government and impose needed reforms. But the Lancastrians, with a much larger army than the Yorkists could muster at that time, pursued them. The Lancastrian army, nominally led by the king himself, decisively defeated the Yorkists at the Battle of Ludford Bridge on 12 October 1459. The Earls of Salisbury and Warwick and Richard's oldest son, Edward, the Earl of March, fled into exile at Calais. This Edward was 17 years old, old enough to become a force in his own right. Richard himself sought refuge in friendly Ireland with his son Edmund. Richard's wife, Cecily and their two youngest sons, George, aged 10 and Richard, aged 7 (destined to become King Richard III, one of the most notorious and controversial figures in British history), were captured at Ludlow Castle and imprisoned in Coventry.

The victorious Lancastrians called for a parliament to be held in Coventry in November 1459. Later called the "Parliament of Devils," it was stacked with Lancaster supporters and, especially, adherents of Queen Margaret. Richard and the Nevilles were not invited to participate. The Parliament officially recognised Henry VI's son, Edward, as the heir and future king. Edward would soon receive nominal governance of Wales. Parliament's main order of business, however, was to pass bills of attainder for treason against both Neville earls as well as Richard and his two oldest sons, Edward and Edmund, the Earl of Rutland. The bills deprived them of their rights to own property or possess any title of nobility, as well as the right to bequeath property or nobility to their heirs. It also came with a death sentence, one that, however, would be difficult to execute given that the targets were far away. Yorkist fortunes appeared to have reached a nadir. But fortune could shift rapidly during these wars.

The only way for the Yorkists to reverse the bills of attainder was by military action. A successful invasion of England was necessary. The Irish offered Richard, still the crown's lieutenant in that country, support both militarily and financially. His earlier solicitation of friendship there was paying dividends. The Duke of Somerset was appointed governor of Calais, centre of English naval might in the English Channel, but he failed to dislodge the Earl of Warwick from the city. Warwick, still acting as the Captain of Calais and in charge of the naval forces there, controlled the English Channel. He was able to sail to Ireland in March 1460 to confer with Richard before returning to Calais.

In June 1460, the Neville earls and Edward, Earl of March, sailed from Calais and landed at Sandwich, where the people of Kent welcomed them and offered their support. With their forces bolstered, they marched on London, where the populace also welcomed and aided them. With their augmented army, they marched north. Aided by treachery—Edmund Grey, later made Earl of Kent, who commanded part of the Lancastrian army, switched sides from Lancaster to York—they won a resounding victory on 10 July 1460, at the Battle of Northampton. The Yorkists captured King Henry once again, although they again took care to treat him well. The king was taken to London, where he remained a prisoner. However, Queen Margaret and her son were not at the scene of the battle and were safe from harm. Cecily and her young sons were quickly released from their captivity.

Richard remained in Ireland during these events, returning to England only in September. He reunited with his wife in early October. They entered London together in grand, almost regal, style and moved into the royal palace. Fortune had indeed changed. Richard now had choices. He could merely become Protector again, as he had been before. He could assert his claim to be Henry's heir, displacing Henry's son Edward. Or he could seek the throne immediately himself. Subsequent events demonstrated that he had opted for the last choice. Dramatic events were soon to occur.

A new Parliament met in London in October 1460. Because of the changed circumstances, this Parliament's composition was much different than the previous year's Parliament of Devils. It repealed that Parliament's acts, including the acts of attainder against Richard and his family and allies. Seeking more, Richard reiterated the Yorkist claim that the Lancastrian line of kings, descended from Edward III's third son, was illegitimate and that only Richard, descended from that king's second son, was the legitimate king. At an early session of Parliament, Richard, "with the pomp of a great following, arrived in no small exultation of spirit; for he came with horns and trumpets and men at arms and very many other servants." He strode straight towards the unoccupied "royal throne and there he laid his hand on the cushion or bolster, like a man about to take possession of his right and kept his hand there for a short while. At last, drawing it back, he turned his face towards the people, and...he looked attentively at the gazing assembly."[74] He undoubtedly hoped they would urge him to sit on the throne and preside over Parliament as their king.

But the ploy failed. Richard's seeking the throne himself contradicted the Yorkists' long insistence that they were loyal to King Henry and merely wanted to rid him of his incompetent and corrupt advisors. Most of the lords in Parliament, including Richard's own supporters, wanted reform and new men around the king, but they were not ready to overthrow the king. The Archbishop of Canterbury asked Richard if he wished to see the king. Richard responded, "I know of no person in this realm whom it does not behove to come to me and see my person, rather than that, I should go and visit him." This response impressed few, both within and outside Parliament. "And when the news of the duke's high-handedness was published among the people and they heard how he had entered thus of his own ill-considered presumption without any weighty discussion, everyone…at once began to murmur against him and say that he had acted in a rash manner."[75] Regime change would not come so easily; much more blood would have to be shed before it would happen.

On October 16, Richard presented to Parliament a formal, written statement of his dynastic claim to the throne, asserting that his descent from Edward III's second son gave him legal priority over Henry VI, descended from the third son. After due deliberation, Parliament decided it could not adjudicate the matter and refused to accept his claim.[76] In the face of this opposition, Richard abandoned his claim to kingship. But a compromise was reached, one similar to the 1153 Treaty of Westminster between King Stephen and the future King Henry II (Chapter 3). By the Act of Accord, passed on 25 October 1460, Henry remained king for the rest of his life. But Richard and his heirs would inherit the throne when he died. Edward of Westminster, Henry and Margaret's son, was disinherited. The same Parliament made Richard Prince of Wales and, again, Lord Protector of England. In the latter role, Richard was able to govern on Henry's behalf. The arrangement was the best result Richard could achieve at the time and it satisfied most Parliament members. King Henry had no say in the matter. The Act of Accord made Richard an heir to the throne of England, a

---

[74] *Registrum Abbatiae Johannis Whethamstede*, compiled in *EHD, vol. IV*, p. 283. John Whethamstede, who died in 1465, was an abbot at St Albans Abbey.

[75] *Registrum Abbatiae Johannis Whethamstede*, compiled in *EHD, vol. IV,* p. 284.

[76] For the parliamentary proceedings regarding Richard's claim to the throne, see *EHD, vol. IV*, pp. 415-9.

throne he was destined never to occupy. He was again in the ascendant, but the fates would see to it that fortune shifted yet again.

Although the Act of Accord was similar in many respects to the Treaty of Westminster, the circumstances were different in one significant way. In 1153, the indomitable Queen Matilda, who had been Stephen's main support and a woman determined to see her son succeed to her husband's crown, was dead. She could not fight against the Treaty of Westminster. Queen Margaret, equally indomitable and equally determined that her son not be disinherited, was very much alive and, at the age of 30, in her prime. She very much opposed the Act of Accord. Her son's council in Wales protested the agreement and vowed to fight on.

After the defeat at Northampton and with the king still a prisoner, the queen and her son, then less than seven years old, fled to Lancastrian territory in Wales. From there, after many adventures—including seeking and obtaining aid from brigands and other outlaws—they made their way to Scotland. There, she negotiated for Scottish help. Other Lancastrians who refused to accept the Act of Accord, including the Duke of Somerset and the Percys, raised forces in the north of England. Richard and the Duke of Salisbury, accompanied by Richard's son, Edmund, moved north that December to meet the threat, arriving at Sandal Castle near the town of Wakefield shortly before Christmas. Despite its name, the nearby city of York was a Lancastrian stronghold. Most of the northern barons, some put off by Richard's regal aspirations, joined the Lancastrian side. Thus, the Lancaster forces, numbering in total perhaps 18,000 troops, badly outnumbered the Yorkist forces in the area. They were led by Richard's bitter enemies, including sons of the nobles killed at the First Battle of St Albans. Trapped in their castle, Richard and his allies were in serious trouble. Christmas that year was, for them, not a happy time.

For reasons that are far from clear, perhaps due to treachery or deception, perhaps due to a misunderstanding of how badly outnumbered they were, possibly because they were running out of provisions, Richard and his forces sortied from the castle on 30 December. That day, in a field near Wakefield, the Lancaster army surrounded, attacked, overwhelmed and then destroyed the Yorkist forces. The Battle of Wakefield was a complete rout. Richard himself was killed, either in the battle itself or immediately afterwards by beheading. A mocking paper crown was placed on his head. His son, Edmund, attempted to escape but was captured and, his pleas for mercy unheeded, was also killed. One account, quite credible, was that the son of Lord Clifford who had died at the First Battle of St Albans stabbed Edmund in the heart in revenge for his father's death. The Earl of Salisbury escaped but was soon captured and summarily executed. Other Yorkists, including close relatives of the leaders, were also beheaded. The war's viciousness had escalated. Now, in a spiralling cycle of revenge, not only were the major leaders of the losing side executed after battle, but their kindred also.

Queen Margaret, still in Scotland with her son, was overjoyed when she heard the news from Wakefield. Reportedly at her instructions, the heads of Richard, his son Edmund and the Earl of Salisbury were hung as a warning over Micklegate Bar, a gate guarding the city of York. The mocking paper crown remained on Richard's head.

Richard's death made him another heir who never reigned. Although a product of his violent times, he was a capable man. He could be moderate in temperament and at times cautious, perhaps excessively so. Considered a hawk when it came to the war in France, he could also excel in the arts of peace. But he sometimes misjudged the political climate, like the occasion in October 1460, when he approached the throne during a session of Parliament and expected (or hoped) to be proclaimed king by acclimation, only to be met with silence even from his supporters. In his role as the crown's lieutenant in Ireland, he managed to win the Irish to his side, a difficult feat in that fractious country. King Henry's mismanagement and the queen's bitter enmity forced Richard to oppose the government while he still protested, apparently sincerely at first, his loyalty to the king himself. The circumstances that caused the conflict to escalate into open warfare and later caused him to seek to become king himself, were largely beyond his control. If he had succeeded in becoming king, he would have been far more capable than the pious Henry. Given the implacable enmity between the opposing sides, however, it is unclear to what extent he might have ruled in peace.

Richard's death did not mean the death of the Yorkist cause. The Act of Accord was still in effect; it had not (yet) been repealed. Richard's oldest son, the 18-year-old Edward, was now, legally at least, King Henry's heir. This son was determined to fight for his rights and do something about the heads hanging over Micklegate Bar in York. He was in the Welsh Marches raising an army. The Earl of Warwick was also still alive and commanded an army in London.

Moreover, the king himself was still a Yorkist prisoner. Margaret acted to do something about that. She and her son joined the Lancastrian leaders and marched south towards London with their army. As it moved, the army looted some of the relatively prosperous areas in the region, actions that cost the queen much support in the south and in London. The Earl of Warwick, with the king in his possession, moved to intercept them. At the Second Battle of St Albans, fought in February 1461, the queen's forces defeated Warwick and forced him to flee the field with the surviving remnants of his army.

The victorious Lancastrians found the king sitting under a tree singing a song. The king was reunited with his wife and son, whom he knighted on the battlefield. Two knights, Lord William Bonville and Sir Thomas Kyriell, both veterans of the Hundred Years' War and members of the Order of the Garter, had guarded the king during the battle. When the rest of the Yorkist army fled, they had agreed to remain behind to protect him in return for the king's promise that they would not be harmed. However, the queen considered the knights merely two more traitorous Yorkists and disregarded the king's wishes. Reportedly, the morning after the battle, she put the two on trial, during which she asked her seven-year-old son—entrusted for the first time with the appearance of personal authority—how they should die. Edward responded that they should be beheaded. Despite the king's impassioned pleas to spare the knights, as he had promised, it was done.

The Second Battle of St Albans was the high point of the Lancastrian cause in the early stages of the wars. But once again, fortune shifted. Warwick had been defeated but not so the Earl of March. Displaying an energy and competence belaying his young age, he defeated an army led by Owen and Jasper Tudor, father and son, at the February 1461 Battle of Mortimer's Cross, in the west near the Welsh border. Owen Tudor had been the second husband of Henry V's queen consort, Catherine of Valois and was the grandfather of the future King Henry VII, the first King of the Tudor dynasty. (Chapter 9.) He was captured and beheaded after the battle. Jasper Tudor, who survived the battle, was the future king's uncle.

The victorious Edward moved west, where he joined his army with the remnants of the Earl of Warwick's army. Edward and Warwick entered London, where they were greeted enthusiastically. At this point, it was clear that Edward sought to obtain the throne itself and not merely to rid Henry of bad advisors. When the question of who should be king was raised, the London populace shouted, "King Edward!" Parliament, or at least as many of the lords as were present in London at the time, agreed and proclaimed him king. He was not yet crowned, however. Formal coronation would await a military validation of his right to be king.

After her victory at St Albans, the queen moved towards London. The Londoners, however, frightened by the reports of her army's looting and plundering, barred her entry. Not wanting to take the city by storm, Margaret retreated north with her son and the king. The Earl of March, now claiming to be the king, and Warwick followed her with their greatly augmented army. The Yorkist and Lancastrian armies, with a combined total of well over 50,000 troops, clashed on 29 March 1461, in a snowstorm near the town of Towton in Yorkshire. The resulting Battle of Towton was the largest and deadliest of the Wars of the Roses and, indeed, the largest and deadliest ever fought on English soil. Somewhere between 20,000 and 30,000 men lost their lives. With the Earl of Warwick one of the heroes of the day—beginning his legend as the Kingmaker—the battle was a complete Yorkist victory. It confirmed what the Londoners had decreed: The Earl of March was now King Edward IV. Regime change had come at last.

Numerous Lancastrian leaders were executed after the battle. The Duke of Somerset (the successor of the one killed at the First Battle of St Albans) escaped. (He was later temporarily reconciled with King Edward but, after raising a new insurrection against the king, he was captured and beheaded after the 1464 Battle of Hexham.) Margaret and Henry and their son were not present at the battle and the Yorkists were unable to capture them. The new King Edward promptly marched to York, where he removed the heads of his father, his brother and the Earl of Salisbury from Micklegate Bar and replaced them with the heads of executed Lancastrians, including the Clifford blamed for killing Edmund. Edward was formally crowned in London to great acclaim that June. In December 1461, King Edward's first Parliament attainted the former Queen Margaret and her son, Edward. Once again, Margaret, queen no longer, and her son, now accompanied by former King Henry, had to flee after a military defeat. Like before, they went to Wales and then on to Scotland, where they remained for three years. The queen, determined as ever to see her son on the throne, plotted with the Scottish King James III and the few remaining Lancastrian nobles still supporting her to stir up rebellion in the border region. She had little success. Eventually, when King Edward and James III reached an agreement, the former queen and Edward were forced to move on to France. Henry stayed behind. He and Margaret never saw each other again. In 1465, Henry was, again, captured by the Yorkists and imprisoned in the Tower of London.

Margaret and her son languished in exile in France for several years, most of the time at the court of her father, Rene of Anjou, in Lorraine, with some of her last few remaining Lancastrian allies. With King Edward consolidating his power, there was nothing she could do but dream of a reversal of fortunes and the chance for revenge. She inculcated her son with the same dream of revenge and cutting off of heads, but, for the present, it appeared the opportunity would never present itself. Events in England—in which she played no role—would change that.

The Earl of Warwick, who had played a major role in making Edward King, was now the power behind the throne, or at least he believed he should be. He wanted England to ally itself with France. To this end, he negotiated with the French King to have King Edward marry a suitable French bride. But, unbeknownst to him, in 1464, Edward married—either for love or lust— Elizabeth Woodville, a woman who had a middling rank in society (far lower than a Queen Consort should have) and a scheming family. The marriage would have fateful consequences for his dynasty. Edward kept the marriage secret for several months before he was forced to divulge it. The marriage, obviously, aborted Warwick's efforts to have him marry a Frenchwoman. Embarrassed by news of the marriage and resentful of the growing influence of the Woodville family, the king's new in-laws, which undercut his own position, Warwick considered switching sides.

Warwick made an agreement with King Edward's treacherous brother George, who also resented the growing Woodville power. George agreed to oppose his own brother, possibly in the hopes of becoming king himself. To cement an alliance between himself and Warwick, George married Warwick's daughter Isabel. Previously, King Edward had opposed the marriage. The two raised rebellion in England and, for a while, Warwick even held King Edward prisoner. But, in the face of heavy opposition from other magnates, he was forced to release the king. Eventually, in 1470, Warwick fled to France.

Warwick met with the exiled Margaret in France in July 1470. The French King, Louis XI—hoping to gain England as an ally—negotiated an alliance between Warwick and Margaret. Doing so was an impressive act of diplomacy. Margaret and Warwick were bitter enemies. Warwick had been instrumental in overthrowing her husband and depriving her son of his birth right. Margaret had rejoiced when her forces captured and executed Warwick's father after the Battle of Wakefield. Both were reluctant to work together. But no other opportunity presented itself. Eventually, the French King persuaded them to put aside personal feelings and forge a cynical alliance of convenience. Just as Warwick and George had cemented their alliance by George's marrying Warwick's older daughter, Warwick and Margaret agreed that her son Edward, now 17 years old, would marry Warwick's younger daughter, Anne. They were married in December 1470.

The new alliance was fruitful, for a while. In the fall of 1470, Warwick landed in England with a small army. King Edward was in the north of England suppressing an uprising and was unprepared to oppose Warwick. Gaining support on the way, Warwick marched on London, entering the city in October. He proclaimed Henry the restored king and paraded him around London. Warwick thus made Henry king once again. Henry's son, Prince Edward, was heir to the throne again. When other nobles defected to Warwick's side, Edward was forced to flee the country with his youngest brother, Richard, Duke of Gloucester, who had remained loyal to him. They went into exile in Burgundy. Margaret and her son remained in France until the following spring. They sailed for England in March 1471.

Warwick's triumph did not last long. He had overreached. With Burgundian help, both financial and military, the deposed Edward raised an army. With the loyal Richard at his side, Edward invaded England in his turn. He forgave his traitorous brother George, who, sensing the shift in fortunes, switched sides again. Meeting little initial resistance, Edward entered a welcoming London, where he seized the supposedly restored Henry VI. In London, Edward reclaimed the throne. But he had to fight to make good his restoration.

On Easter Sunday, 14 April 1471, the day Margaret and Prince Edward landed in England on their return from France, Edward's forces met Warwick's army north of Barnet, near London, in a thick fog. Edward had brought Henry—whose status as either king or deposed king was at stake—and placed him among his army. In the fog and confusion of war, some of Warwick's troops inadvertently attacked others of his troops. Fearing treachery, much of Warwick's army fled. As a result, Edward won a major victory. Warwick, the man called the Kingmaker, was kingmaker no longer; he was killed trying to flee the battlefield. One of Edward's commanders was his youngest, most faithful, brother, the 18-year-old Richard, Duke of Gloucester. Henry was captured and once again became a Yorkist prisoner, later incarcerated in the Tower of London.

When Margaret and her son heard of the debacle at Barnet, they considered the prudent step of returning to France. But they did not do so. Instead, they sought to join Lancastrian supporters in Wales. But Margaret was unable to cross the River Severn, as the city of Gloucester blocked her path. Edward pursued her with his army. On 4 May 1471, Margaret's army, commanded by the latest Duke of Somerset, was brought to heel near the town of Tewkesbury in Gloucester. The Lancastrian army probably slightly outnumbered the Yorkists, but the Yorkist army was more experienced. The inexperienced Prince Edward was put in nominal command of the centre of the Lancastrian forces. The Battle of Tewkesbury, fought that day, was the final battle of the first portion of the Wars of the Roses. It was a complete Yorkist victory and ensured King Edward of many more years of rule. And once again, one of the heroes of the day was Richard, Duke of Gloucester.

The 17-year-old Prince Edward was killed. A contemporary account stated that he "was taken, fleeing towards the town and slain in the field." Later accounts claimed he was killed after the battle. One account stated that troops under George, the Duke of Clarence (who had allied himself with the prince only a few months previously before switching sides for the second time) found the prince among a grove of trees. Despite Edward's pleas, he was summarily beheaded. In *Henry VI, part 3*, Shakespeare dramatized a different and dubious account that first appeared in the sixteenth century. In this account, the captured prince was brought before King Edward and his brothers, George and Richard, and questioned about why he had fought against them. He responded, "To recover my father's kingdom and heritage, from his father and grandfather to him and from him, after him, to me lineally descended." At these words, King Edward struck Prince Edward with his gauntlet, after which the king's brothers and others killed him.[77] In whatever manner he died, his body was buried at Tewkesbury Abbey.

Other Lancastrians captured in the battle were beheaded shortly afterwards. These included the latest Duke of Somerset, the third successive man with that

---

[77] For the various accounts of Edward's death, see *EHD, vol. IV*, pp. 313-5. For Shakespeare's dramatization, see *Henry VI, part 3, act V, scene v*. Because the Shakespearean account first arose in the sixteenth century and reflects Tudor propaganda, it is unlikely to be true.

title to die in the wars (the others at the 1455 First Battle of St Albans and the 1464 Battle of Hexham). The defeated Margaret, broken in spirit by the death of her only son and now without hope for the future, was taken prisoner a few days later. Because she was a woman, she was not executed. Instead, King Edward ordered her imprisoned and she remained an English prisoner for the next few years. In 1475, the French King Louis XI ransomed her. She spent the rest of her life in France, dying there in 1482 at 52 years.

The former King Henry VI died in the Tower of London on 21 May 1471, "of pure displeasure and melancholy," the Yorkists claimed, but probably by murder, as most people have believed, then and today.[78] Now that Henry's only heir was dead, the Yorkists had no reason to keep the former king alive and a strong motivation to have him dead. Henry had been restored to the throne once and might become the focus of future attempts at a second restoration. Henry's death was too convenient to believe it was natural.

It is difficult to determine what Edward of Lancaster would have been like as King had he become one. His mother dominated him his entire life and his individual personality does not readily appear. But he was very different from his pacific, pious father. Warfare fascinated him, although he never experienced it first-hand until the day he died. His mother imbued him from an early age with a strong sense of vindictiveness and brutality, as indicated by his decision, at the age of seven, that the two Yorkist captives should be beheaded after the Second Battle of St Albans.

A sixteenth-century account of his death described him at the time as "a goodly girlish looking and a well-featured young gentleman."[79] But when he was thirteen years old, during his exile in France, an Italian ambassador to the French court wrote of him that he "already talks of nothing but cutting off heads or making war, as if he had everything in his hands or was the god of battle or the peaceful occupant of that [English] throne." A man who knew the prince well in exile said that "as soon as he became grown-up, [he] gave himself over entirely to martial exercises; and, seated on fierce and half-tamed steeds urged on by his

---

[78] *EHD, vol. IV,* pp. 316-7.

[79] Edward Hall, compiled in *EHD, vol. IV,* p. 315. Hall, an English historian who lived from 1497 to 1547, generally presented the Tudor view. His work was a major source for Shakespeare's history plays.

spurs, he often delighted in attacking and assaulting the young companions attending him."[80]

With this background and character, it is hard to imagine that Edward of Lancaster would have been anything other than a brutal and vindictive king, at least at first. Whether, when he matured, he might also have become a wise and judicious one is impossible to say.

---

[80] The last two quotations in this paragraph are found in *ODNB, Edward of Westminster*.

Chapter 8
The Wars of the Roses, Part II:
Two More Edwards

After his victory at the Battle of Tewkesbury, King Edward IV managed to rule as King of England for the rest of his life. But his life was far shorter than it should have been, both for the good of the realm and the good of his dynasty. After the struggles and deprivations of his earlier years, once he had his reign secured, the king settled down to a life of luxury and dissolution. In 1483, when he was only 40 years old, but overweight and in poor condition, he died suddenly and unexpectedly in bed of natural causes—a rare event for the men in his family (and many other noble families of the era). His premature death set the stage for the final acts of the Wars of the Roses. He left behind an unpopular queen, who had an even more unpopular family. Fatefully, he also left behind a 12-year-old son who, as a boy-king, would inevitably have been dominated by that queen and that family. These circumstances would lead to two more heirs who never reigned, both named Edward. The first was Edward IV's son, who was immediately declared king, but who never actually reigned in any significant way. The second was the son of Edward IV's youngest brother, Richard, Duke of Gloucester.

After the 1470 restoration of Henry VI and Edward IV's flight into exile in Burgundy, Edward's wife, Elizabeth, fled into sanctuary at Westminster Abbey with her three daughters. There, on 2 November 1470, her and King Edward's first son, named for his father, was born. It was good news for the Yorkist succession, if any were to be had. When fortune changed again and Edward, the father, entered London on his way to battle with Warwick in April 1471, he rushed to Westminster to rescue his wife and family. There he met his infant son and heir for the first time. It was a joyful reunion for the family. Prince Edward, as we will call him, was declared Prince of Wales in June 1471, after his father's restoration was complete. Two years later, he became nominal president of the newly created Council of Wales and the Marches, although, obviously, others exercised the real authority. Prince Edward's only brother to survive infancy, called Richard of Shrewsbury after his birthplace, was born on 17 August 1473. The following year, this Richard was named Duke of York.

As a youth, Prince Edward resided primarily at Ludlow Castle, in Shropshire near Wales. His maternal uncle, Anthony Woodville, Earl Rivers, himself a noted scholar, was entrusted with his upbringing and education. Rivers was the primary person who exercised authority in Edward's name. Edward was raised to become a king, taught to read and write and schooled in literature and other subjects. He seemed to have been raised well. Domenico Mancini, an Italian visitor and close observer of the English scene during this time, described him as he appeared shortly after his father's death when he was 12 years old: "In word and deed he gave so many proofs of his liberal education, of polite, nay rather scholarly, attainments far beyond his age...[H]is special knowledge of literature...enabled him to discourse elegantly, to understand fully and to declaim most excellently from any work whether in verse or prose that came into his hands, unless it were from among the most abstruse authors. He had such dignity in his whole person and in his face such charm, that however much they might gaze, he never wearied the eyes of beholders."[81] Young as the prince was, King Edward already made plans for his marriage, negotiating for the expected dynastic advantages of a royal marriage. In 1480, at the tender age of 10, he was betrothed to Anne, the four-year-old daughter of the Duke of Brittany. They were to be married when they came of age. Events, however, were to intervene and the marriage never occurred.

Even after King Edward's restoration, turbulent times remained. The king's brother, George, was forgiven after his treasonous alliance with the Kingmaker that helped bring down King Edward and temporarily restored Henry VI. But George later became involved in yet more treasonous affairs. He was tried in Parliament and convicted of treason and, in 1478, executed, supposedly by drowning in a butt of Malmsey wine. Tudor propaganda later blamed the other brother, Richard, Duke of Gloucester, for George's death. In fact, Richard was in the north of England during the trial and execution and, if anything, actively

---

[81] *EHD, vol. 4*, p. 333. Mancini visited England around 1482 to 1483 and later reported his observations. He is considered a neutral and fairly reliable source. His report was lost and not rediscovered until 1934.

opposed George's execution. Mancini wrote that Richard "was so overcome with grief for his brother, that...he was overheard to say that he would one day avenge his brother's death."[82]

But George's death did benefit Richard. Richard was now King Edward's only surviving brother. George left behind a son, also named Edward. But George and his family had been attainted when he was executed, which meant that this son could not inherit and was removed from the line of succession. This made Richard next in line to the throne after Edward's sons. In 1472, he married Warwick the Kingmaker's younger daughter, Anne. Anne had previously and briefly been married to the doomed Edward of Lancaster, King Henry VI's son. Richard spent most of his time during the rest of his brother's reign in the north of England, primarily at York and his nearby castle of Middleham. During Edward' reign, Richard was the first Lord President of the Council of the North, a council Edward had established to bring better government to that region. Richard essentially governed the north in Edward's name, a position that carried substantial military obligations; the nearby Scots always posed a threat. It is, generally, acknowledged that Richard did well; he was popular, especially in York.

By 1483, the queen's grasping family, the Woodvilles, previously of middling rank in the English aristocracy, had worked its way into wealth and influence through appointed positions and profitable, albeit cynical, marriages. Her brother, Earl Rivers, had control of the heir to the throne at Ludlow Castle. The queen had two sons by a prior marriage, Thomas Grey (made Marquis of Dorset in 1475) and Sir Richard Grey. (Her first husband had been killed at the Second Battle of St Albans fighting on the *Lancastrian* side.) As an example of the cynical marriages, Elizabeth's 19-year-year-old brother, John Woodville, married the dowager Duchess of Norfolk, the aunt of Warwick the Kingmaker. John's bride was 65 years old and a four-time widow. The Earl of Warwick was outraged; this marriage was one more insult among many that led him into treason against King Edward. Much of the rest of the country was also outraged.

This was the situation when King Edward died on 9 April 1483. Dramatic events were to occur over the next few months. On his deathbed, King Edward named Richard, the prince's uncle, as the Lord Protector of the Realm; in this role, Richard was to oversee Prince Edward's coronation. The prince himself lived at Ludlow Castle with his guardian, Earl Rivers (the queen's brother).

---

[82] *EHD, vol. 4,* p. 330.

When news of the king's death reached Ludlow, the prince was immediately declared King Edward V. Earl Rivers and the queen's younger son by her first marriage, Sir Richard Grey, escorted the prince west towards London to be crowned. Accompanying the prince and his guardian were some 2,000 troops, allegedly heavily armed.

While Richard was still in the north, the Woodville family took steps in London in an apparent attempt to consolidate their power and marginalise Richard. They and those who sided with them decided there should be no Protectorate. Instead, they formed a council to govern England until Edward's coronation. They also planned a prompt coronation, scheduled for May 4. Richard was to be a member of the council, but he would not act as the sole Protector. William Hastings, the Lord Chamberlain of England, a man who had been one of King Edward's most trusted and capable friends and advisors, opposed these steps but, outvoted, could do nothing. One of the queen's sons, the Marquis of Dorset, seized the royal treasury. One of her brothers, Edward Woodville, got himself appointed a naval captain and took to sea with a fleet of 20 ships.

Richard was at Middleham Castle when he heard of Edward's death. Lord Hastings was the first to notify Richard of the King's death. Concerned about what was going on, Hastings advised Richard to come to London immediately with a substantial armed retinue. From Richard's perspective, the situation was ominous. With the treasury, the army and the navy in their control, the Woodvilles appeared determined to rule England with the soon-to-be-crowned boy, Edward, also in their control, acting as their puppet. Richard was threatened with being excluded entirely. To meet the threat, Richard collected around 600 troops and, accompanied by his cousin and ally, Henry Stafford, Duke of Buckingham, moved south to intercept the prince.

Richard arranged with Earl Rivers to meet with him and Prince Edward at Stony Stratford, a small town in Buckinghamshire. Richard and the Duke of Buckingham met Rivers and Grey near the town the evening of April 29 and dined with them, apparently amicably. But the next day, Richard arrested Rivers, Grey and Prince Edward's chamberlain, Thomas Vaughan, on charges of treason. The three were transported north to Pontefract Castle in Yorkshire. There, they were tried for treason in a proceeding conducted by Henry Percy, Earl of Northumberland. All three were convicted and, on 25 June, they were beheaded.

Richard took custody of the prince and dismissed his retinue. Richard told him that Rivers, Grey and Vaughan were guilty of treason and that he would take him to London to be crowned. Mancini reports that Edward replied that "he merely had those ministers whom his father had given him…he had seen nothing evil in them and wished to keep them unless otherwise proved… As for the government of the kingdom, he had complete confidence in the peers of the realm and the queen."[83] Richard and Prince Edward entered London on May 4, the day originally set for the coronation. There, Richard displayed to the populace wagons containing weapons that he claimed Rivers' 2,000 troops had been armed with.

Preparations continued for the coronation, but it was now postponed to 22 June. On May 19, the prince was placed in the Tower of London. The Tower has a dark reputation today as a place where prisoners, often of high station, were sent to be incarcerated until they were executed on charges of treason. Many were. But the Tower also had comfortable residences and royal heirs often resided there before their coronation. So, placing Prince Edward in the Tower of London was not, by itself, a sinister act. But no record exists that the prince was ever seen again outside the Tower gates.

When Elizabeth heard of the events at Stony Stratford, she entered sanctuary at Westminster with her other son, Richard, and her daughters, much as she had done in 1470 when her husband fled into exile. She and her family hoped for a prompt coronation, which would end Richard's term as Lord Protector. But much happened in between. On 10 June, Richard wrote to the city of York pleading for additional troops to be sent to London to meet the Woodville threat. Three days later, a stormy meeting of the council was held. Richard and Lord Hastings were among those present. The meeting was peaceful at first. But after a recess, Richard suddenly accused Hastings and others of conspiring with the Woodvilles against him. Some, including John Morton, the Bishop of Ely, were merely arrested and later released. According to most accounts, Hastings was taken into a nearby courtyard and summarily beheaded. (One biographer has argued that Hastings's beheading occurred a week later, after a trial.[84])

---

[83] Dan Jones, *The Wars of the Roses: The Fall of the Plantagenets and the Rise of the Tudors*, Viking (2014), p. 270.

[84] Clements Markham, *Richard III: His Life and Character*, Smith, Elder and Co. (1906), pp. 99, 212–214 (hereafter Markham, *Richard III*).

Despite this ominous turn, the Archbishop of Canterbury persuaded Elizabeth to release her younger son, Richard, Duke of York, from sanctuary, possibly so he could attend the coronation, still planned for 22 June. Richard joined his brother in the Tower of London on 16 June.

Suddenly, plans changed. An informant, identified as Robert Stillington, the Bishop of Bath and Wells, revealed a secret that, if true, was a game-changer. Before King Edward IV married Elizabeth Woodville, the Bishop stated, the king had made a pre-contract to marry a young widower named Lady Eleanor Butler. The Bishop presided over the ceremony himself. A pre-contract to marry was legally binding and, in medieval times, it prohibited the parties to it from marrying anyone else in the future.[85] This meant that the marriage between the king and Elizabeth was invalid, which in turn meant that their children, including Prince Edward himself, were illegitimate. An illegitimate child could not inherit the crown. Richard was now the only legal, living heir to his brother's throne.

Matters moved quickly now. The planned coronation was postponed indefinitely. On 22 June, the date the coronation as supposed to have occurred, a certain Dr Ralph Shaw, brother of the Mayor of London, preached a public sermon outside Old St Paul's Cathedral. Shaw told the crowd about the pre-contract to marry, after which he declared that Prince Edward was illegitimate and Richard was now the legitimate king. The sermon was widely accepted, both among the common people and the nobles, either because they believed it, or because it provided a legal excuse to do what they wanted to do: make Richard king and avoid having a child King dominated by the hated Woodville family. The citizens of London petitioned Richard to become king. He accepted and was declared King Richard III on 26 June. He was formally crowned in a ceremony at Westminster Abbey on July 6. To the extent Prince Edward was ever king, he was now deposed. In January 1484, Parliament issued a document called the *Titulus Regius* that formally declared the issue of King Edward IV and Elizabeth Woodville illegitimate and Richard the legitimate king.

Prince Edward and his brother Richard, popularly known today as the "Princes in the Tower," were occasionally seen playing in the Tower of London, but by the end of summer 1483, they were seen no more. Domenico Mancini, the Italian observer, wrote that Prince Edward "and his brother were withdrawn into the inner apartments of the Tower proper and day by day began to be seen more rarely behind the bars and windows, till at length they ceased to appear

---

[85] *Black's Law Dictionary*, 10th ed. (2004), p. 396.

altogether. Dr Argentine, the last of his attendants whose service the king enjoyed, reported that the young king, like a victim prepared for sacrifice, sought remission of his sins by daily confession and penance, because he believed that death was facing him."[86] There is some indication that in July, when Richard was away from London on a royal progress, an attempt was made to rescue the princes from the Tower. The attempt was thwarted.

As is well known, King Richard's reign proved to be a short one. In August 1485, a new claimant to the throne, Henry Tudor, invaded England, defeated Richard at the Battle of Bosworth Field and took the crown as King Henry VII. Richard was killed in a wild mounted charge trying to reach Henry, his mortal enemy. The Plantagenet dynasty, which had begun over three centuries earlier with the ascent of King Henry II, came to an end. The Tudor dynasty began.

These are the basic facts behind Prince Edward's deposition and Richard's obtaining (or usurping, depending on one's point of view) the throne that, according to the official Tudor version, should have belonged to Prince Edward. These facts give rise to two basic questions that have been debated over the centuries and are central to Prince Edward's story. First, was Richard's becoming king justified or was it a tyrant's usurpation? A subsidiary question is when did Richard first seek to become king—as soon as he learned of Edward's death, or not until later when events overtook him? Second, what was the ultimate fate of the Princes in the Tower?

No definitive conclusion can be reached on either question. The Tudor view, which predominated during the Tudor regime and beyond—the victors usually write the history—is that Richard was a faithless tyrant who treacherously seized the throne in violation of his duty to oversee his nephew's coronation and that he committed many heinous crimes, capped by his pitiless murder of the two Princes in the Tower. Sir Thomas Moore's early sixteenth-century account, *The History of King Richard III*, exemplifies this view. Later Tudor accounts added evermore to Richard's supposed villainy, culminating in the Shakespeare tragedy where the great playwright has Richard himself declaim, "I am determined to prove a villain."[87]

In more recent times, beginning shortly after the end of the Tudor dynasty, when it was safe to challenge the official position, many historians have taken a different view, one far more favourable to Richard. The revisionist position

---

[86] *EHD, vol. 4*, pp. 332-3.

[87] *The Life and Death of King Richard III, act I, scene i.*

reached its zenith in Sir Clements Markham's 1906 biography, *Richard III: His Life and Character*. In Markham's version, Richard could do no wrong. The biography is almost hero-worshipping: "There was nothing mean or sordid in his nature; he was liberal, open-handed and generous. Richard's Parliament was the best that had met since the time of Edward I." Markham believed that the "battle of Bosworth was a calamity from which England did not soon recover."[88] More recent historians have generally taken a more nuanced and moderate position. Richard was no saint. But a dispassionate review of the historical record shows substantial justification for Richard's becoming king.

The *legal* basis for making Richard king instead of the prince was the Bishop of Bath and Wells' revelation (or allegation) that the marriage between Edward IV and Elizabeth Woodville was invalid due to Edward's prior pre-contract to marry. The basis seems rather technical and unsatisfactory from today's perspective. But, if true, in the fifteenth century, it would have been a legally valid basis to declare the prince ineligible for kingship. An invalid marriage made the issue of that invalid marriage illegitimate. An illegitimate son could not inherit his father's throne. This was the reason Robert of Gloucester, the natural but illegitimate son of King Henry I, could not himself seek the throne when his father died without a legitimate male heir, despite Robert's great abilities. (Chapter 3.)

Was it true? The pre-contract was not documented. All we have to go by is the statement attributed to Robert Stillington, the Bishop of Bath and Wells. The revelation was very convenient for Richard and was belatedly made, nearly two decades after the Bishop must have known of King Edward's allegedly invalid second marriage. Perhaps the revelation was part of a scheme devised between Richard and a compliant clergyman to ease Richard's path to the throne. But Robert Stillington was not just any clergyman. He was a high church official, the kind who might have presided over a king's secret pre-contract. He had become the Bishop of Bath and Wells back in 1465 and had been loyal to King Edward IV. No clear reason appears why he would tell such an egregious lie with such egregious consequences for that king's oldest son. Moreover, the Bishop's revelation was, to many at least, credible. King Edward IV was a known womaniser. He had married Elizabeth Woodville in secret in 1464, very possibly, as many believed, because Elizabeth insisted on marriage as the price for allowing him into her bed. He kept the marriage secret for several months. Might

---

[88] Markham, *Richard III*, pp. 160, 163.

he not have done something similar a few years previously and then conveniently forgot about it when sexual temptation arose again?

We will probably never know. What was important in 1483 was that people believed it, or wanted to, which, at the time, amounted to much the same thing. And, ultimately, legal points like this were not dispositive in an era of power politics. The revelation provided an excuse to do what the people, at least the nobles and populace in London, wanted to do. Richard had the popular backing to seize the throne and he did it. As a practical matter and setting aside legal issues, given the then-existing circumstances, there were arguably good reasons for Richard to become king rather than a child dominated by the Woodvilles. As a nineteenth-century biographer (who also believed Richard guilty of later murdering the princes), summarised it: "One individual only there was who, from his exalted rank, his high reputation as a statesman and a soldier, his independence of faction, the friendly terms on which he had ever associated with men of all parties, his profound knowledge of human character and of the motives of human action…was capable of grappling with every emergency and of thus preserving his country from the horrors of civil war. That man was Richard Duke of Gloucester."[89]

Once he became king, Richard worked hard to be a good one. He and his sole Parliament, which he largely controlled, enacted some of the most enlightened legislation of the Middle Ages. He created an institution called the Court of Requests, where poor people could present legal grievances inexpensively and have them heard quickly. He made a pretrial release on bail more accessible for those charged with crimes and prohibited the confiscation of their property before trial. He ordered laws to be translated from French, the traditional language of law, into English. He prohibited the use of "benevolences"—theoretically voluntary donations of money to the king but in reality coerced payments, a practice his brother, Edward, had engaged in regularly to raise money. He made it illegal, when selling property, to conceal that some or all of the property was subject to legal obligations benefiting other parties. He also enacted detailed restrictions on foreign merchants in the country. But, tellingly, the same enactment specifically and unambiguously exempted from all restrictions the importation, printing, or selling "of any kind of books,

---

[89] John Heneage Jesse, *Memoirs of King Richard III*, L.C. Page and Co. (1892), p. 122.

written or printed."[90] When printing was in its infancy, Richard wanted to encourage the reading of books of any kind. A tyrant would not have so acted.

When they came to power, the Tudors promptly repealed much of this legislation (but not the Court of Requests, which survived into the seventeenth century). King Henry VII perfected the use of benevolences to raise money.[91]

But Richard's benevolent acts as a king can be viewed two ways: As the acts of a usurping king trying to win others to his side despite his dastardly deeds, or as the acts of a good man working to be a good king. The former view is exemplified by the *Great Chronicle of London*, written by a contemporary observer but during, and possibly coloured by, the reign of the Tudors: "When this feast [after Richard's coronation] was finished, the king sent home the lords into their countries... And also, unto such as went home he gave strait commandments that they should see the countries where they dwelt well guided and that no extortions should be done to his subjects. And thus, he taught others to exercise justice and goodness which he would not do himself."[92]

Not all of Richard's contemporaries shared this view. During Richard's reign, Thomas Langton, Bishop of St David's, wrote in a letter that King Richard "contents the people wherever he goes better than ever did any prince; for many a poor man that has suffered wrong many days has been relieved and helped by him and his commands in his progress. And in many cities and towns were given to him great sums of money which he has refused. Upon my word, I never liked the qualities of any prince so well as his; God has sent him to us for the welfare of us all."[93] Langton was a credible source and not just another Ricardian partisan. He had been chaplain to King Edward IV and survived into the reign of

---

[90] "An act to control Italian merchants in England, 1484," compiled in *EHD, vol. 4,* pp. 1051-2

[91] John Morton, Bishop of Ely under Edward IV and Richard III and promoted to Archbishop of Canterbury and Chancellor under Henry VII, implemented what was later called "Morton's Fork" to coerce the payment of benevolences into King Henry's treasury. If a person lived lavishly, he clearly had plenty of money and could afford to give some to the king; if a person lived frugally, he clearly had saved plenty of money and could afford to give some to the king.

[92] *EHD, vol. 4,* p. 335. The *Great Chronicle of London* was attributed to Robert Fabyan, a London draper who died around 1512.

[93] *EHD, vol. 4,* pp. 336-7.

Henry VII. He rose to be elected Archbishop of Canterbury under Henry, although he died before assuming the office.

It is not known exactly when Richard decided to occupy the throne himself. He was always ambitious, but the probabilities suggest this decision occurred late during the events of the spring of 1483. He had been faithful to his brother and, probably, intended to be faithful to his nephew. However, he also intended, beginning immediately after King Edward's death, to remove the prince from the influence of the Woodville family. This latter intent was reasonable, even necessary from Richard's perspective. His nephew was 12 years old, an age at which he might be expected to make some governmental decisions himself. But his age also meant that whoever had control over him would have great influence over those decisions. With Edward in Woodville hands, Richard could reasonably fear he would be excluded and, given the tenor of the times, perhaps destroyed.

Over time, Richard's attitude no doubt changed until finally, due to events, he sought to be king. The temptation these events presented became too much for him to resist. The sudden arrest of Lord Hastings on 13 June and his execution, which was never satisfactorily explained, suggests that by that time, 13 days before he was declared king, Richard had decided to seek the throne himself and to remove someone who might have been an obstacle to that ambition. On the other hand, it is possible that Richard had some concrete information that Hastings had sided with the Woodvilles against him, although, if so, it seems likely he would have made the information public.

The circumstances under which Richard became king and the short duration of his reign deprived him of the opportunity to exercise his authority peacefully and demonstrate what kind of a king he might have been over the long term. He could never overcome the stigma of having seized the throne from a child who many believed was the lawful king and later the suspicion that he murdered that child. The record shows that he acted well as a king, whatever his motivation. Had he been born the oldest son of a reigning king and assumed the monarchy without controversy and lived a normal life span, he might have become one of England's great kings. Prince Edward might also have made a fine king. He appeared to be intelligent, cultured and well-spoken. Again, we will never know.

We can also draw no firm conclusion about what happened to Prince Edward and his brother, Richard, after they were placed in the Tower of London. The only thing we know for certain about the fate of the Princes in the Tower is that we don't know anything for certain about the fate of the Princes in the Tower. All we can do is examine the evidence and determine what the probabilities are.

The Tudor party line was that Richard had them murdered. In his *History of King Richard III*, Sir Thomas More described in lurid detail how Sir James Tyrrell, acting at Richard's command, had two of his henchmen, Miles Forrest and John Dighton, smother the princes in their bed. According to More, Tyrrell confessed to the murders in 1502 after he was charged with treason. Tyrrell was then beheaded before anyone could look into the circumstances of the alleged confession or inquire into its credibility. No written confession exists or, so far as anyone knows, ever existed. Thomas More was known for his integrity, which added credibility to his account. But historians, and people generally, are rightfully sceptical when a government announces a confession that supports that government's party line and then summarily executes the alleged confessor. Many reasons exist to doubt the story, partly because some of the details are incredible and some contradict other known facts. As the editors of English Historical Documents stated, More's account is "full of difficulties."[94] Indeed, More himself had his doubts (perhaps his integrity showing?). In this same *History of King Richard III*, he acknowledged that the princes' "death and final misfortune have nonetheless so far come in question, that some remain yet in doubt, whether they were in his [Richard's] days destroyed or no."[95] The story of Tyrrell's villainy, although possibly true, cannot be accepted at face value.

Discounting a specific story of how Richard supposedly murdered the princes does not, of course, mean that Richard was innocent. It just means we do not know. Virtually all historians today recognise that no one knows for sure. Given the scarcity and vagueness of the evidence and the number of possibilities, it is not surprising that historians disagree on what most likely happened to the Princes in the Tower.[96]

---

[94] *EHD, vol. 4*, p. 338.

[95] J. Rawson Lumby, ed., Sir Thomas More's, *History of King Richard III*, Cambridge University Press (1883), p. 80, converted into modern English by the author.

[96] A recent book describing the discovery of Richard's skeleton in Leicester in 2012 contains an interesting debate between the book's two authors, who disagree regarding Richard's guilt. Philippa Langley and Michael Jones, *The King's Grave: The Discovery of Richard III's Lost Burial Place and the Clues It Holds*, St Martin's Press (2013), pp. 237-53.

Several possible scenarios exist. Obviously, one is that the princes were murdered in the summer of 1483 at Richard's command. Another is that some official under Richard, believing the king wanted them dead, murdered them on his own initiative (somewhat like the way four of Henry II's knights murdered Thomas Becket, Archbishop of Canterbury, in the cathedral in 1170).

Some have suggested that Richard's cousin, Henry Stafford, Duke of Buckingham, murdered the princes. Although Buckingham had been Richard's strong ally in the months leading to Richard's coronation, he rebelled against him in the fall of 1483—unsuccessfully; he was captured and executed for treason. Buckingham was descended from Edward III in several ways and may have wanted to seize the throne himself. In that event, he would have been motivated to have the princes killed. As a major magnate and Richard's right-hand man, he might have had sufficient access to the Tower of London to have contrived to kill them.

Another suspect is King Henry VII, the Tudor claimant who seized the throne after defeating Richard in 1485. If the princes had been alive when he became king, Henry would probably have needed to kill them to secure his shaky claim. Henry did execute several persons he perceived to be threats to him. He appears to have been morally capable of just about anything, including murdering the two princes. However, Henry's guilt requires that the princes had lived in the Tower of London (or some other place where Henry could have found them) for two more years, which seems unlikely. No report exists of anyone seeing them after the summer of 1483.

Another possibility is that Prince Edward simply died a natural death. Children often did in those days. Domenico Mancini stated that a "Dr Argentine" was the last person to attend the prince. Perhaps he was treating him for a disease that eventually killed him. This scenario, although possible, also seems unlikely. It is too convenient. Moreover, if Edward died a natural death, why all the secrecy? Murder generally occurs in secret, a natural death generally not. If the doctor had treated Edward for a serious illness, surely someone would have known and commented on it. And if Edward had died naturally, it would have been in Richard's best interest to make that publicly known. Additionally, what about Prince Richard? If Edward had died, his younger brother would have remained a possible heir and threat to the king. It is hard to credit that *both* would have died naturally—although it is possible; both could have died of the same illness. Such an event would have been extraordinarily convenient for Richard. And, surely, Richard would have publicised their deaths.

Another possibility that some have suggested is that after Buckingham's rebellion showed how shaky Richard's position was, the king quietly secreted the princes out of the country for their own protection, perhaps to Burgundy into the custody of his sister, Margaret, Duchess of Burgundy, the princes' aunt. Proponents of this scenario argue that Richard must have known that if he were overthrown, whoever succeeded him would need to kill the princes to consolidate his position. But they could be murdered only if they were available. To guard against this danger, Richard might have sent them away. Then, after Henry VII seized the throne, their identity would have to be kept a secret indefinitely, again, for their own safety. They might have died natural deaths while living incognito wherever they were. In 1674, two skeletons were discovered in the Tower of London in a location where the princes' bodies might have been secreted. The skeletons have been presumed to be those of the princes. If true, this would disprove this theory. But it has never been proven that the skeletons were, in fact, those of the princes. Nevertheless, this scenario, while also possible, seems farfetched. Could Richard have removed them from the country without anyone knowing or even suspecting? How long could a secret like that have been kept? And would Richard really have been so concerned for his nephews' welfare that he would risk moving them from his own custody?

Of the theories suggesting that Richard was not the culprit, the guilt of Buckingham seems most likely. But it is not clear that he *could* have killed the princes. They were in the Tower of London, guarded by Richard's people. Moreover, although little is known for sure about his motivation in rebelling against Richard, it does not appear it was on his own behalf. More likely, he rebelled on behalf of the princes, at least at first and then, when he became convinced they were dead, he shifted his allegiance to Henry Tudor. Or, he might have learned at some point that Richard had killed the princes and, for this reason, rebelled on behalf of Henry Tudor. Buckingham had little reason to kill the princes unless it was to further his own claim, a claim that would have been doubtful at best. Buckingham may have been involved in the princes' murders, but it seems unlikely he acted without Richard's knowledge and consent.

The most obvious and simplest explanation of the princes' fate seems the most likely: They were murdered on Richard's order, or at least under his watch by men acting on his behalf. He had the most to gain from their deaths. Rumours began to circulate that Richard had murdered them shortly after their disappearance. The Chancellor of France even so stated in a speech in that country. Their supposed deaths at Richard's hands were the focal point of later rebellions and Henry Tudor's successful invasion of England in 1485. Surely, if they had remained alive after the summer of 1483, Richard would have displayed them to the world to squelch any belief that he had killed them. Presenting the princes alive would have deflated the Tudor campaign leading to Bosworth.

One circumstance that argues against Richard's guilt is that Elizabeth Woodville, the former queen who had had her marriage declared invalid under Richard, came out of sanctuary with her daughters in March 1484 and resumed her place in Richard's court, apparently reconciled with the king. Surely, the argument goes, Elizabeth would not have been on friendly terms with him had she known, or even suspected, that he had murdered her sons. This is a weighty argument, but not enough to exonerate Richard in this author's view. To entice Elizabeth to come out of sanctuary with her daughters, King Richard swore publicly that they would not be harmed or imprisoned and that he would find suitable marriages for her daughters. Elizabeth accepted the promise of safety, which Richard kept. Perhaps she felt she had no choice. She could not stay in sanctuary forever. And with Richard in power, she could hardly accuse him of murder. She and her daughters probably simply made the best they could out of a bad situation. (However, as far as we can tell, Elizabeth *never* accused Richard of murdering her sons, even after Richard was dead and Henry was king, which seems odd if she did believe or suspect Richard was guilty. Perhaps she simply did not know.)

Ultimately, this author concludes—reluctantly, for he was an ardent Ricardian in his youth—the probability (not the certainty) is that the Princes in the Tower were murdered during the summer of 1483, either at Richard's instigation or by someone acting on his behalf and probably with his knowledge. Exactly when and how is unknown. Readers can, of course, make up their own mind.

Assuming, as seems likely, that Edward was murdered, his fate was particularly tragic. The boy had grown up, taught that he was destined to become King of a great nation. When his father died, he was but twelve years old. He was told he was now the king and his future appeared assured. The world seemed to be his, truly. But he had no control over subsequent events. Within a few days, everyone dear to him was removed from his presence. He came into the custody of a stern uncle he barely knew. He was placed, friendless, into the intimidating Tower of London, from which he never emerged. His brother soon joined him, which probably provided a measure of solace. At least the two brothers could provide companionship and try to comfort each other. But, as their circumstances became even more constrained and as it became increasingly apparent, even to a 12-year-old, that matters would not end well, the sense of foreboding must have been overwhelming. Then the brothers were murdered. We do not know exactly how or when they died, but the fate of the Princes in the Tower still tugs at people's hearts some five centuries later.

King Richard had one son who was supposed to succeed him. In December 1473 (or sometime later; the date is not certain), Queen Anne gave birth to the couple's only child, named Edward, at Middleham Castle. Edward was the king's great hope for a peaceful succession. Little is known of him. He was crowned Earl of Salisbury in February 1478 and he acquired other titles when his father became king. A sickly child most of his life, he lived primarily at Middleham Castle, even after his father became king. He did not attend Richard's coronation, possibly because of illness. On 8 September 1483, while Richard and his queen were on a royal progress through the north, Richard had Edward invested as Prince of Wales. The king chose to give the city of York, his primary base of support, the honour of holding the ceremony in its cathedral. In January 1484, members of Parliament swore an oath of allegiance to Edward as Richard's heir.

Edward died after a short illness—exactly what kind is unknown—at Middleham Castle on 9 April 1484, almost exactly one year after the death of his uncle, King Edward IV. He was around ten years old. It is unknown where he was buried. The most likely location is the parish church near Middleham Castle.

When they heard the news, his parents were devastated. Richard's hopes and dreams largely died when his son died. A contemporary chronicler stated that "you might have seen his father and mother in a state almost bordering on madness, by reason of their sudden grief."[97] No one, not even Richard's enemies, ever disputed the genuineness of Richard's grief for the death of his son. The young Edward's death was almost the only death of a major English figure during Richard's adult life, including that of his wife, that Tudor propaganda (and Shakespearian drama) did not blame on Richard. But some of the king's

---

[97] Henry T. Riley, ed. and transl., *Chronicle of the Abbey of Croyland*, Henry G. Bohn (1854), p. 497. This chronicle was produced at the Abbey of Croyland in Lincolnshire.

contemporaries believed his heir's early death was divine retribution for his seizing the throne and murdering the Princes in the Tower.

Richard might have believed it himself. If so, a picture of the events and his character emerges that is likely to be far more accurate than the Shakespearean one—a picture, moreover, that would help explain Richard's lacklustre defence of his realm against Henry Tudor. At first, after King Edward IV's death, Richard sincerely intended to faithfully play his proper role as Lord Protector and see Edward crowned king. But circumstances, mixed with temptation, eventually caused him to seize the throne himself. This act was contrary to all that he had stood for. His motto had always been "loyaulte me lie": Loyalty binds me. He had remained fiercely loyal to his brother, King Edward, in 1470 when others, including the other brother, George, turned against him, even going into exile with the deposed king in Burgundy. Seizing the throne, alone, would have created strong feelings of guilt in the new king.

But, as happens so often when one irrevocably chooses a dark path, seizing the throne was not enough. When the princes became, or appeared to become, a threat to the peace and safety of his reign, especially after the July 1483 attempt to rescue them, Richard was forced (he believed) to order, or at least acquiesce in, the murder of the princes—how and when being still unknown, but, possibly, with Sir James Tyrrell acting as Richard's agent, as he supposedly confessed two decades later. Events simply overtook Richard.

In this likely scenario, Richard tried to atone for what he had done by being a good king. But the death of his only son and heir, followed by that of his wife and queen, Anne (who died at the age of 28 in March 1485, probably of tuberculosis), might have seemed like divine retribution for his sins. The dramatic night of August 21-22, the night before the Battle of Bosworth Field— when, under Shakespeare's version, he was tormented by visits from the ghosts of his many victims—he might instead have struggled with feelings of guilt over his usurpation and murder of the princes. The next day, during the battle itself, Richard might have decided to leave matters to divine will by a mad personal charge against Henry Tudor, a reckless act in which he was killed. This would mean Richard was essentially a good man who was led to do bad things by circumstances and temptation and who was tormented onto death by feelings of guilt over what he had done.

A modern playwright with Shakespearean talent could write a truly great play about *that* Richard.

What is the historical significance of Prince Edward's early death? As always, it is impossible to say for sure. His fate, which was directly attributable to Edward IV's premature death and Richard's failure to perpetuate the Plantagenet dynasty, allowed the Tudor family to establish a new ruling dynasty. The Tudors went on to provide a seemingly inexhaustible mass of material for historians, novelists, playwrights and screenwriters to write about. While they might not have been quite the calamity Sir Clements Markham believed them to have been, England probably would have been better off had the Plantagenets continued to rule and the Tudors remained a minor family of no political significance.

Chapter 9
The Second Non-King Arthur

The high mortality rate among the nobility during and after battles in the Wars of the Roses meant that no one on the Lancastrian side survived who had a strong claim to the throne. By 1485, only one man remained who had even a plausible claim: a member of the formerly obscure Tudor family, Henry Tudor, called the Earl of Richmond.

It is not easy to describe briefly and simply Henry's dynastic claim. He had two connections to England's royal family, both tenuous. First, his mother was Lady Margaret Beaufort, a member of the Beaufort family that had so bitterly opposed Richard, Duke of York, before and during the Wars of the Roses. (Her father was the Duke of Somerset who had been installed as a rival commander to Richard, Duke of York, in the 1440s and who died in 1444. (Chapter 7.)) Margaret was descended from John of Gaunt, third son of King Edward III, through his mistress and eventual wife, Katherine Swynford. When John of Gaunt and Katherine married, their four children, including their firstborn, Margaret's grandfather, were retroactively declared legitimate. The act legitimizing the four children also stipulated that they and their descendants were not to be included in the line of succession to the throne. Rules were made to be broken, however, especially when no other Lancastrian claimant remained.

Second, Henry's paternal grandfather, Owen Tudor, a Welsh adventurer, married King Henry V's widow, Catherine of Valois (a daughter of the French King Charles VI). This meant that Henry Tudor's father, Edmund Tudor, Earl of Richmond, was King Henry VI's half-brother. The English crown was not supposed to be conferred on a descendant of a dowager queen consort (as Catherine of Valois was when she married Owen Tudor) by a later marriage. But, again, rules were made to be broken as necessity required.

Henry Tudor and the remnants of the Lancastrian opposition invaded England in the fall of 1485 in a longshot attempt to overturn Richard III. They landed in Wales. Seeking help in that country, land of his ancestors, Henry promised the Welsh that if they supported him and he became king, he would name his first son Arthur, so that another King Arthur might one day rule over them. They supported him, he won the throne by defeating Richard III at Bosworth Field, and, now called King Henry VII, he kept his word.

But before Henry could have a son, he had to get married. Long before he invaded England to become king, Henry promised that he would marry Elizabeth of York, the oldest daughter of Edward IV, niece of Richard III and the older sister of the two Princes in the Tower. Because Henry had become king by conquest rather than dynastic right, his position was vulnerable, just as Richard III's position had been vulnerable. A marriage between Henry, leader of the Lancastrian branch of the Plantagenets, and Elizabeth of York was supposed to unite the red rose of Lancaster and the white rose of York and lend unchallengeable legitimacy to its issue. The two were married at Westminster Abbey on 18 January 1486.

The new Queen Elizabeth performed her dynastic duty promptly. During the night of 19-20 September 1486, almost exactly eight months after the marriage, she gave birth to a son, born about a month premature. As King Henry had promised, the couple named the child Arthur. Arthur was born at Saint Swithun's Priory (now Winchester Cathedral Priory) in Winchester, England's former capital. The location was not chance but the result of careful political calculation. In the fifteenth century, the story of King Arthur and his Round Table fascinated the English. Sir Thomas Malory's classic recounting of the legend, *Le Morte d'Arthur*, had recently been published. But it was merely the most recent of the Arthurian accounts. King Henry sought to gain acceptance of his dynasty as a worthy successor to the legendary king. He had genealogists trace his ancestry back to Arthur and other British rulers. In those days, Winchester was closely associated with Camelot, King Arthur's fabled capital. So, when Elizabeth was ready to give birth, the king ordered her transported to Winchester—or, as he hoped everyone would view it, Camelot.

Although born premature, Arthur was a healthy baby. Everyone exulted at the birth of an heir with unassailable credentials and had high hopes for him. Beginning the day he was born, major titles of nobility and positions within the government, although obviously not the actual responsibility, came his way. He was invested as Prince of Wales when he was three years old in a ceremony at Westminster. A year later he was made a Knight of the Garter. Arthur's brother, named Henry after the king, was born on 28 June 1491. The two brothers became quite close when they were children.

When Arthur was still very young, King Henry began making plans for his marriage. The king wanted to negotiate a marriage alliance that would make the Tudors one of the great dynasties of Europe. He turned his attention to Ferdinand and Isabella, separately the King of Aragon and Queen of Castile, and, after their marriage, together the joint rulers of the fledgeling nation of Spain. He wanted to forge an alliance with Spain against their mutual enemy, France. In March 1489, the countries agreed to the Treaty of Medina del Campo, by which Arthur was to marry Catherine of Aragon, Ferdinand and Isabella's youngest daughter, when they were old enough. Catherine was about eight months older than Arthur. The two were betrothed by proxy at Woodstock in 1497. By that time, the Spanish Reconquista (reconquest) of the Iberian Peninsula had been completed. The Emirate of Granada, the last Moorish bastion on the peninsula, was defeated in 1492 and its ruler was forced to flee across the water to modern-day Morocco. In that same year, an unheralded navigator named Christopher Columbus, acting on Ferdinand and Isabella's behalf, made an epic voyage and discovered a new, unsuspected, world. The Reconquista and the discovery of America would soon make Spain the richest and most powerful nation in Europe. It made sense for King Henry to want to ally himself with such a country.

Like Edward IV's oldest son before him, Arthur was raised from birth to be a king. Also, like Prince Edward, he resided primarily at Ludlow Castle near Wales. His great uncle, Jasper Tudor, long one of King Henry's most trusted and loyal aides, was his primary guardian. Arthur's education was entrusted to a scholar named Bernard André. André taught him the classics and other traditional disciplines a lord should learn, including grammar, rhetoric and history. André reported to the king that Arthur was an adept student and was well versed in the classics. Also, like Prince Edward, Arthur became the nominal head of the Council of Wales and the Marches, although Jasper Tudor exercised his authority for him.[98] All seemed ready for Arthur to become a great king.

---

[98] In 1493, King Henry formally gave Arthur specific powers in Wales and the Marches. See "The Council in the Marches of Wales," compiled in C.H. Williams, ed., *English Historical Documents, vol. V, 1485-1558,* Oxford University Press (1967), pp. 552-3 (hereafter *EHD, vol. V*).

By 1501, Arthur and Catherine of Aragon were considered old enough to marry. The two had corresponded for years, writing in Latin, the only language they had in common. The letters, more formal at first, became love letters as the date for the wedding approached. Arthur professed great love for his intended bride. Catherine sailed with a large entourage from her native Spain to England, landing at Plymouth on 2 October 1501. Her journey from Plymouth to London was a well-publicised progress. Celebrations and ceremonies were held at every opportunity, as King Henry wanted everyone to know about, and to marvel at, the marriage between their future king and the Spanish princess. On 4 November 1501, Prince Arthur and Princess Catherine of Aragon met for the first time in a small town in Hampshire. To their chagrin, they discovered that they had been taught different pronunciations of Latin. So, they had difficulty speaking to one another at first. But they soon overcame the problem, as each became used to the other's pronunciation and as the princess gradually learned English. By all accounts, they got along well.

Both were well educated, especially in the classics, which gave them common ground to build a relationship. Catherine entered London with great fanfare on 9 November. A mere five days later, with even greater fanfare, the two fifteen-year-olds were married at St Paul's Cathedral, with the Archbishop of Canterbury presiding over the ceremony. Arthur's eight-year-old brother, Henry, played a prominent role in the proceedings. Afterwards, the couple was given a royal send-off, as they moved on to Baynard's Castle, long a royal residence in London, for the night.

At Baynard's Castle, Arthur and Catherine were prepared for what was expected to follow by what was called a "bedding ceremony," presided over by Arthur's grandmother, Margaret Beaufort. Very publicly and ceremoniously, the marital bed was prepared for its occupants and blessed, hoping it would be fruitful. Just as publicly, the newly married princess and prince were led to that bed by their ladies-in-waiting and gentlemen. Then they were left alone. The purpose was to view, as much as decency permitted, the consummation of the marriage and aid the bride, in the beginning, to carry out her primary duty—to produce an heir.

What happened that night and other nights over the next few months when the couple were left alone, was to become, years later, a critical question that would have major repercussions for England and, indeed, the world. Did the fifteen-year-olds consummate the marriage, that is, have sexual relations? A marriage not consummated could be annulled, which effectively would mean it never occurred and either party would be free to marry someone else. According to testimony years later, on the morning after the bedding ceremony, Arthur supposedly said to his servant, "Willoughby, bring me a cup of ale, for I have been this night in the midst of Spain." He said to others, "Masters, it is a good pastime to have a wife." After that first night, they had many more opportunities to have sexual relations but, because no pregnancy resulted, whether they did so was known only to them.

The couple soon set up residence in Ludlow Castle. Unlike Henry, the Young King, who was never given any real authority despite his nominal crown, Arthur was installed as the effective ruler of Wales. That country, often the scene of unrest and rebellion, was quiet just then, so administering it was not particularly difficult. Arthur and Catherine settled into their daily regime, enjoying life as the centre of attention and preparing for Arthur's anticipated kingship. Christmas that year was enjoyed in the traditional way. Then tragedy struck.

It does not appear that Arthur was sickly as a boy; he seems to have been reasonably healthy and robust, although there is some indication to the contrary. In any event, both Catharine and Arthur became ill in March 1502. Catherine recovered; Arthur did not. He died at Ludlow Castle on April 2, only fifteen years old. Catherine was a widow at sixteen years of age, after five months of marriage. Arthur's body was embalmed, then transported with great ceremony and sadness along the Severn River to Worcester, where he was buried after a sombre funeral at the great cathedral in that city.

As is often the case when dealing with medieval or early modern times, what illness took Arthur's life is uncertain. It might have been the "sweating sickness," a mysterious malady that first appeared in England in 1485, the year the Plantagenet dynasty ended and the Tudor dynasty began. The sweating sickness took many lives, then mysteriously disappeared in the middle of the sixteenth century. Arthur might instead have died of tuberculosis or something else. We will never know for sure.

What is known for sure is that Arthur's death devastated his parents and all of England, which had placed high hopes on having a second, perhaps even more glorious, King Arthur.[99] King Henry's policy of maintaining an alliance with

---

[99] It is a moot, but interesting, question whether, had Arthur lived to become king, he would have been called King Arthur II, to connect him ever closer to his supposed predecessor; or whether the Tudors would have followed the precedent set when Henry

Spain was now in tatters. His hopes for his dynasty's future now centred on his only remaining son, the then eight-year-old Prince Henry. The king immediately proposed that, when Prince Henry came of age, he would marry Catherine of Aragon in his turn. Ferdinand and Isabella were willing. Without a papal dispensation, the marriage would violate church law; a man was not allowed to marry his brother's widow. To be more precise, marriage between Catherine and Henry would violate church law if, but only if, the prior marriage between Catherine and Arthur had been consummated. Catherine testified under oath that it had not been consummated. Her *duenna*, or primary lady-in-waiting, supported this testimony.

The question was not conclusively determined at that time. If the previous marriage had not been consummated, a papal dispensation would not be needed; an invalid marriage would pose no impediment to Prince Henry's marrying Catherine. But King Henry and the Spanish monarchs decided that, rather than rest everything on Catherine's testimony, they would seek a papal dispensation for the marriage. The application was based on the understanding that the marriage *had been* consummated. Pope Julius II granted the dispensation and permitted Henry and Catharine to marry "even if," as it was phrased, Catherine's earlier marriage had been consummated.[100] Prince Henry and Catharine were married on 11 June 1509, after Henry had become King Henry VIII. As everyone knows, Catherine was not to be Henry's only wife. He would have five more.

Henry and Catherine had one child who survived infancy, a girl named Mary and later Queen Mary I. Catherine produced no surviving male heir. This circumstance worried Henry more and more over time, especially after Catharine reached the age of 40 and it became clear she would bear no more children. Around 1526, Henry became disenchanted with Catharine and infatuated with a lady in her entourage, Anne Boleyn. Anne was a young woman who knew what she wanted and refused to become merely his mistress. Henry also became convinced that Arthur and Catherine had consummated their marriage and that, therefore, his own marriage was incestuous. He obsessed about the biblical injunction, "And if a man shall take his brother's wife, it is an unclean thing: he

---

III's son become King Edward I (not II) in the thirteenth century, even though Edward the Confessor had been King of England for some 24 years in the eleventh century, just before the Battle of Hastings.

[100] "Negotiations for the marriage of Prince Henry and Catherine of Aragon," compiled in *EHD, vol. V,* pp. 697-8.

hath uncovered his brother's nakedness; they shall be childless."[101] Catherine and Henry were not exactly childless, but they were without a male heir, a situation Henry blamed on what he believed to be his incestuous marriage. He believed, or wanted to believe, that Pope Julius II should never have granted the dispensation permitting him to marry Catherine.

Henry decided to obtain an annulment of his marriage to Catharine so he could marry Anne Boleyn. The asserted grounds were that Catherine had previously married his brother. Confident that the annulment would be granted, he requested it from Pope Clement VII in 1527. Popes have sometimes complied quietly with such requests, as when the Pope granted Eleanor of Aquitaine an annulment from King Louis VII on the grounds of consanguinity. (Chapter 3.) But the situation this time was not so simple. Catherine did not go quietly but continued to insist, as she did her entire life, sometimes under oath, that she and Arthur had not had a sexual relationship and that she had been a virgin when she married Henry. For complex diplomatic and political reasons, the Pope wanted neither to grant nor deny the annulment, nor to decide definitively whether Henry's marriage to Catherine was valid.

Unfortunately for Henry, his request for an annulment came at a time of historic events on the European mainland. The new King of Spain, Charles I (also Holy Roman Emperor Charles V), Catharine's nephew, took his aunt's side. Troops under his command captured and sacked Rome in 1527 and gained effective control over the Pope. Thus, the Pope was in no position to anger Charles. But he also did not want to anger Henry. Another concern was that he did not want to undo the dispensation the earlier Pope had issued; doing so would weaken the force of dispensations in the future. So Clement chose to delay. The delay went on for years.

Angered by the Pope's lack of cooperation and tired of endless delays, Henry eventually chose to act independently of the church in Rome. He took steps that began the separation of the English church from the Roman Catholic church, a historic process called the English Reformation. He married Anne Boleyn in January 1533. That May, Henry's newly appointed, and compliant, Archbishop of Canterbury, Thomas Cranmer, annulled Henry's marriage with Catherine and declared valid his marriage with Anne. The Archbishop crowned Anne Queen of England on June 1. The church in Rome had nothing to do with any of this. The Archbishop acted on his own, independently of Rome. The English Reformation

---

[101] *Leviticus*, 20:21.

was well underway. Henry got what he wished, but from his own people in England, not from the Pope.

The Pope prepared documents to excommunicate Henry for disregarding Rome and instituting the English Reformation. Theoretically, and in reality in past times, excommunication had drastic consequences for the target. But given the religious developments in England, it would have had virtually no effect in that country. The Pope never actually issued the excommunication, possibly because he did not want the world—including especially those parts of Europe where the Protestant movement, led by Martin Luther and others, was rampant—to note how ineffective it was.

Arthur's premature death had the immediate consequence of causing his brother to become the royal heir in his place, leading to Henry's becoming king on Henry VII's death in 1509. Years later, the controversy over whether Arthur had consummated his marriage contributed, in a substantial way, to England's break with the Roman Catholic Church and the establishment of the independent Church of England. The breakup was monumental and revolutionised the religious landscape in England. It led to centuries of religious strife in that country.

Did Catherine and Arthur consummate their marriage? Obviously, we do not know. No one was watching the marriage bed after the two were left alone. Only they knew for sure. Catherine consistently denied it, sometimes under oath. A statement under oath was a very serious undertaking, especially in those days, which lends credence to Catherine's testimony. Arthur's supposed statement that he had been "in the midst of Spain" the morning after his wedding implied that they had had sex. But, assuming he said it, he might merely have been bragging, saying what he thought the others would expect him to say. Young boys mature sexually at differing ages. Arthur was a little over fifteen years, five months old when he died. He was born prematurely, so his physical age was even younger. He might not have been sexually mature enough to have consummated his marriage. The question is unimportant today, but at one time it had great consequences. It is an overstatement to say that the question of whether Arthur and Catherine had had sexual intercourse caused the English Reformation. But the question and the Reformation were closely intertwined.

As with any heir who died so young, we cannot confidently say what kind of a King Arthur would have made had he lived. He was well educated, appeared intelligent and sober-minded and he would have had an intelligent, sober-minded queen. He was trained to be a king and entrusted from an early age with administrative duties. He seemed to be a reasonably gentle and thoughtful young man. He might have done well.

What does seem safe to say is that Arthur's reign would not have been as tumultuous (to use an unduly benign adjective) as the actual reign of his brother, King Henry VIII. After a relatively promising start to his reign, Henry had six wives, two of whom he ordered beheaded. He forced the English Church to break with the church in Rome. He plundered the country's many monasteries, small and large, strict and not so strict, rich and poor (concentrating on the rich); then he promptly squandered the riches thereby obtained in obscenely wasteful and egotistical spending. He left untold numbers of monks and nuns without a way to make a living, many of whom, along with other citizens, were executed for treason or heresy. In what can only be described as judicial murders, he oversaw the execution of many of his own, generally loyal, officials on dubious, or entirely specious, grounds of treason or heresy, with or without a show trial.

A supine Parliament passed the Treasons Act of 1534 that expanded the definition of treason, a crime punishable by hanging, drawing and quartering, to include wishing, desiring, or imagining harm to the royal family, or calling the king a tyrant or just about anything else that could be considered derogatory. Additionally, it was considered to be heresy, a crime punishable by burning at the stake, not to agree with whatever the king happened to believe at any moment in time, including that the king was, by divine right, the supreme, indeed sole, authority on all matters of theological and civil law. Because of these changes and given these new definitions, the charges of treason and heresy might actually have been factually supported in many cases. Among Henry's many victims from within his own government were Sir Thomas More who, earlier in his career, had hewed to the Tudor line in his biography of Richard III; and, in what many no doubt viewed as poetic justice, the man who, as Henry's chief minister for many years, had masterminded most of the judicial murders, the ingenious and clever Thomas Cromwell.

Whatever one thinks of Sir Clements Markham's opinion that the Battle of Bosworth Field was a calamity for England (chapter 8), Arthur's early death almost certainly had calamitous consequences for the country. Had he lived, his hypothetical reign would surely been preferable to Henry's. He would not have been the vile and murderous tyrant Henry became in the later years of his reign.

Chapter 10
Mary, Queen of Scots

Everyone has heard of Mary, Queen of Scots. Everyone also knows that, as the name implies, she was the Queen of Scotland. Less well known is that, although never formally recognised as such, she was effectively the heir presumptive to Queen Elizabeth I. When it became apparent that Elizabeth would never produce her own heir, this meant Mary was in effect the heir apparent. All she had to do to become Queen of England was to outlive Elizabeth. As she was younger by nine years, she could expect to assume the throne in the natural course of events. But events did not take a natural course. Mary's life would be dramatic—and tragic. (If it had been fiction, it would have been considered melodrama.)

Mary's life began auspiciously. She was born on 8 December 1542, at Linlithgow Palace, about 15 miles west of Edinburgh, the only legitimate child of the Scottish King James V. Her mother, Mary of Guise, was a member of one of the most powerful and most strongly Catholic families in France. Her father, the king, was sick and dying when she was born. When he heard he had a daughter and knowing he would have no other children, he reportedly exclaimed, "Woe is me! My dynasty came with a lass. It will go with a lass." (His ancestor, Robert II, had been the son of Robert the Bruce's daughter and the High Steward of Scotland. When Robert II became king—inheriting through a woman (or lass)—he named his new dynasty Stewart, a variation of the word steward.) James apparently believed the dynasty would not continue without a male heir. He was mistaken. The Stewart dynasty, better known today by the French variant, Stuart, would see far more glorious days in the future.

James V died six days after Mary was born and, suddenly, at less than a week of age, Mary was Queen of Scots. An auspicious beginning, indeed, if she had only been aware of it. Hers would prove to be a contentious and turbulent inheritance. She was born into royalty and was to become famous. But she would pay a heavy price.

Obviously, the infant Mary could not rule, so a regency was formed. By 1542, the Protestant Reformation, led by John Knox, had arrived in Scotland. As in so many places in Europe, religious strife—Roman Catholics versus Protestants and different Protestant faiths versus other Protestant faiths—existed throughout the kingdom. Two nobles vied to become the Regent, one Protestant, one Catholic. The Protestant, James Hamilton, the Earl of Arran prevailed. He was the closest relative of King James and was next in line to become the monarch of Scotland after Mary. In 1554, Mary's mother managed to replace him as Regent. By that time, however, Mary was living in France.

When Mary was still an infant, the English King Henry VIII proposed a marriage between her and his only surviving son, Edward, later King Edward VI. He hoped such a marriage would lead to a united England and Scotland. On July 1, 1543, representatives of the two countries agreed to the Treaty of Greenwich, whereby Mary and Edward were to marry when she was ten years old. The Earl of Arran signed the treaty on Scotland's behalf. However, the Scottish Parliament rejected it, which led to several years of warfare between England and Scotland known as the "Rough Wooing," in which King Henry tried to force the Scots to agree to the proposed marriage. Additionally, religious conflict continued in Scotland. In July 1543, for her safety, Mary was moved to the more secure castle at Stirling. A large armed escort escorted her. There, she was crowned Queen of Scots on 9 September 1543. She was nine months old.

After Scottish defeats in the Rough Wooing, Scotland turned to France for help, as it often did. Scotland and France had long been allies against their mutual enemy, England. The French King, Henry II (in French Henri), was amenable to another alliance. He proposed that, when they became old enough, Mary would marry his son and heir, the Dauphin Francis (in French Francois). The Earl of Arran agreed. So, later, did the Scottish Parliament. In July 1548, to further the marriage plans (and to escape the ongoing warfare in Scotland), the five-year-old Mary sailed from Dumbarton Castle to France, avoiding, with French military help, English ships along the way. They arrived in August. There she was raised at the French court and essentially became French. Fatefully, she was raised as a Catholic. She had no say in how she was raised, but she remained a faithful Catholic all her life, although she was always willing to tolerate other religions.

Mary was accompanied by a large entourage, including four daughters of Scottish noble families, who would remain with her for many years. All bore the same name as the queen and thus were known as the "Four Marys": Mary Fleming, Mary Beaton, Mary Seton and Mary Livingston. The French King, Henry II, welcomed Mary as the royalty that she was and he treated her like a daughter. He was reportedly delighted with her. His delight was understandable. She was vivacious, pretty and intelligent. She and the Dauphin, a little more than a year younger than she, got along well when they were children. From the time they first met, both knew they were intended to marry when they got older. They lived in various royal palaces in France.

When Mary was seven years old, her mother came from Scotland to visit her. After the mother left, they were destined never to see each other again. Mary was given a classical education, learning French, Italian, Spanish, Latin and a smattering of Greek. She befriended and became close with, her future sister-in-law, Elizabeth of Valois, later Queen of Spain as the wife of the Spanish King Philip II. When Mary was a child and later, when she was an adult, she was described as beautiful. In those days, virtually all princesses were described as beautiful, but surviving portraits suggest she was at least very attractive, with bright auburn hair and hazel eyes. She was very tall, especially for a woman in those days, attaining a height of five feet, eleven inches, or one meter, 80 centimetres.

Mary and Francis were married on 24 April 1558, in a magnificent ceremony at the Cathedral of Notre Dame in Paris. He was fourteen years old and she fifteen. Given Francis's age and delicate health, they probably never consummated the marriage, although the question had no political significance then or ever and, mercifully, was never the subject of litigation. (Cf. Chapter 9.) With the marriage, Francis became king consort of Scotland, although he never actually visited the country.

Meanwhile, the Tudor dynasty in England continued. When Henry VIII died in 1547, his son by his third wife, Jane Seymour—Henry's only son to survive infancy—became King Edward VI at the age of nine years. Edward was doomed to die at fifteen. Edward's half-sister, Mary—Henry VIII's daughter by his first wife, Catherine of Aragon—succeeded Edward as Mary I. Mary, a Catholic, tried to reverse the English Reformation and restore Catholicism to its accustomed position in England. She succeeded temporarily, but in the process, she oversaw the burning at the stake of hundreds of unrepentant Protestants charged with heresy—most prominently Thomas Cranmer, Henry VIII's Archbishop of Canterbury, one of the leaders of the English Reformation and the man who had declared invalid the marriage between Mary's mother and Henry. Her brutal suppression of Protestantism earned her the sobriquet by which she is known to this day: Bloody Mary. After a five-year reign, Mary died at the age of 42, only a few months after the marriage between Francis and Mary. On 17 November 1558, Henry's daughter by his second wife, Anne Boleyn, succeeded to the throne as Queen Elizabeth I. To understate matters, Elizabeth and Mary, Queen of Scots, would have a strained relationship.

Unlike both her sister Mary and Mary, Queen of Scots, Elizabeth was Protestant. Most, if not all, Catholics considered Elizabeth ineligible to be queen. In Catholic eyes, Henry's first marriage to Catherine was valid and remained valid until her death, which occurred in 1536, well after Elizabeth was born. He was never lawfully married to Anne Boleyn, which meant that their issue, Elizabeth, was illegitimate. As noted before (chapters 3, 8), an illegitimate child could not inherit the throne. With Elizabeth ineligible to inherit Henry's crown and King Edward VI and Queen Mary I having died childless, the rightful monarch, in the Catholic view, was the next closest living relative to Henry VIII. That happened to be Mary, Queen of Scots. Mary's paternal grandmother, Margaret Tudor, was Henry VIII's sister, making Henry her great-uncle and Elizabeth her cousin.

With both Mary I and Elizabeth I having been recognised as queen regnant of England, a precedent was set four centuries after Matilda, Henry I's only surviving legitimate child, unsuccessfully tried to be recognised queen regnant (see chapter 3): a woman could wear the crown of England in her own right. Thus, the Catholic world considered Mary, Queen of Scots, to be the rightful Queen of England. This meant that Mary was, or might be viewed as, a threat to Elizabeth's position as Queen of England and would remain a threat as long as she lived. The situation was fraught with danger for Mary. But for now, she was safe in France.

When Elizabeth became Queen, Mary's father-in-law, the French (and Catholic) King Henry II, declared that his son, Francis, and Mary were the legitimate king and queen of England. He ordered the royal arms of England be added to their heraldry. Other than the change in heraldry, nothing came of this declaration. Henry himself died of injuries suffered in a jousting accident in July 1559, at the age of 40. (His death in a jousting tournament did not make him an heir who never reigned, unlike the similar death of Geoffrey, the English King Henry II's third son [chapter 4], but it certainly shortened his reign, probably significantly.) Mary tried to persuade Elizabeth that her father-in-law's action was his own doing and not her wish, which helped ease the relationship between them. But Elizabeth probably never forgot the French King's actions and never fully trusted Mary.

King Henry's death meant that his son, the Dauphin, became King Francis II. The sixteen-year-old Mary became queen consort of France while she was simultaneously queen regnant of Scotland. Conversely, Francis became king regnant of France while he was simultaneously king consort of Scotland. While she was queen, she and Francis entertained as a guest one of her future husbands, James Hepburn, Earl of Bothwell, when he was visiting the French court. They apparently got along well. The new king and queen seemed happy living together in France in these circumstances. Events were to ensure this happiness would not last long.

In June 1560, Mary's mother, Mary of Guise, still acting as regent, died. She had succeeded in maintaining her position as regent against Protestant opposition only with the support of French troops who came to Scotland to assist her. Her death left an uncertain situation in that country. Quarrels and sometimes open warfare between Catholics and Protestants were endemic. The Protestants were led by an institution called the Lords of the Congregation. By this time, both English and French troops were in Scotland. The French supported the Catholics. The English supported the Protestants. One of the leaders of the Lords of the Congregation was Mary's half-brother, James Stewart, later called the Earl of Moray, King James V's illegitimate son (of whom we will hear much more later).

France and England sought to reach an agreement to extricate themselves from Scotland. A month after Mary of Guise died, English and French diplomats, representing Queen Elizabeth and King Francis, with the agreement of the Lords of the Congregation, negotiated the Treaty of Edinburgh. The French and English agreed to withdraw their troops from Scotland. France recognised Elizabeth as the lawful Queen of England. Mary and Francis were to renounce any claim to the English throne and remove the English heraldry from their own heraldry. There was to be peace between England and Scotland and between England and France. However, Mary herself, acting as Queen of Scotland, refused to ratify the treaty, possibly because she did not want to formally recognise Elizabeth as the legitimate Queen of England.

Francis died of an ear infection on 5 December 1560, leaving Mary a widow three days before her eighteenth birthday. Mary was devastated by the twin blows of her mother's, then her husband's, deaths. Now she had to decide what to do with her life and her position as Queen of Scots. Her former mother-in-law, Catherine de Medici, became regent during the childhood of the ten-year-old new King of France, Charles IX. As Catherine had always disliked Mary, Mary's position in France was precarious.

Mary did what she effectively had to do; she returned to Scotland to begin to rule personally over her country. She left France in August 1561, accompanied by the four Marys and arrived five days later at Leith, the port of her capital of Edinburgh. Her situation there was also precarious. She had virtually no experience with the situation in Scotland. Because she had not lived in that country since she was five years old, it was, to her, essentially a foreign country. She was also essentially a foreigner to her people, having been raised in France and primarily speaking French. The withdrawal of French troops from Scotland under the Treaty of Edinburgh deprived her of much-needed military support. The Scottish Parliament also proclaimed Scotland to be a Protestant country. For *any* Catholic to rule Scotland effectively would have been a challenge. Under Mary's circumstances, it would be even more challenging.

Mary's relationship with Elizabeth was ambiguous, an ambiguity fraught with danger for her and even, to a lesser extent, for Elizabeth. When she arrived in France and for the rest of her life, Mary insisted, both publicly and in letters to Elizabeth, that she wanted to coexist peacefully with the English Queen, a fellow woman and someone Mary professed to view as a sister. She was probably sincere. But Elizabeth and especially her advisors, always had doubts, doubts no doubt fuelled by memories of Mary's father-in-law, the French King Henry II, claiming that Mary was the rightful Queen of England when Queen Mary I died. Additionally, whatever Mary might have felt and intended, she was to a large extent a pawn in international power politics. England's traditional enemy France, the land of Mary's mother and her strongly Catholic Guise family, the country where Mary had once been queen consort, might again claim Mary was the legitimate English queen. France might even lead an invasion of England to make good this claim.

The position of Catholic Spain was more ambivalent. It naturally wanted a Catholic on the English throne, but it was often at odds with France during this period and did not wish a French-English alliance that could threaten its position.

But Spain's sympathy for Mary was always an undercurrent of European politics. The papacy, which viewed Elizabeth as the illegitimate offspring of a whore (Anne Boleyn, who purported to marry Henry VIII while, in Catholic eyes, Henry was still married to Catherine of Aragon), also claimed Mary was the legitimate Queen of England. All of these circumstances made Mary at least an implied threat to Elizabeth, whatever Mary might have personally wanted. This implied threat was to colour the relationship between Mary and Elizabeth for the rest of Mary's life.

When she first returned to Scotland, Mary was greeted with joy and celebration as a returned queen. But, as a Catholic, she was also viewed with suspicion by the new Protestant establishment. The Scottish reformer, John Knox, founder of the Presbyterian Church of Scotland, preached against her and her Catholic ways. Three years previously, in 1558, he had written and circulated a political tract—"The First Blast of the Trumpet against the Monstrous Regiment of Women"—fulminating against the whole idea of women as sovereigns.[102] Mary met with him several times in an unsuccessful attempt to win him over, or at least to find some common ground. He criticised her to her face for adhering to Catholicism. She held her ground in the theological debate, although the meetings often reduced her to tears. Her interviews with the stern Knox accomplished little, but they show her at her moderate, but determined and intelligent, best.

Mary also adopted—or tried to adopt—a policy that, given the times, satisfied neither the Catholics nor the Protestants. She preached and practised religious tolerance—let the Catholics live in peace with their religion and let the Protestants live in peace with theirs. She sought to have all treated fairly. This was quite a novel attitude in the sixteenth century. But both sides of the religious divide agreed on one thing; they could not tolerate tolerance. They were united against that policy; some opposed Mary herself for adopting it. One side or the other had to win and suppress the other. Catholic and Protestant could not co-exist. Mary also sought to strengthen the power of the crown and diminish that of the nobles, a policy the nobles resisted, although it tended to be popular with the commoners.

---

[102] Jayne Elizabeth Lewis, *The Trial of Mary Queen of Scots: A Brief History with Documents*, Bedford/St Martin's (1999), pp. 53-63 (hereafter Lewis, *The Trial of Mary Queen of Scots*).

As part of her effort to rule over a religiously neutral state, or perhaps merely accepting the fact the Protestants were in the ascendant, Mary chose as one of her chief advisors her half-brother, the Protestant James Stewart, whom she made the Earl of Moray. She created a privy council of sixteen men to advise her, one dominated by Protestants. The Catholics, expecting Mary to favour her co-religionists, were not happy. In 1562, a leading Catholic nobleman, George Gordon, Earl of Huntly, rebelled against her in the Scottish Highlands. With Mary's support, the Earl of Moray defeated Huntly at the October 28 Battle of Corrichie. Huntly died soon thereafter. Over the next year, in an attempt to solidify her position, Mary travelled widely throughout Scotland. These royal progresses helped her make personal friends and potential allies among many Scottish nobility, including some who were Protestant.

In foreign policy, Mary managed to maintain peace with France and Spain and even England. She urged Queen Elizabeth to name her the heir presumptive to the English throne, something her bloodline warranted. Although it appears Elizabeth privately wanted Mary to succeed her, she chose to name no heir formally. She wanted no named heir and especially not Mary, around whom her enemies could conspire to replace her. Mary continually sought to meet Elizabeth face to face. Presumably, she wanted to urge her position as Elizabeth's heir, but also to reassure Elizabeth that she had no designs on her throne as long as she lived. The meeting could never satisfactorily be arranged and the two never actually met.

Soon it became time for Mary to marry for a second time and produce an heir to ensure her dynasty's continuation. Negotiations for marriage with someone outside Scotland came to nothing. She made her choice from within her own family. In July 1565, she married a cousin, Henry Stewart, Lord Darnley, at Hollyrood Palace in Edinburgh. He had been raised in England and, like Mary, was a grandchild of Henry VIII's sister, Margaret. The two had met briefly several years earlier in France. Mary was attracted to him and married him at least partly due to this attraction. He could be charming and, what must have been especially alluring to her, he was actually taller than she. He was a fellow Catholic, although his religious views were flexible enough to accommodate whatever beliefs were most convenient at any given time. He was also vain and immature. The marriage would prove turbulent. Darnley demanded power. He wanted to be a co-equal monarch of Scotland. Mary refused, leading to tension. The marriage also worried Queen Elizabeth. Both Darnley and Mary had credible claims to her throne and their children would have an even stronger claim. The marriage added to Elizabeth's latent distrust of her cousin.

The marriage between the two Catholics also caused dissension within her own country, fuelled by fears that the couple intended to try to return Scotland to Catholicism. Soon after the marriage, Mary's half-brother and former advisor, the Earl of Moray, and other Protestant lords rebelled and raised troops against her. Mary raised her own army. She found important allies in the son of the Earl of Huntly who had rebelled against her three years previously and the Earl of Bothwell. In an episode derisively called the Chaseabout Raid, the two sides circled around each other in the Scottish Lowlands without ever coming to grips. Eventually, as Mary's forces were stronger, Moray fled to England, where he sought, but did not receive, help from the English Queen. Mary survived this time. The rebellion, however, portended trouble for the future. To try to strengthen her government, she added new members to her privy council, both Protestant and Catholic.

Soon after her marriage to Darnley, Mary became pregnant. But shocking events were about to happen. During this time, she had an Italian private secretary and confidant named David Rizzio (sometimes spelt Riccio), whom she valued highly. Her husband, frustrated by his lack of recognised power and believing Rizzio had too much influence over her, decided to have him murdered. Although Rizzio was short and ugly, Darnley may also have believed that the two had a romantic relationship and possibly even that Rizzio was the one who had gotten her pregnant. In March 1566, around 8:00 pm on a Sunday, when Mary was some six months pregnant, Darnley and several Protestant lords, including some who had opposed her in the Chaseabout Raid, broke into her dining room at Hollyrood Palace, where she was dining with Rizzio and some of her ladies-in-waiting. The intruders stabbed Rizzio to death, either in front of Mary or in an adjoining room, inflicting some 57 stab wounds. She claimed later that one of the intruders even pointed a gun at her pregnant body.

At the time, some believed the Protestant lords hoped the experience would cause Mary to miscarry, which, given the state of medical skill at the time, might also have caused her own death. Some suspected Darnley himself had the same hope, believing that Mary's death would allow him to become king in her place. This has, however, never been proven. In any event, any such hope did not come to fruition, as Mary, despite becoming understandably distraught, survived the incident in reasonably good health.

The lords kept Mary a prisoner in her own palace. Startlingly, two nights later, a desperate Mary won Darnley back to her side, possibly convincing him that he himself was in danger from the Protestant lords. The two escaped together from the palace around midnight and fled to nearby Dunbar Castle. Later, they were able to return to Edinburgh, although they did not occupy Hollyrood Palace. In a sign of how fluid the situation was and possibly out of sympathy for her plight, the former rebel (and, earlier, her chief advisor), the Earl of Moray, also came back to her side. She restored him and other former rebels to her privy council. Once again, Mary survived. But these events also did not bode well for the future.

Three months later, on 19 June 1566, Mary peacefully gave birth in Edinburgh Castle to her son and heir. He was to be her only child. The boy was named James, like his maternal grandfather. Giving birth to a healthy son and remaining in robust good health herself, might have been the high point of her life. She was 23 years old and could look forward to many more years as Queen of Scotland. As she gazed upon her long-desired son, she might have forgotten her problems with her divided country and maybe even with her husband, at least for a while. But only for a short while. The storm clouds soon returned.

A few weeks after James's birth, Mary, accompanied by several others, rode a horse several hours through the Scottish countryside to visit the Earl of Bothwell, the man who had been her guest in France several years previously and had aided her during the Chaseabout Raid. Bothwell had been seriously wounded in a local affair and Mary was told he might die. Bothwell recovered, but the visit had consequences for both. To discredit her, Mary's enemies later used this episode to claim that Bothwell and Mary had been lovers. However, it appears that the visit was innocent; it may have involved state business, as well as a friend's simple concern for a friend and ally who might have been dying.

When Mary returned from visiting Bothwell, she became seriously ill. By late October 1566, it appeared she might be dying. On what she thought was her death bed, she gave an emotional speech to those surrounding her and prepared for her upcoming death. But she recovered; by the next month, she was active again. On 17 December, her son was baptised at Stirling Castle. The baptism was part of a Catholic service.

Although Darnley had helped Mary to escape, obviously Rizzio's murder strained their relationship. She discussed a possible divorce with her leading nobles. But some of the nobles might have preferred another solution. As one account later stated, "It was thought expedient and most profitable for the common wealth, by the whole nobility and lords under scribed, that such a young fool and proud tyrant should not reign or bear rule over them;…that he should be put off by one way or another; and whosoever should take the deed in hand, or do it, they should defend and fortify as themselves."[103] The Protestant lords who participated in Rizzio's murder also felt betrayed by Darnley's helping Mary to escape their clutches. Many people, including Mary herself, had a motive to want him dead.

In January 1567, Darnley lived in a house at a former abbey called Kirk O'Field, just within Edinburgh's city walls, a short walk from Hollyrood Palace. Mary visited him often. In the evening of 9 February, she visited him then went to a wedding celebration for one of her servants. Early the next morning, a violent gunpowder explosion destroyed the house. Darnley's body, along with a servant's, was found in a nearby garden. Darnley, however, was not killed in the explosion. He had been smothered or strangled, either before or after the explosion.

Darnley's murder was never solved. It remains one of the great mysteries of Scottish history. The reaction was swift. Suspicion fell on many people, including Mary and her half-brother, the Earl of Moray. Not all suspected Mary, however. Queen Elizabeth wrote to her expressing sympathy and support. The main suspect was the Earl of Bothwell. Bothwell was tried for the murder in the privy council in April 1567, but he was acquitted after a seven-hour trial for want of evidence—and maybe for less worthy reasons; the trial was conducted quickly, arguably too soon for anyone to have time to gather the necessary evidence.

Bothwell wanted much more than just an acquittal; he wanted to marry the queen. At his instigation, around 20 April, many major Scottish lords and bishops signed what was called the Ainslee Tavern Bond, named for a tavern in Edinburgh where the group had met and discussed the matter over supper. The document expressed approval of Bothwell's acquittal of Darnley's murder. More significantly, it stated that Bothwell would make a good husband for the now-widowed queen. The signatories pledged to defend such a marriage.

Around this time, Mary visited her ten-month-old son at Stirling. Sadly, it would be the last time she would see him. She then went on the road to return to

---

[103] Antonia Fraser, *Mary Queen of Scots*, Delta (1969), p. 279 (hereafter Fraser, *Mary Queen of Scots*).

Edinburgh. On the way, Bothwell, accompanied by some 600-armed men, intercepted her. Telling her she would be in danger in Edinburgh, he offered to escort her to his castle at Dunbar. Either voluntarily or involuntarily (it remains uncertain whether it was an abduction), she agreed. There, the two may have had sexual intercourse, again either consensually or not (if not, then it was rape). On May 6, the two returned to Edinburgh. At some time during these events, Mary agreed to marry Bothwell, apparently willingly. She also made him the Duke of Orkney. One problem was that Bothwell had married another woman the previous year. Mary had even attended the wedding. But Bothwell quickly began divorce proceedings and a divorce was granted on May 7. Eight days later, Mary and Bothwell were married in a small, private Protestant ceremony, probably at Hollyrood Palace. Her third husband would be her last.

Given the circumstances, Mary's decision to marry Bothwell seems odd. Although they knew each fairly well and she was apparently impressed by him (indeed, her enemies claimed they had been lovers), love probably had nothing to do with it. With all the turmoil in her country and with her having a young, vulnerable son, she may have felt the need to have a strong man at her side, a need that Bothwell seemed to fill. The Ainslee Tavern Bond, with all of its signatories, may have convinced her that the country would endorse the marriage. Mary defended her action to the outside world. She wrote that she was in danger and Bothwell was a strong warrior and defender of Scotland who could aid her in a time of crisis. That was the reason she said that she married him. Whatever the reasons, it was a serious mistake and would lead to her undoing.

To the extent Mary believed the country would embrace the marriage, she badly miscalculated. The marriage, which elevated Bothwell far higher than others wanted, proved unpopular. Catholics did not believe the marriage was valid because they refused to recognise Bothwell's quick divorce. To some of them, Mary was a bigamist and a whore. Many were dismayed that Mary took as her third husband a man strongly suspected of murdering her second husband. Some even believed Mary and Bothwell had together arranged the murder so that Mary would be free to marry him. Within weeks of the marriage, many of the nobles, including some who had signed the Ainslee Tavern Bond, raised an army against Mary and Bothwell. Mary raised her own forces. The two armies confronted each other on 15 June at a place called Carberry Hill near Edinburgh, ready for battle. But there was no battle; instead, negotiations ensued. During the negotiations, many of Mary's troops deserted the field.

With dwindling support and to avoid further bloodshed, Mary agreed to surrender to one of the opposing nobles. Bothwell was given safe passage from the field. The married couple never saw each other again. Bothwell eventually made his way to Norway, where he was arrested. He was imprisoned in Denmark for the remaining ten years of his life. Mary was taken to Edinburgh and escorted to Hollyrood Palace. On the way, enemy soldiers taunted her with cries of "burn the whore."[104] In Edinburgh, where Mary was once welcomed, the reception was now quite different. "The people yelled insults, but Mary shouted back that she was innocent and that they had been deceived by false and cruel traitors."[105]

Mary was imprisoned at Loch Leven Castle, on an island on Loch Leven. There, she miscarried after a short pregnancy (it would have been twins) sometime between July 20 to 23. It is not clear when she had become pregnant, whether it was before or after she married Bothwell. She survived the miscarriage, but, on July 24, 1567, despondent and ill, she was forced to sign papers abdicating her throne in favour of her one-year-old son. At the age of 24 years, she would never again truly be Mary, Queen of Scots. She had personally ruled Scotland for less than six years.

The infant James was crowned King of Scotland on July 29. John Knox preached a sermon at the coronation. In contrast to his mother, who lost all control over him, James was to be raised a Protestant. Mary's mercurial half-brother, the Earl of Moray, her sometimes chief advisor, sometimes bitter enemy, was named regent during James' minority. The Protestant opposition, led by the Earl of Moray, thus took from Mary her only child, as well as her throne.

In the meantime, the former Queen of Scots was kept a prisoner at Loch Leven Castle. But she still had supporters who did not believe she was part of the conspiracy to murder Darnley. On May 2, 1568, she escaped from the castle with the help of the brother of the man entrusted with keeping her imprisoned. Many of the Scots welcomed her escape. She was determined to regain her crown, which meant she sought to overthrow her own son. (The infant James, of course, was oblivious of these events.) Over the next few days, she quickly raised an army of some 6,000 men, a decent size under the circumstances. Many of the leading nobles joined her and signed a document calling for her restitution as

---

[104] Julian Goodare, *Oxford Dictionary of National Biography, Mary Stewart*, Oxford University Press (2007) (hereafter *ODNB, Mary Stewart*).

[105] Alison Weir, *Mary, Queen of Scots and the Murder of Lord Darnley*, Ballantine Books (2003), p. 449 (hereafter Weir, *Mary, Queen of Scots*).

Queen of Scotland. They declared that Mary had abdicated only under duress and remained the rightful queen. The Earl of Moray raised his own army. While Mary was trying to reach the relative safety of Dumbarton Castle, the forces met at the town of Langside, then a few miles south of Glasgow, today within that city. On May 13, the Battle of Langside, nominally contested between Mary and her infant son (represented by the Earl of Moray) was fought. Although Mary had a larger army, the battle was a decisive defeat for her. Many of her supporters were captured. Her last chance to regain her crown was lost.

Mary fled south. After great difficulties, including a frantic overnight ride on horseback, she arrived at the coast. Her advisors recommended she flee to France, where the French King, Henry III, her former brother-in-law (Francis II's brother, who became king when the other brother, Charles IX, died childless), would surely welcome her and champion her cause. However, she decided to go to England where she was confident, Elizabeth, her cousin and fellow queen, would come to her aid. Elizabeth's letter to Mary after Darnley's death expressing sympathy and support might have encouraged this confidence. Mary would soon learn she was tragically mistaken. She sailed for England on a fishing boat on May 16, 1568, landing in Cumberland. There, English forces took her into custody. She would never again be free.

In Scotland, the struggle on Mary's behalf continued for several years. Her remaining supporters fought a bitter civil war, called the Marian War, to support her cause. But it was all for nought and the struggle eventually ended in defeat for the cause. James ruled over Scotland for the rest of his life. Never again did Mary set foot in Scotland, the country over which she had been queen since she was one week old.

Elizabeth was uncertain what to do with Mary. Although Mary posed no immediate threat to her throne, many, even in England, viewed her as Elizabeth's proper heir. Disaffected subjects in England could rally around her and she remained a symbol of Catholic opposition throughout Europe. Elizabeth and her advisors viewed a free Mary as an unacceptable threat. Acting as she was advised and rather reluctantly, Elizabeth ordered her kept in custody in the north, at a safe distance from London. Mary repeatedly demanded to meet with Elizabeth face to face. Elizabeth refused, possibly worried that the younger and, at that time of their lives, more glamorous, Mary would upstage her. She established a commission to inquire into the matter of Mary's abdication and the question of her guilt of Darnley's murder. Thomas Howard, Duke of Norfolk, presided over the inquiry, which was held at York and later Westminster in 1568 and 1569. Mary did not attend, but she sent representatives to the proceedings in York.

In December 1569, the Earl of Moray, who had come to England to effectively act as prosecutor against Mary, presented as evidence the so-called "Casket Letters" (named for the box in which one sometimes stores things of value, not for the container in which a body is placed for burial). The letters had allegedly been secreted in a silver casket found among Bothwell's personal effects. They consisted of eight letters, written in French, supposedly from Mary to Bothwell, that implied she was involved in the conspiracy to murder Darnley; two marriage contracts (supposedly showing that Mary had agreed to marry Bothwell even before he had divorced his current wife); and some love sonnets that Mary supposedly wrote for Bothwell's benefit. None of the letters was signed. The letters had been known in Scotland for a year or so, but this was the first time they were produced publicly against Mary.

The letters contained no smoking gun, nothing directly stating that Mary was involved in Darnley's murder. But they did contain language that, depending on how it was interpreted, might refer to plans to kill Darnley and that suggested Mary had a romantic relationship with Bothwell while still married to Darnley. Three examples from the letter viewed as constituting the strongest evidence of Mary's guilt are as follows: (1) "We are tied to with two false races. The good year untie us from them. God forgive me and God knit us together forever for the most faithful couple that ever he did knit together. This is my faith. I will die in it." (2) "Think also if you will not find some invention more secret by physick, for he is to take physick at Craigmillar and the baths also. And shall not come forth of long time." (3) "Burn this letter, for it is too dangerous, neither is there anything well said in it, for I think upon nothing but upon grief if you be in Edinburgh."[106] If genuine, the letters and marriage contracts could be considered evidence of Mary's moral laxity and her guilt of Darnley's murder.

The Casket Letters constitute another mystery of Scottish history. It has never been definitively determined whether they were genuine. Mary, who was never allowed to see them, always denied she wrote them. She claimed they were a forgery intended to discredit her. Some believed her and some did not. Many of the commissioners accepted the letters as genuine. Historians today still debate the question. The modern trend favours finding that they were forgeries,

---

[106] John Guy, *Queen of Scots: The True Life of Mary Stuart*, Houghton Mifflin Company (2004), p. 401 (hereafter Guy, *Queen of Scots*). "Physick" means medicine or a drug.

or at least that they had been tampered with or contained excerpts from letters Mary actually wrote to others that were used in a deceptive way; and that Mary was probably not complicit in her husband's murder.[107] If the letters were not genuine, it seems more likely that they were tampered with rather than outright forgeries. If they had been outright forgeries, the forger would surely have used more clearly incriminating language than the letters contained. If, instead, they were tampered with, or some of Mary's actual letters to others were used deceptively (as seems likely to this author), the clearly less incriminating language might have been the best the culprit could achieve. Ultimately, as with the fate of the Princes in the Tower, all we can say for certain is that we cannot be certain. The originals were destroyed, under unclear circumstances, apparently in 1584. The letters exist today only in copies and translations. The destruction of the originals makes it impossible today to compare the handwriting in the letters with Mary's own known handwriting, or to use other modern forensic techniques developed to examine the genuineness of questioned documents.

The upshot of the commission's inquiry was that it reached no conclusion. That was how Elizabeth wanted it. For political reasons, she wanted neither a finding that Mary was guilty nor that she was not. Elizabeth declared that "there had been nothing sufficiently produced nor shewn by them against the queen their sovereign, whereby the Queen of England should conceive or take any evil opinion of the queen her good sister, for anything yet seen."[108] A recent biographer described the inquiry as "one of the strangest judicial proceedings in the history of the British Isles, with a verdict of not proven given to both parties, yet one plaintiff [Moray] allowed to return freely to rule in the place of the other plaintiff, who in the meantime continued to be held a prisoner."[109] Moray returned to his position as regent to Mary's son. He would pay the price for his

---

[107] Fraser, *Mary Queen of Scots*, pp. 391-408; Guy, *Queen of Scots*, pp. 384-423; Weir, *Mary, Queen of Scots*, p. 535 ["In the light of all the evidence, it is impossible to resist the conclusion that the Casket Letters were fabrications."]; see *id.*, pp. 525-535; *ODNB, Mary Stewart* ["It is obvious…that they have been extensively tampered with, largely by blending Mary's genuine letters with existing material from other sources. The sonnets date on stylistic grounds from about 1520."].)

[108] Fraser, *Mary Queen of Scots*, p. 390.

[109] Fraser, *Mary Queen of Scots*, p. 391.

duplicitous dealings with Mary. One of Mary's diehard supporters, a man named James Hamilton of Bothwell Haugh, assassinated him the next year.

Although charged with no crime, Mary was kept a prisoner in various strongholds in the north of England, all of which, to deter rescue efforts, were at a safe distance from Scotland, London and the ocean. Although perhaps somewhat sympathetic with Mary's plight and unwilling at this time to charge her with a crime that could lead to her execution, Elizabeth also did not trust her enough to set her free. She wanted to be able to keep a close eye on her cousin and a potential rival. She, or her advisors, saw to it that spies were placed within Mary's entourage to keep her informed of any dangerous activities.

Mary was generally kept in reasonably comfortable and sometimes luxurious confinement. She had a large personal staff to tend to her needs and generally had sumptuous clothes and room decorations and good food served on the finest of dinnerware. She usually had all the comforts she could desire except for her freedom. She was sometimes allowed outside, although always under strict supervision. Over the years, she was allegedly involved in, or at least was the intended beneficiary of, various plots to gain her freedom and win Elizabeth's crown—and maybe even to assassinate Elizabeth. All came to nothing.

One early plot involved the same Duke of Norfolk who had presided over the commission of inquiry. Norfolk was a Protestant. He concocted a scheme whereby he would wed Mary himself (presumably after obtaining an annulment of her current marriage to the imprisoned Bothwell). Some in England liked the idea of Mary's being the wife of the leading Protestant lord in the country. Any children of the marriage could be raised Protestant, which might solve the succession problem. Intertwined with this scheme was an aborted revolt in 1569 against Elizabeth by lords in the north of England, who hoped to replace Elizabeth with Mary. Mary was moved into custody farther south, in Coventry, to discourage any attempts by the northerners to rescue her. Elizabeth's forces easily suppressed the revolt. Norfolk was arrested for his involvement in the northern rebellion but later released.

Two years later came the so-called Ridolfi Plot, named after Roberto Ridolfi, an Italian banker who facilitated it. The plotters allegedly sought to assassinate Elizabeth and replace her with Mary. Norfolk was involved in this plot also. This time he was arrested, tried for treason and executed. The extent of Mary's involvement, if any, was unclear. She wanted to obtain her freedom and maybe reclaim her Scottish throne. But she always professed her loyalty to Elizabeth.

She claimed to be Elizabeth's heir after she died but, she insisted, never sought to overthrow her during her lifetime. Documents that supposedly incriminated her in the plot mysteriously disappeared. Many of Elizabeth's adherents wanted Mary condemned as well as Norfolk. Elizabeth refused. She still probably felt sympathy for her incarcerated cousin and did not want to kill a fellow monarch. She also might have believed a live Mary (who would succeed to the throne should something happen to her) would deter any schemes against her by Protestants.

Another aborted plot was the 1583 "Throckmorton Plot," named for the main conspirator, Sir Francis Throckmorton. The idea here was that the French Duke of Guise, with Spanish help, would invade England, inspire a Catholic revolt in that country, free Mary, overthrow Elizabeth in Mary's favour and restore Catholicism to England. The Duke of Guise would wed Mary and become the King of England. It sounds preposterous today and it was preposterous then. Elizabeth's agents easily thwarted it. Throckmorton was captured and executed. Mary was not charged with a crime, but the plot added to Elizabeth's distrust of her. At some point, the English Queen must have begun to wonder if it was a good idea to keep her alive.

One result of the Throckmorton Plot was that, in 1584, Elizabeth's Privy Council drafted a document, which many men signed, called the Bond of Association. The document required the signatories to avenge any "wicked attempt against" Elizabeth or her throne. In language clearly targeting Mary, it specifically referred to such an act committed by "any that have, may or shall pretend title to come to this crown by the untimely death of her majesty." It required all of the signatories, and there were many, "to prosecute such person or persons to death, with our joint and particular forces and to act the utmost revenge upon them, that my any means we or any of us can devise and do, or cause to be devised and done for their utter overthrow and extirpation." "The Bond of Association was essentially a lynch law, for it licensed the speediest possible punishment for an alleged crime."[110]

Outside events did not aid Mary's cause. In 1584, a Catholic supporter of Spanish rule in the Netherlands assassinated William the Silent, the Protestant leader of the Dutch, who were rebelling against their Spanish overlords. Concerned by the plots against Elizabeth, which were given credence by William's assassination, Parliament enacted the Act for the Queen's Safety in

---

[110] Lewis, *The Trial of Mary Queen of Scots*, pp. 20, 92-3.

1585. It established a tribunal to investigate any rebellion or attempt on the queen's life and made such action a capital offence. The act was also primarily directed against Mary.

Mary's incarceration continued year after year until, ultimately, she spent almost as much time an English prisoner as she had spent as Queen of Scotland. During these years, she and Elizabeth often corresponded in French, Mary's primary language. Mary, naturally, wrote to Elizabeth more often than Elizabeth to her, but both wrote letters to the other. Mary complained about her endless incarceration and, sometimes, about her conditions of confinement. She also pleaded for Elizabeth to help her regain the Scottish throne. Elizabeth, while sometimes seeming to be a bit sympathetic, refused to help. She might have believed that two queens on one island was one queen too many. Mary also asked her son James, now King of Scotland, to help her regain her freedom. He also refused, possibly considering the probability that he would succeed Elizabeth if he did not antagonise her.

Matters came to a head in 1586 with the so-called "Babington Plot," named for Sir Anthony Babington, a Catholic conspirator. This was another Catholic plot to assassinate Elizabeth and place Mary on the throne. Like the other plots, it had no chance of success. It was never a serious threat to Elizabeth. Her agents knew about the plot essentially from the beginning and, indeed, actively furthered it. It is not clear today how much the plot was self-generating and how much it was created, or at least encouraged, by Elizabeth's agent provocateurs. Many of Elizabeth's officials, including above all her influential Secretary of State and leading advisor for four decades, William Cecil, were determined to convince the queen that Mary had to be eliminated; uncovering and, if necessary, encouraging plots like this seemed like a good way to do it. Her agents entrapped others into involvement, including Mary herself. Believing her letters were secure, when, in fact, Elizabeth's agents were reading them, she allegedly exchanged letters with Babington in which she sought to be rescued and also appeared to sanction Elizabeth's overthrow and assassination. (As will be seen, Mary denied writing the letters.)

Babington and the other conspirators were eventually captured and executed for treason. This time, Mary herself was also charged with treason under the 1585 Act for the Queen's Safety. The allegations were that she had plotted against the queen's throne and even her life. The Bond of Association was invoked against her. She was moved to Fotheringhay Castle, about 70 miles northwest of London.

There, beginning on October 14, 1586, she was tried before a tribunal of 36 nobles appointed by Elizabeth (two of them Catholic), including some members of Elizabeth's own Privy Council. Elizabeth was not physically present, but she was symbolically represented by a large empty chair at the head of the room covered with a cloth of state. She wrote a letter to Mary, stating, "You have in various ways and manners attempted to take my life and to bring my kingdom to destruction by bloodshed. I have never proceeded so harshly against you, but have, on the contrary, protected and maintained you like myself. These treasons will be proved to you and all made manifest. Yet it is my will, that you answer the nobles and peers of the kingdom as if I were myself present. I therefore require, charge and command that you make answer for I have been well informed of your arrogance. Act plainly without reserve and you will sooner be able to obtain favour of me."[111]

The trial (if it can be called that; it bore little similarity to trials as we know them today) lasted two days. The outcome was preordained. Elizabeth—and even more strongly, her advisors—wanted a conviction, so a conviction it would be. By this time, after 18 years of captivity, Mary's health had deteriorated, largely due to lack of exercise. She suffered greatly from rheumatism and appeared prematurely old. The trial was utterly unfair. Mary was denied legal counsel, had no friends present during the trial and was not allowed to preview the evidence against her. She confronted a legal system she was unfamiliar with and all the proceedings were conducted in English, essentially a foreign language to Mary. (French was her primary language.) No live witnesses were produced; therefore, none could be cross-examined. Cross-examination of witnesses has long been described as "the greatest legal engine ever invented for the discovery of truth."[112] Yet, alone and undoubtedly aware of what the outcome would be, Mary defended herself vigorously and eloquently.[113]

---

[111] Lewis, *The Trial of Mary Queen of Scots*, pp. 89-90.

[112] *Wigmore on Evidence, vol. 5* (Chadbourn rev. 1974), sec. 1367, p. 32.

[113] Readers familiar with the heresy trial of Joan of Arc, before a nominally French tribunal but with the conquering English effectively in charge, will see strong parallels to Mary's trial. Both women suffered similar handicaps—including having no counsel or friends, no right to see the evidence, no live witnesses against them—yet both defended themselves eloquently, intelligently and—given the inevitable outcomes— courageously. Neither trial was England's finest hour.

Before the proceeding began, Mary said she would not attend, arguing that the tribunal had no jurisdiction over her, a sovereign queen. She insisted that she should be tried before Parliament. She also protested the unfairness of the procedures, stating that she did not know whether she had already been "condemned by forejudging, to give some shew and colour of a just and legal proceeding." She argued that, because she was a queen of a foreign country and had never been an English subject, she could not be guilty of *treason* against England or its queen. Mary also played to the outside world and posterity. She warned the commissioners "to look to their consciences and to remember that the theatre of the whole world is much wider than the kingdom of England." One of Elizabeth's officials tried to convince her to appear personally. He told her, "You are accused (but not condemned) to have conspired the Destruction of our lady and queen anointed." He said the tribunal would try her with or without her presence. Ultimately, on condition that her protests would be noted "in writing," she agreed to appear and defend herself.[114]

At the beginning of the trial, the sergeant at law read the charge: Mary "knew of [Babington's conspiracy], approved it, assented unto it, promised her assistance and shewed the way and means." She answered "with stout courage" (according to the record of the trial) that she did not know Babington and had not corresponded with him. (Clearly, at this point, Mary was still unaware that Elizabeth's officials knew about what she thought was secret correspondence.) Tearfully, she admitted that "many also, which were to her utterly unknown, had offered her their help and assistance"; but she insisted that she had "excited no man to commit any offence; and being shut up in prison, she could neither know nor hinder what they attempted."[115] Copies of the alleged letters between her and Babington were read in court. No one claimed the original letters, which were said to have been written in code, were in her handwriting. The claim was that Mary had dictated them to her secretaries, who wrote them in *their* handwriting.

As read at the trial, the alleged letter from Babington to Mary clearly stated the conspirators' intent to overthrow and assassinate Elizabeth: "And for the dispatch of the Usurper [Elizabeth],…six noble gentlemen, all his [Babington's]

---

[114] *Record of the State Trial of Mary Queen of Scots*, compiled in Lewis, *The Trial of Mary Queen of Scots*, pp. 96, 98-9. This document, considered the definitive record of the trial, is derived from notes of various persons who were present and that were compiled into one document in the nineteenth century. *Id.*, at p. 94.

[115] Lewis, *The Trial of Mary Queen of Scots*, pp. 100-1.

private friends, would undertake that tragical execution." Mary's alleged letter in reply was mostly directed to the question of how she could be freed from her captivity. But it also seemed to show her agreement to the entire scheme, including Elizabeth's assassination. She advised how to go about summoning military forces, both domestic and foreign, to aid the affair. Then, as read in court, "The affairs being thus prepared and forces in readiness both without and within the realm, she saith, that then shall it be time to set the six gentlemen to work; taking order, upon the accomplishing of their design, that she should be suddenly transported from the place of her restraint and all their forces to be at the same time in the field and meet her, in tarrying for the arrival of the foreign aid, which must be hastened with all diligence."[116]

If genuine, the letters and especially Mary's reference to setting "the six gentlemen to work," indicated her agreement to Elizabeth's assassination. She denied that she had written any of the letters attributed to her. When she was told that Babington himself had confessed that she wrote them, she insisted it was a lie. "And now, again, she burst forth into tears: I would never, said she, make shipwreck of my soul by conspiring the destruction of my dearest sister."[117]

After a midday break, the commissioners "pressed...her with the Testimonies of her Secretaries, Nau and Curle, out of Babington's Confession and the Letters sent to and fro betwixt her and Babington and the whole credit of their Proofs rested upon their testimony; yet were not they produced before her face to face." Mary argued that her secretaries might have put statements in her letters without her knowledge. She pleaded, "The majesty and safety of all princes falleth to the ground if they depend upon the Writings and Testimony of Secretaries." She admitted that she had sought to escape (and why not? she had never been charged with a crime), stating, "I delivered nothing to them [her secretaries] but what nature delivered to me, that I might at length recover my liberty." She added, "And I am not to be convicted but by mine own Word or Writing. If they have written anything which may be hurtful to the queen, my sister, they have written it altogether without my knowledge and let them bear the punishment of their inconsiderate boldness. Sure, I am, if they were here present, they would clear me of all blame in this Cause."[118] But they were not

---

[116] A. Francis Steuart, ed., *Trial of Mary Queen of Scots*, William Hodge and Company, Limited (1923), pp. 69-70 (hereafter Steuart, *Trial of Mary Queen of Scots*).

[117] Lewis, *The Trial of Mary Queen of Scots*, pp. 102-3.

[118] Lewis, *The Trial of Mary Queen of Scots*, pp. 103-4.

present and could not clear her of blame. Other than their alleged hearsay statements, not subject to cross-examination, they also could not condemn her.

The proceeding continued the next day. Mary again protested that the tribunal had no jurisdiction over her. As the Lord Treasurer, William Cecil replied that the tribunal received its authority from the queen herself. Mary requested "that an advocate might be granted unto her to plead her Cause." Cecil refused to give Mary counsel. Instead, he insisted the letters that had been openly read in court proved her guilt. Mary responded, "Letters may be directed to others than those to whom they are written and many things have been often inserted which she never dictated. If her papers had not been taken away and she had her Secretary, she could better confute the things objected against her." When Cecil continued to rail against her, Mary interjected, "Ah..., you are my adversary." He responded, "Yea...I am adversary to Queen Elizabeth's adversaries."[119]

In a plea for mercy, Mary noted her own practice of mercy and tolerance for the Protestants while Queen of Scotland. She said that her subjects "now complain that they were never so well off as under my government." She also reiterated her wish to be heard by Parliament or to meet personally with Elizabeth. (Both wishes were denied her.) Then the proceeding ended. "And now rising up with great confidence of countenance," she conferred privately with some of the commissioners. Before leaving the hall, Mary had one final shot at the commissioners, telling them, "May God keep me from having to do with you all again."[120] (This final wish was granted; she never saw them again.)

Despite Mary's reported "confidence of countenance" at the end of the trial, and as she must have anticipated, her pleas were ignored. After a delay caused by the tribunal communicating with Elizabeth, she was convicted and sentenced to death on October 25. Of the 36 judges, only one, the 30-year-old Edward, Baron of Zouch, an English diplomat, dissented. Mary heard of the verdict calmly, saying she did not fear to die in a good cause. She insisted to the end that she was innocent of any earthly crimes. In a letter to Sir Amyas Paulet, her jailer, she wrote, "As a sinner, I am truly conscious of having often offended my Creator and I beg him to forgive me, but as a queen and Sovereign, I am aware

---

[119] Lewis, *The Trial of Mary Queen of Scots*, pp. 105-6.

[120] Fraser, *Mary Queen of Scots*, pp. 515, 516; Lewis, *The Trial of Mary Queen of Scots*, p. 107.

of no fault or offence for which I have to render account to anyone here below."[121]

Was Mary in fact guilty as charged of treason? Her entire life she insisted publicly that she had no designs on Elizabeth's throne as long as the English Queen lived. At her trial, she admitted she was trying to escape, but she continued to insist she had no intent beyond that and that she did not intend to overthrow Elizabeth. In her own mind, she may have thought she was telling the truth. The problem—a problem inherent in her entire situation—was that, as Mary must have known and certainly should have known, the intent to free Mary was *not* all that the Babington conspirators (and, more generally, other conspirators) intended. Mary's release, although possibly all that *she* wanted, would accomplish nothing for the conspiracy if Elizabeth continued to rule. The conspirators wanted to overthrow Elizabeth and replace her with a Catholic, ideally Mary.

In the unlikely event that the Babington conspiracy, or any other conspiracy, had succeeded, Elizabeth would have been deposed. Given the times, deposition would also have meant her death; she would almost certainly have been murdered. A deposed monarch did not live long in those days. Thus, to the extent Mary cooperated with the Babington conspirators in the hope of gaining her release—and it appears she did cooperate at least to that extent—she was effectively conspiring to have Elizabeth deposed and murdered, whatever she personally might have wished. She could not be part of a conspiracy to gain her freedom without also being part of a conspiracy to overthrow Elizabeth. Thus, even if Mary was truthful in saying she merely wanted her freedom, she might still have been guilty of treason as it was defined at that time.

Elizabeth hesitated to order the final step. She did not want to be involved in regicide; it might set a bad example. She might also have been aware that her propaganda machine had substantially overstated the extent to which Mary was really a threat to her or Protestant England. At one point, she wrote to Mary's jailer, Paulet, suggesting he have her secretly murdered to avoid a public execution. He declined, writing back, "God forbid that I should make so foul a shipwreck of my conscience, or leave so great a blot on my poor posterity, to shed blood without law or warrant."[122] Parliament forced Elizabeth's hand, castigating Mary and demanding her execution. One impassioned speech in

---

[121] Fraser, *Mary Queen of Scots*, pp. 501, 517.

[122] Fraser, *Mary Queen of Scots*, p. 529.

Parliament portrayed her as "the daughter of sedition, the mother of rebellion, the nurse of impiety, the handmaid of iniquity, the sister of unshamefastness."[123]

Finally, on 1 February 1587, Elizabeth signed the death warrant. Her officials immediately dispatched it to Fotheringham Castle and put it into effect. On the evening of 7 February, Mary was informed she was to be beheaded the next morning. The three months between the death verdict and this announcement must have been agonizing for her. She could not have known exactly what was occurring with Elizabeth and the death judgment, but she always knew that at any time she might be told, on short notice, that she was about to die. When she received the news, "[s]he undauntedly and with a composed spirit, made this Answer, 'I did not think the queen, my sister, would have consented to my death, who am not subject to your law and jurisdiction; but, seeing her pleasure is so, Death shall be to me most welcome, neither is that soul worthy of the high and everlasting joys above, whose body cannot endure one stroke of the executioner.'"[124]

Mary spent her last hours praying, writing a will, providing for her household staff and writing a letter to Henry III, the King of France and her former brother-in-law. She asked for, but was denied, the services of a Catholic chaplain. She was offered a Protestant chaplain instead. She declined, stating she wished to adhere to her lifelong faith when preparing to die. Thus, the woman who, as queen, had allowed others to practice their own faith, even if it was not hers, was denied the same right. She also expressed her wish to be buried in France; that wish, too, was denied.

Mary also presumably spent the evening of 7 February mentally rehearsing her role the next day. Although she was the intended victim, she would also be the central figure of a dramatic production. She intended to take full advantage of the situation. To a large extent, Mary orchestrated—and starred in—her own execution. She had had ample time to think about it in the months since she heard of the death judgment.

On the morning of 8 February, the sun rose just as on any other day. But it was to be the last day of the life of Mary, the former Queen of Scots. With the help of her servants, she arose early and carefully dressed and prepared herself for what was to come. Wearing black satin and velvet, and with all the quiet dignity she could muster, she entered the Great Hall of the castle in full view of

---

[123] Lewis, *The Trial of Mary Queen of Scots*, p. 32.
[124] Steuart, *Trial of Mary Queen of Scots*, p. 60.

the large number of spectators (perhaps as many as 300) who were present to witness the execution. The witnesses included envoys of Queen Elizabeth, who were present to ensure that Mary did, in fact, die. One eyewitness described Mary as "being of stature tall, of body corpulent, round-shouldered, her face fat and broad, double-chinned and hazel-eyed, her borrowed hair aborne."[125]

The scaffold where Mary was to die, draped in black, had already been set up in the hall. Mary was forced to listen to the reading of the execution warrant. Then, in front of the entire audience, she prayed aloud for her son and for the church; she did not forget to add a prayer for Elizabeth. Very publicly, she did her best to comfort her weeping servants and friends. She told one servant to "carry this message from me, that I die a true woman to my religion and like a true Queen of Scotland and France, but God forgive them…that have long desired my end and thirsted for my blood." She asked the servant to tell her son "that I have not done anything prejudicial to the State and Kingdom of Scotland."[126]

Mary approached the scaffold, which had a cushion for her to kneel on in front of the block where she was to lay her head. The executioner, a man named Bull, asked her to forgive him for what he was about to do, a customary practice for executioners in those days. She replied, "I forgive you with all my heart; for I hope this death shall give an end to all my troubles." Two servants, aided by the executioner and his assistant, helped her take off her outer garments. When she did so, it was revealed to all that, underneath her black gown, Mary wore a blood-red petticoat with red sleeves. Mary chose the colour carefully; red is the liturgical colour of martyrdom in the Catholic Church. The audience probably reacted with astonishment or anger when it saw that, underneath her black attire, Mary was wearing red, a reaction that probably nurtured her spirit during the few minutes of life left to her. As she undressed, she smiled and joked that "she never had such grooms before to make her unready, nor ever did put off her clothes before such company."[127] One of her servants blindfolded her. Then she knelt on the cushion and positioned her head. Before the axe descended, her last words

---

[125] "*A Circumstantial Account of the Execution of Mary Queen of Scots*," compiled in Lewis, *The Trial of Mary Queen of Scots*, p. 114. Much of the following description of the events is taken from this famous account.

[126] Lewis, *The Trial of Mary Queen of Scots*, p. 115.

[127] Lewis, *The Trial of Mary Queen of Scots*, pp. 118-9.

were a Latin prayer: "*In manus tuas, Domine, commendo spiritum meum.*" (Into thy hands, O Lord, I commend my spirit.)

Even at this point, with her head on the block, all of Mary's troubles were not yet at an end. She did not receive the "one stroke of the executioner" she anticipated when told she would be executed. The guillotine, a reliable way to chop off a head with one stroke, had not yet been invented. Whether the beheading would be a single, quick stroke depended on the skill of the axman. Bull was not skilful. Or perhaps he was just nervous, having to kill a queen in front of a large audience. One likes to think that he was also dismayed by what he was being ordered to do. When the axe first came down, it did not sever Mary's head cleanly. Instead, it missed her neck and struck the back of her head. One spectator reported hearing Mary utter, "Sweet Jesus," although, in reality, she was probably unconscious after the first blow. Then a second swing of the axe nearly severed the neck and finally made an end of her troubles. It took a third, lighter, blow to sever the head from the neck entirely. It was around 10:00 am, 8 February 1587. Mary had become another heir who never reigned.

The spectators, however, had still another macabre scene to witness. The executioner raised the severed head aloft to show it to the spectators and shouted, "God save the queen!" He held it by its auburn hair. The hair, however, was a wig. The head fell out of his grip and landed on the floor, revealing Mary's real hair. The eyewitness reported that her head "appeared as grey as if she had been threescore and ten years old, polled very short, her face much altered. Her lips stirred up and down almost a quarter of an hour after her head was cut off." He also reported that Mary's favourite dog, a Skye terrier—Mary had always loved dogs—emerged from under her petticoat, where it had managed to secrete itself (presumably with Mary's assistance, intended to be part of the show). The dog "would not be gotten forth but with force; and afterwards would not depart from the dead corpse, but came and lay between her head and shoulders."[128] It could not comprehend what had occurred.

Thus died Mary, Queen of Scots, as courageously and well as she had lived (in this author's view). She was 44 years old. She was buried, following a Protestant, not Catholic, service, at the nearby Peterborough Cathedral. In 1612, her son, now King James I of England and Ireland, as well as James VI of Scotland, ordered her body reinterred at Westminster Abbey. It was placed in a lavish tomb near the tomb of Elizabeth's body, where it lies today.

---

[128] Lewis, *The Trial of Mary Queen of Scots*, p. 119-20.

After the execution, a Latin prayer was said to have been found in Mary's devotional book in her handwriting. She might have written it the evening before she died. In English translation, it states:

"O Lord my God, I have trusted in thee;

O Jesu my dearest one, now set me free.

In prison's oppression, in sorrow's obsession,

I weary for thee.

With sighing and crying bowed down as dying,

I adore thee, I implore thee, set me free."[129]

Elizabeth reacted angrily when she was informed of the execution. She claimed the death warrant was not supposed to have been delivered to Fotheringham Castle without her authorization and she had not intended to have Mary actually executed. How sincere she was is questionable. In truth, she was probably ambivalent and possibly relieved that her rival had finally been removed from the scene. Mary's execution was extraordinarily convenient for Elizabeth. It seems likely she was simply trying to evade responsibility for the death of her kinswoman and fellow queen while reaping the benefit.

If Elizabeth was ambivalent about Mary's death, the people of London were not. They celebrated the death of the Catholic abomination they had been taught to view as a threat to their country. The reaction in France, where she had been queen consort and then dowager queen, was different. Anger and dismay were the prevalent reactions. A few weeks after her death, a requiem mass was celebrated in her memory at Notre Dame Cathedral. The Archbishop of Bourges gave an eloquent sermon, recalling that Mary had been married in that same cathedral some three decades previously.

The reaction in Scotland was mixed. Many felt anger and grief over the death of their former queen. Others, like the people of London, celebrated the end of the woman who was a Catholic in a Protestant country. Her son James, not yet King of England, expressed public feelings of grief and regret. But it is doubtful that he sincerely had any such feelings for a mother he had never personally known other than in tiny infancy. He had done little to try to prevent, or even discourage, her execution, much less to gain her release. He knew that his

---

[129] As quoted in *Bartlett's Familiar Quotations*, 16th ed., Little, Brown and Company (1992), p. 147. This prayer is traditionally attributed to her, but it is not certain that she actually wrote it. If not, it at least speaks eloquently of her situation and how she no doubt felt.

mother's death paved the way for him to succeed to Elizabeth's throne when that monarch died, something that might have been more important to him than his mother's life.

In Spain, the death of the last Catholic claimant to the throne was met with anger. Not entirely coincidentally, the next year, 1588, the Spanish King Philip II, who had been married to Elizabeth's older sister, Queen Mary I, and was himself directly descended from the English King Edward III, unleashed the mighty Spanish Armada on England in an attempt to enforce his own claim to the throne. As the world knows, the attempt failed.

Mary's motto had been, "*En ma fin est mon commencement*" (In my end is my beginning). In one sense, that became true. Her end was the beginning of her legacy. Her character, as well as the unsolved questions of whether she was involved in Darnley's murder and had really sought Elizabeth's death, have been debated ever since. She certainly chose her second and third husbands poorly and both marriages worked out badly for her. But did she commit any crimes? Of course, the Tudor line was that Mary was guilty of all she was charged with and richly deserved to die. Subsequent historians, as well as more casual observers, have been far less certain. Many, including this author, believe that Mary's evil fate was due far more to evil fortune than to evil character.

Like most of the subjects of this book, Mary was fortunate in her birth. She was a queen at less than one week of age. But she was unfortunate to be a faithful Catholic when Protestantism became dominant in her country. Her idea of religious tolerance was considered a weakness, not a virtue, and she lost everything in the religious struggles that overwhelmed her. She lost her crown and her freedom. She even lost to her enemies her infant son, the only child she ever bore. Then, after 18 years of imprisonment (even though she was charged with no crime), she lost her life. Her head was brutally chopped off for actions that, even if they technically constituted a capital offence, were understandable under her circumstances. Even if she had been involved in the conspiracy leading to Darnley's death—something never proven; it is easy to believe Mary's many enemies forged or tampered with the Casket Letters—that, too, was at least somewhat understandable under the circumstances.

Today, it is virtually impossible to read (or write) about Mary's life and death without feeling sympathy for this often-gentle woman, a sympathy that is far stronger than any feeling of condemnation.

Chapter 11
Henry Frederick

Queen Elizabeth I died in 1603. She was succeeded by the son of Mary, Queen of Scots, the safely Protestant James, who became King James I of England and Ireland. (Thus, Mary gained a measure of posthumous revenge against her adversary. All subsequent British monarchs have been descended directly from Mary; none is descended from Elizabeth.) James had also been King James VI of Scotland since infancy. He married a Danish princess named Anne in 1589. The couple had several children. The oldest was formally named Henry Frederick, after his two grandfathers, Henry Stuart, Lord Darnley (Mary's second husband) and Frederick II, King of Denmark. Henry was James's highly regarded heir apparent. He seemed destined to become King Henry IX. But there has not yet been a ninth King Henry. This Henry was destined, instead, to become yet another heir who never reigned.

Prince Henry was born on 9 February 1594, at Stirling Castle, some six years after his grandmother was beheaded. His younger brother, Charles, was born six years later. At his birth, Henry automatically received several Scottish titles of nobility. The Scottish people celebrated the birth enthusiastically, as it seemed to ensure the continuation of the Stuart dynasty. James was not yet King of England, so Henry was raised in Scotland early in life. His father decided that his mother, Anne, who was suspected of having Catholic sympathies, would have nothing to do with the prince's upbringing. Instead, he entrusted Henry's care to the Earl of Mar and his wife at Stirling Castle. Needless to say, this decision did not sit well with Anne. She continually tried to regain custody and her failure to do so placed a great strain on their marriage.

Like other princes who never reigned, this Henry was trained from birth to become a king. King James literally wrote the book on how he should act as king. He wrote the *Basilicon Doron* (Greek meaning royal gift), the advice in the form of a letter to his son. The book exhorted Henry to be a good king and described in detail how to go about it. The king also wrote detailed instructions for his son's education and training. The prince was taught physical pursuits such as hawking and hunting. His tutors gave him a classical education.

Henry was raised strictly as a Protestant; his tutors and staff indoctrinated him with Calvinism. He was devout and became strongly anti-Catholic. The prince seemed particularly interested in military and national affairs. He became a fan and champion of the courtier, adventurer and poet Sir Walter Raleigh. During Raleigh's long imprisonment in the Tower of London for imagined crimes against King James, Henry lamented, "Who but my father would keep such a bird in a cage!"[130] The Scottish and later English, populace loved him, probably more than they loved his father.

The course of Henry's life changed dramatically in 1603 when his father became King of England. He moved with his family to London, where he became a Knight of the Garter. In his new home, he impressed everyone with his apparent ability and his serious, even strict, outlook on life. His years in England were a dramatic time for the country. Soon after James's coronation as King of England came the Gunpowder Plot of November 1605. The plotters, which included the notorious Guy Fawkes, were Catholics angered by anti-Catholic persecution in England. As all English schoolchildren know, they attempted to blow up the Parliament building with gunpowder and to assassinate King James. They actually collected enough gunpowder to blow the House of Lords to smithereens. Then they intended to seize custody of Henry's nine-year-old sister, Elizabeth, raise a rebellion and make her a Catholic queen under their control. Unsurprisingly, the plot (like the various plots against Queen Elizabeth I) failed miserably and the plotters were captured, tried and executed. But the plot must have had a strong influence over Henry and reinforced his anti-Catholic feelings. His father was the primary target, but Henry's future was also at stake. He was eleven years old at the time, an age when national events can have a special impact.

Henry seemed to prefer sports over studying, something not rare among the young, then and today. The French ambassador reported of him in 1606, "He is a particular lover of horses... He studies two hours a day and employs the rest

---

[130] Frank Cheney Hersey, ed., *Sir Walter Raleigh: "The Shepherd of the Ocean,"* The Macmillan Company (1916), p. viii.

of his time in tossing the pike, or leaping, or shooting with the bow, or throwing the bar, or vaulting."[131] Later he also became a patron of the arts.

Henry was invested as Prince of Wales in 1610 when he was 16 years old. As he grew older, he took an active interest in national affairs, showing a particular interest in England's overseas ventures. He recommended that Sir Thomas Dale, a naval commander, be assigned deputy-governor of England's new colonial venture in Virginia. Because he was heir apparent to the throne, his recommendation carried great weight and Dale received the position. When Dale arrived in Virginia in 1611, he helped reinvigorate the struggling colony at Jamestown. Dale also established a new, second, colony nearby, which he named Henricus, in the prince's honour. In further recognition of Henry's interest in England's colonization of America, the cape at the southern end of the entrance to Chesapeake Bay was named Cape Henry, after him.

Given his interest in governmental affairs, his obvious intelligence, regal upbringing and enthusiastic Protestantism, everyone (except, presumably, Catholics) looked with cherished hopes on his becoming a great king. He was considered a national treasure and the world seemed to be his to do with as he wished. But, in the space of a few days, it all came to an end. In late October or early November 1612, he went for a swim in the Thames. He caught a water-borne bacteria and contracted typhoid fever. He died on 6 November, aged 18 years.

Great was the mourning following Henry's death, both in Britain and abroad. If he had been considered a national treasure in life, his death was considered a national tragedy. Sir Walter Raleigh "perhaps best captured the gloomy mood, claiming his *History* (1614) was 'left to the world without a master.' "[132]

The next in line to succeed to the throne was Henry's sickly younger brother, the not-quite-twelve-year-old Charles, who had never been raised to be a king and who was not viewed as anywhere near as capable or as promising as Henry. However, King James did now provide Charles with a copy of the *Basilikon Doron* for his edification. It is not clear how much it helped, if at all.

Henry's body lay in state for four weeks at the Palace of St James. His funeral was held on 7 December at Westminster Abbey, with the Archbishop of Canterbury presiding. Thousands of mourning spectators lined the streets of

---

[131] James M. Sutton, *Oxford Dictionary of National Biography, Henry Frederick, Prince of Wales*, Oxford University Press (2008), (hereafter *ODNB, Henry Frederick*).
[132] *ODNB, Henry Frederick*.

London to watch as the funeral procession slowly made its way from St James to Henry's final resting place inside Westminster Abbey. Younger brother Charles was the chief mourner, as neither of Henry's parents could bear to attend. Henry was buried in the same vault as his paternal grandmother, Mary, Queen of Scots. One wonders what he thought of this grandmother he never knew. As a pious Protestant with strong anti-Catholic views, he had probably been raised to regard her with horror. But perhaps, somewhere along the line, someone also presented him with a more sympathetic view of the woman he would share a vault with in death.

If upbringing and good intentions meant much, Henry would have made a good king, maybe even one of Britain's best. The main ground for concern was his strong, even puritanical, religious views and his antipathy for Catholicism, which might have made him especially intolerant of other religions. But, much as with Prince Arthur, the first son of King Henry VII, it is unlikely his reign would have been worse than the actual reign of his younger brother. This brother would become King Charles I in 1625. His reign was far from peaceful or successful. Charles would go on to quarrel with Parliament, fight the English Civil War and lose his throne and, eventually, his life. He would be beheaded in 1649 on the orders of the so-called Long Parliament. Indeed, monarchy as the British form of government came to an end under Charles, supplanted by the English Commonwealth led by Oliver Cromwell as Lord Protector. (The end of the monarchy turned out to be only an interruption. The monarchy was restored in 1660, when Charles's son was crowned as King Charles II.)

It seems probable that Henry's hypothetical reign would have been more successful and peaceful than his brother's was. As is so often the case, we will never know.

Chapter 12
James, the Old Pretender

Charles II, the first King of the restored monarchy, died in 1685 and was succeeded by his younger brother, James II (and James VII of Scotland). James had two wives. He married the first, Anne Hyde, in 1660. They had two children who survived into adulthood, both daughters, named Mary and Anne. Anne Hyde died in 1671. Two years later, James married Mary of Modena. They had two children who lived into adulthood, one daughter and one son. The son, formally named James Francis Edward Stuart, was born in 1688. As the oldest, indeed only, surviving son of the king, he became the heir apparent to the throne the day he was born. He was expected to become King James III (and VIII of Scotland) in due course.

It was not to be. The young James was fated to become another heir who never reigned. His father, James II, was overthrown when young James was an infant. The younger James spent the rest of his long life doggedly seeking to recover his inheritance. After his father died, he claimed the throne himself, a claim that he maintained for the remaining 64 years of his life. He became known as the Old Pretender. Few remembered that, when he was an infant, this James was not a mere pretender; he was the recognised heir apparent to the throne, if only for a short time.

Religion underlay these events. As we have seen before (chapters 9, 10), religious strife had been endemic in England since Henry VIII tore the Church of England away from the Church in Rome. The main quarrel (not the only; there was also a strife among differing forms of Protestantism) was between Catholics and Protestants. King James's first wife, Anne Hyde, was born a Protestant but, soon after the marriage, she converted to Catholicism. Fatefully, she influenced James himself to convert to Catholicism long before he became king. Their two daughters, however, were raised as Protestants. Critically, James's only surviving son, by his second wife, a devout Catholic, was raised Catholic.

England did not want a Catholic king. The country was firmly Protestant, although it had a substantial Catholic minority. The memory of Protestant persecution under Queen Mary I lingered into the late seventeenth century. When Charles II died childless, the country was not happy that his heir, James, was Catholic. But his only two children, Mary and Anne, were Protestants. James was 51 years old when Charles II died, so his reign was not expected to be long. Then the crown would pass to the Protestant Mary (or Anne). Under the circumstances, the country was willing to temporarily accept a Catholic king in the anticipation that a Protestant monarch would follow reasonably soon.

But the situation changed dramatically on 10 June 1688, when, to everyone's surprise and Protestant consternation, James II produced a son, also named James, who was born at St James Palace. Although it had become accepted that, if no male heir were available, a woman could become queen regnant, a son, even a younger son, took precedence over any daughter. Suddenly, James's heir was not a Protestant but a boy who would be raised Catholic. England was prepared to have a Catholic monarch for a while. It was not prepared to have the succession remain in Catholic hands indefinitely. Accordingly, the infant baby's birth was controversial from the time it was first announced. Rumours, or a tale concocted by the king's enemies, circulated immediately that the baby was an imposter, smuggled to the mother in a warming pan. The story was surely false, but many wanted to believe it. The king publicly presented proof that the baby was indeed born to Mary of Modena. A month after the birth, on 4 July, the infant James was created Prince of Wales, to designate him as the heir apparent officially.

The reaction came swiftly. The so-called "Glorious Revolution" (not so glorious in Catholic eyes) erupted in November 1688. In its initial stages, the revolution was nearly bloodless. William, the Stadtholder of Holland (essentially the leader of the Dutch Republic) was the husband of King James's older daughter Mary (who had been James's heir until the infant James was born). Many in England wanted William and Mary to become joint rulers in James's place as King William III and Queen Mary II. William invaded England with a large army and marched on London. James's army largely dwindled and the navy switched its allegiance from James to William. By December, after a few minor skirmishes, it became apparent James could not defeat the invading force. To avoid useless bloodshed, he went into exile in France. On 9 December, Mary of Modena also fled with the baby James to France. In France, the deposed James was welcomed by the French King Louis XIV, known as the Sun King. Louis and James were cousins, both being grandsons of the French King Henry IV, Louis through his father and James through his mother.

The following year, Parliament, asserting its supremacy, declared William and Mary joint monarchs of England, Ireland and Scotland. It enacted the Bill of Rights of 1689, entitled, "An act declaring the rights and liberties of the subject and settling the succession of the crown." The act declared that "the late King James the Second, by the assistance of divers evil counsellors, judges and ministers employed by him, did endeavour to subvert and extirpate the Protestant religion and the laws and liberties of this kingdom…" It stated that James II had abdicated the crown and specifically excluded the infant James from the succession. William and Mary's heirs and, if they had none, Anne's heirs would succeed to the crown. To make abundantly clear that England and Scotland should never again be ruled by a Catholic, the act added, "And whereas it hath been found by experience that it is inconsistent with the safety and welfare of this Protestant kingdom to be governed by a popish prince, or by any king or queen marrying a papist,…[it is enacted] that all and every person and persons that is, are or shall be reconciled to or shall hold communion with the see or Church of Rome, or shall profess the popish religion, or shall marry a papist, shall be excluded and be forever incapable to inherit, possess or enjoy the crown and government of this realm…"[133]

Although William and Mary thus replaced James as dual monarchs rather easily, matters would not remain so nearly bloodless. With the deposed James and his infant son in exile in France, pro-Catholic forces in Scotland and Ireland rose against the deposition. Those who wanted to restore James as king or, later, supported his heirs' claims to the throne were called Jacobites, from the Latin version of the name James.[134] When a Jacobite uprising flared in Ireland, the deposed king went to that country to try to win his throne back. James returned into exile in France following the Jacobite defeat at the Battle of the Boyne in 1690. Thereafter, James continued to assert his claim until his death in 1701.

---

[133] Andrew Browning, ed., *English Historical Documents, vol. VIII, 1660-1714*, Oxford University Press (1953), pp. 122-7 (hereafter *EHD, vol. VIII*).

[134] The Jacobites should not be confused with the Jacobins, the radical political faction during the French Revolution.

In the meantime, the young James—who was born the heir apparent, made the Prince of Wales and then deposed, all before he was aware of it—was raised in exile in France. Louis XIV treated the deposed king and his family as royalty and supported their claim to the English and Scottish crowns. He granted the family as their home the Château de Saint-Germain-en-Laye, a short distance west of Paris. In addition to living in the chateau, the young James was a frequent visitor with his family at the magnificent French court at Versailles. He was thus raised in style and wealth. Significantly, he was imbued from a young age with the belief that he was the legitimate heir to the throne.

Queen Mary died childless in 1694, leaving William to rule alone until he died in 1702. On his death, Anne ascended to the throne. Even before then, by the year 1701, it had become apparent that Anne would also not produce an heir. (Chapter 13.) To ensure that no Catholic, particularly not the young James, would succeed to the throne, Parliament enacted the Act of Settlement, 1701, entitled, "An Act for the further limitation of the crown and better securing the rights and liberties of the subject." The act specifically disinherited the young James. It made clear the succession would go to the heir of William or Anne if either should, against all expectations, produce one. But if neither produced an heir, the act declared that the crown would pass to a distant relative, the Protestant Sophia, Electress of Hanover and her heirs, provided they were Protestant. (Chapter 14.) As did the Bill of Rights of 1689, the act specifically excluded Catholics from the succession. To make the point abundantly clear, the act further provided that "whosoever shall hereafter come to the possession of this crown shall join in communion with the Church of England as by law established."[135]

The deposed James died in 1701. After his death, the young James asserted his claim to be King James III of England and Ireland and King James VIII of Scotland. Louis XIV, as well as Spain and the Papal States, recognised him as the legitimate king and refused to recognise King William. In reaction, Parliament passed a bill of attainder for treason against him in his absence. The act was a death sentence, plus forfeiture of all property and titles as well as the ability to pass his titles to his descendants. Obviously, the death sentence was not carried out because James was in exile in France. In time, James became known as the "Old Pretender."

---

[135] *EHD, vol. VIII*, pp. 129-35.

In 1707, Parliament acted again, this time to make it treason to support James's claim. It enacted the Regency Act of 1707, entitled "An act for the security of her majesty's person and government and of the succession to the crown of Great Britain in the Protestant line." (In separate legislation, Parliament also united the kingdoms of England and Scotland into the Kingdom of Great Britain.) The act provided that "if any person or persons shall maliciously, advisedly and directly, by writing or printing, maintain and affirm that our sovereign lady the queen that now is [Queen Anne], is not the lawful and rightful queen of these realms, or that the pretended Prince of Wales, who now styles himself King of Great Britain, or King of England by the name of James the Third, or King of Scotland by the name of James the Eighth, hath any right or title to the crown of these realms,…every such person or persons shall be guilty of high treason and being thereof lawfully convicted shall be adjudged traitors and shall suffer pains of death and all losses and forfeitures as in cases of high treason…"[136]

The next year, James made his first real attempt to make good his claim to the British throne. He intended to go to Scotland and seek his throne from there. Scotland was the land of his ancestors and a continual source of support for the Jacobite cause. In March 1708, after a delay caused by his coming down with the measles, he sailed in French ships, intending to land at the Firth of Forth. But British ships led by Admiral George Byng blocked the way. Bad weather also contributed to James's failure to actually land. He returned to France, having accomplished nothing. He then joined the French army and fought with distinction on the French side during the War of the Spanish Succession.

Beginning in late 1713, when it became apparent that Queen Anne would not live much longer, some English officials secretly corresponded with James about the possibility of his succeeding Anne in contravention of the acts of Parliament. Many of the British did not want the crown to pass to a German branch of the family, which is what the acts decreed. Some urged James to convert to Protestantism to facilitate his succession. He refused. Conversion might not have been sufficient for him to become king. But his refusal doomed any such effort.

In the eighteenth century, it was popular to write character sketches of prominent persons. A supporter of James, one Charles Leslie, wrote a sketch of James in a letter to a member of Parliament in 1714, possibly to try to assuage the fear many had of his Catholicism and attempt to facilitate his possible

---

[136] *EHD, vol. VIII*, pp. 138-9.

succession to the throne. Both because it provides insight into James's character (helping to explain why he refused to convert to Protestantism) and gives a flavour of what eighteenth-century character sketches were like, it is quoted extensively.

"And first for the person of the Chevalier [James], which you desire to know. He is tall, straight and clean-limbed, slender, yet his bones pretty large. He has a very graceful mien, walks fast; and his gait has a great resemblance to his uncle, King Charles II and the lines of his face grow daily more and more like him. He uses exercise more for health than diversion; he walks abroad, shoots or hunts every day, but is not what they call a keen sportsman. Being asked what he most delighted in, he said it would be to hear wise men discourse upon useful subjects.

"He is always cheerful but seldom merry, thoughtful but not dejected and bears his misfortunes with a visible magnanimity of spirit. He frequents the public devotions, but there is no sort of bigotry about him. He has a great application to business, spends much time in his closet and writes much, which no man does better and more succinctly. I have often admired his criticalness in the choice of words. He apprehends readily and gives the direct answer. He is very affable and has something strangely engaging in his voice and deportment, that none whoever conversed with him but are charmed with his good sense and sweetness of temper. Nor can any take it ill even when he grants not their request, for he always gives such a reason as must satisfy. Yet he can show displeasure but without anger…

"He has informed himself of past miscarriages and knows well the difference betwixt the office of a king and a missionary. He will concern himself with no man's religion, but is resolved to defend that which is legally established and whose principles are true to monarchy and safe for government, for whose satisfaction and for his own restoration he thinks himself obliged to do everything that is consistent with conscience and honour… I would not have said so much were it not to do him justice and expose the vile clamours of his enemies that he has no regard to Protestants, which is known to be notoriously false to all who have the honour to attend him. He has given all the demonstrations possible to the contrary except parting with his conscience and honour, which some would have him do that they might object it against him and represent him as unworthy to reign for so doing…"[137]

---

[137] *EHD, vol. VIII*, pp. 910-1. James's refusal to convert to Protestantism should be contrasted with the choice made by the French King Henry IV, who faced the reverse

The letter and other efforts on James's behalf, had no effect. When Queen Anne died in August 1714, the son of the Sophia designated as her successor in the Act of Settlement of 1701 succeeded to the throne as King George I, the first King of the new Hanoverian dynasty. George's main qualification to be king was that he was Protestant. He bypassed many members of the Stuart family who had superior dynastic claims to the throne but were disqualified for being Catholic. Because he was German, was only distantly related to the British royal family and did not even speak English, his succession was unpopular in many quarters. James himself condemned a foreigner coming to rule Britain. George's ascension led to rioting in some places. Ultimately, England's aversion to having a Catholic king proved stronger than its aversion to having a foreign king. The option of dispensing with the monarchy altogether—something tried only half a century before—was not considered.

But George did not secure his throne quietly. Rebellion broke out in Cornwall and especially Scotland. Many Scots dreamed of restoring the Stuart dynasty, their own dynasty. The uprising popularly called "The Fifteen," after the year it began, 1715, ensued. An early advocate of a Stuart restoration, John Erskine, the Earl of Mar, declared James the rightful king. Before James himself arrived in Scotland, the Earl raised nearly 20,000 troops, mostly Scottish, and won some early successes. His forces met an army loyal to King George in the November 1715 Battle of Sheriffmuir, near Stirling. The fighting there was inconclusive, but the Jacobites were defeated at the Battle of Preston, in Lancashire, and their cause waned.

James himself finally arrived in Scotland on 22 December 1715, landing in Peterhead in Aberdeenshire. By this time, the Jacobite cause had crested and become doomed to defeat. To make matters worse, James fell ill in the Scottish winter weather. He moved on to Perth in January 1716 and attempted to establish a royal court to pursue his cause. He hoped to be crowned king at Scone Palace near Perth. But his situation became hopeless. With his support dwindling and strong forces loyal to King George advancing on him, James left Scotland in disguise on 5 February and returned to France. He did not bother to inform his Scottish allies of his departure. The rebellion became a lost cause. The Fifteen was a failure.

---

situation—a Catholic country averse to having a Protestant king. In 1593, he agreed to convert from Protestantism to Catholicism to secure his position as the King of France, supposedly declaring that "Paris is well worth a mass".

Part of the problem was James's failure of leadership. Many in Scotland viewed his unannounced departure as abandoning his allies to their fate. One Scottish rebel wrote of James, "We saw nothing in him that looked like spirit. He never appeared with cheerfulness and vigour to animate us. Our men began to despise him; some asked if he could speak. His countenance looked extremely heavy. He cared not to come abroad among us soldiers or to see us handle our arms or do our exercise."[138]

During these events, James was repeatedly pressured to declare himself a Protestant to aid his cause. As before, he refused. Shortly before James left Scotland, he wrote a letter explaining his refusal. "For it is not to be supposed that men of sense or honour could believe me to play the hypocrite so notoriously as to be a Protestant in exterior and a Catholic in my heart..." He insisted that he had "given sufficient proofs of my moderation, of my kindness for my Protestant subjects and of the happiness they may enjoy under me." Therefore, he argued, Great Britain would have to either receive him as a Catholic or not at all.[139] The British chose not at all.

Back in France, James found a changed political situation, a change greatly to his disadvantage. The War of the Spanish Succession had ended in defeat for France and France officially recognised the Hanoverian branch as the legitimate ruling family in Great Britain. Moreover, James's great sponsor, Louis XIV, had died. James's presence in France became an embarrassment for the French government. Fortunately for him, he had a place to go. The papacy still sympathised with a Catholic who had a stronger dynastic claim to the British throne than the current Protestant occupant. At the Pope's invitation, James moved to the papal territory, first living in Avignon, then eventually in Rome.

Pope Clement XI offered James the use of the Palazzo Muti in Rome as his residence, which he gratefully accepted. On his arrival in Rome, he established a court in exile, which he maintained for the rest of his long life. The Pope awarded him a generous life annuity, which permitted him to live in luxury and entertain friends and visitors in the style he considered appropriate for the rightful British king. He did not abandon his dream of making good on his claim.

---

[138] Edward Gregg, *Oxford Dictionary of National Biography, James Francis Edward Stuart, the Old.*

[139] D.B. Horn and Mary Ransome, eds., *English Historical Documents, vol. X, 1714-83,* Oxford University Press (1957), p. 648.

In 1719 came yet another Jacobite attempt to restore the Stuart dynasty, this time with Spanish help. In late March, a fleet left Spain intending to land some 5,000 troops to support the Jacobite cause. A storm badly damaged the fleet and forced it to abandon any attempt at a large-scale landing. A small Spanish force did manage to land in Scotland, where they were joined by exiles living in France. But the Jacobites and Spanish were decisively defeated at the June 10 Battle of Glenshiels in west Scotland. This ended the uprising. James himself never made it to Scotland. He went to Spain hoping to be able to go on to Scotland. But with the collapse of the rising, he simply returned to Rome in August. This was James's last personal attempt to make good his claim.

James continued to preside over a court in exile in Rome. He acted as if he were the real king, conferring titles of nobility and making other royal decrees, all of which were ignored in Britain. His court became a favourite stop for British expatriates and other travellers, including many who remained loyal to the Hanoverian kings but were simply curious to meet the Old Pretender. In some ways, it acted as a British embassy in Rome.

James finally married at the age of 31. On 2 September 1719, shortly after he returned from Spain, he married Maria Clementina Sobieska, the granddaughter of the Polish King John III Sobieski.[140] She came with a large dowry, which was quite welcome. The couple had two sons. The first, named Charles and later romanticised as Bonnie Prince Charlie (and less glamorously called the "Young Pretender"), was born in December 1720. The second, named Henry, born five years later, became a cardinal in the Catholic Church. The marriage was stormy and the couple lived separately during much of the time. Maria, the titular queen consort of Great Britain, died at 32 on 18 January 1735. James never remarried.

James himself never again personally attempted to gain the throne. But in 1745, his son, Bonnie Prince Charlie, now 24 years old, led one last major rebellion attempting to restore the Stuart dynasty and place his father on the throne. The time seemed ripe, as Charles believed he could count on substantial English Jacobite support. Moreover, the War of the Austrian Succession was raging in Europe and much of the British army was on the European mainland.

---

[140] John III Sobieski was famous as the Polish King who, in 1683, arrived with an army at the gates of Vienna just in time to defeat a large Ottoman Turkish force that was laying siege to the city. He was hailed throughout Christendom as the hero who saved Vienna from capture.

Popularly known as "The Forty-five," this rebellion has been greatly romanticised in history, but in truth it was just tragic. Charles's army consisted mainly of Scottish clansmen, mostly Highlanders, with a few French troops supporting them. The expected English Jacobite support largely failed to materialise.

This rebellion achieved early success in Scotland, just as the rebellion in 1715 had. Charles was able to march into the Scottish capital of Edinburgh at the head of an army to great acclaim. He held court there and continue the struggle. But his hopes were crushed at the 16 April 1746 Battle of Culloden, near Inverness in the Scottish Highlands. The British, led by Prince William, the Duke of Cumberland, younger son of King George II, decisively and brutally defeated the rebels. William viewed the Scots as traitorous rebels. He adopted a policy of showing no quarter and taking no prisoners. He excepted the French forces from this policy, as he viewed them as legitimate enemy combatants. Under this policy, the Scottish clansmen were slaughtered by the hundreds. All Scottish hopes for a restoration of the dynasty that had begun in their country died with them. Many of the clans were ruined forever. Prince William's political opponents later called him "Butcher Cumberland" for his role in the slaughter.

Charles fled the scene of the battle. After numerous adventures, he managed to elude British forces seeking to capture him. He returned to France and never set foot in Scotland again. The Battle of Culloden was the last land battle ever fought on British soil. Never again would there be any serious Jacobite attempt to restore the Stuart dynasty.

James, the Old Pretender, lived on year after year in exile in his palace in Rome, presiding over his pretend court, continually financed by one pope after another. Visitors continued to see him and accept his hospitality, but he became increasingly irrelevant over time. He became largely an invalid in his last years. He finally died at the Palazzo Muti, still honoured by the pope but few others and still an exile from the land of his birth, on New Year's Day, 1766, at 77. He was buried with great pomp and royal ceremony in a crypt at St Peter's Basilica in what is today the Vatican City.

From the time his father died in 1701, James claimed to be King of Great Britain for over 64 years, a time longer than the reign of any British monarch until Queen Elizabeth II exceeded it in 2016. James's son, Charles, the Young Pretender, died in 1788, no longer the romanticised Bonnie Prince Charlie of his younger days. By that time, 42 years after the Battle of Culloden, few remembered the Stuart pretentions. Fewer still cared.

Chapter 13
The Children of Queen Anne, Including William of Gloucester

When the Glorious Revolution of 1688 overthrew King James II in favour of William and Mary, with Mary's younger sister, Anne, becoming the heir presumptive, everyone hoped and assumed that at least one of the sisters would produce a Protestant heir to continue the Stuart dynasty. From the Protestant perspective, a Protestant heir was desperately needed to prevent the Catholic side of the Stuart family from succeeding to the throne. A Catholic succession would defeat the purpose of the Glorious Revolution. But William and Mary had no children. So, it fell to Anne, who would herself ascend the throne in 1702, to produce the needed heir. She tried. Oh, how she tried.

Anne married Prince George of Denmark, a younger brother of the Danish king, in July 1683. Although an arranged marriage, it was a successful and, to all appearances, a loving one. Between 1683 and 1700, Anne became pregnant some 17 times. Her pregnancies went like this: a stillborn daughter; a daughter named Mary, who died of smallpox in February 1687, before the age of two; a daughter named Anne, who also died of smallpox a few days before her sister died; a miscarriage; a stillborn son; a miscarriage; a son named William, who survived infancy; a daughter named Mary, who live about two hours; a son named George, who lived a few minutes; a stillborn daughter; a miscarriage; a miscarriage; a miscarriage; a miscarriage; a miscarriage; a stillborn son; and a stillborn son. Thus, Mary had only one child, the son William, who survived infancy. That says much about the times.

William was born on 24 July 1689, two years after his two sisters died of smallpox and shortly after William and Mary became the joint monarchs. His uncle, King William, for whom he was named, immediately declared him the Duke of Gloucester, the title by which he is known today. After so many disappointments, his live birth was immediately celebrated throughout the country. The English people had high hopes that he would be the boy who would finally ensure the continuation of the Protestant line of the Stuart dynasty, especially when it became apparent that he would survive infancy. But from the beginning, all was not well with him.

William was often ill and possibly suffered from a condition today called hydrocephalus, a build-up of fluid within the brain, resulting in an enlarged head, lack of coordination, difficulty walking and similar symptoms. He did not learn to speak properly until he was three years old. His Welsh bodyguard, who befriended the prince and left a memoir about him, said that when he was five years old, he still could not easily walk up and down stairs. To combat his health problems, the family gave him his own household in Kensington near some gravel pits, where the air was considered purer and healthier. Every day, he was driven outside in a small coach especially made for him and pulled by Shetland ponies. These actions, or perhaps merely the passage of time and its ability to cure, had a positive effect. Within a few years, the boy seemed to be progressing nicely. His education was delayed by his slow development, but when it began, he reportedly did quite well. He was taught the usual subjects for a prince, including mathematics, Latin and French.

The boy William developed a close relationship with his aunt and uncle and especially with his uncle after Queen Mary died in 1694. Before she died, Mary often showered him with toys. King William was devoted to him as the hope of the dynasty. The young William became fascinated with all things military. He presided over his own "Horse Guard," a group of local boys he drilled— sometimes in front of the king and queen—as a sort of mock regiment. The Horse Guard eventually numbered several dozen boys. On his seventh birthday, William was admitted as a Knight of the Order of the Garter in a ceremony at Windsor Castle.

After his initial health difficulties, all seemed to be going well with the boy. That changed on his eleventh birthday. After a birthday party at Windsor Castle, he became ill, complaining of fatigue. At first, his attendants downplayed his complaints, ascribing his fatigue to the strenuous party. But he got worse and doctors were called in. He suffered from headaches, sore throat, chills and then high fever and delirium. His doctors could not agree on what ailed the prince. Some suspected smallpox, or possibly scarlet fever, but the symptoms did not seem to fit either diagnosis. The doctors tried the treatments usual at the time.

The prince was bled and blistered, a practice of literally raising blisters in the affected areas. These treatments probably just made his condition worse. After seeming to rally briefly, Prince William died in great pain early in the morning of 30 July 1700, at Windsor Castle with his distraught parents at his bedside, thus becoming another heir who never reigned. His body lay in state for several days, then was interred in the Henry VII Chapel at Westminster Abbey.

William's death devastated his parents, the king and the entire country. It portended a succession crisis of the first order. By this time, after ten consecutive miscarriages, stillborn births, or infants dying within hours of their birth, it was apparent that Anne, not yet queen, would never produce another heir. Her herculean efforts were for nought. It was up to Parliament to decide what to do after the prince's death.

The next year, Parliament passed the Act of Settlement of 1701, designating a Protestant branch of the royal family—the House of Hanover—as the successor when King William and then Anne died. (Chapter 12.) Parliament's agony, indeed, the country's agony, over the young prince's premature death is reflected in that act's legalese. In explaining why it was necessary to settle the succession, the act stated that it had "since pleased Almighty God to take away our said sovereign lady [Queen Mary II] and also the most hopeful Prince William, Duke of Gloucester (the only surviving issue of her Royal Highness the Princess Anne of Denmark [later Queen Anne]), to the unspeakable grief and sorrow of your Majesty [King William III] and your said good subjects..."[141]

Because he died so young, it is impossible to judge what kind of a king William would have been with any degree of confidence. He would have been a reasonably mature 25 years old when he ascended to the throne on his mother's death in 1714 and probably would at least have been a competent king. What is known for sure is that, had he lived and continued the Protestant Stuart line, the British monarchy would not have passed to a distant and a foreign branch of the family. Much internal strife, including the Fifteen and the Forty-Five, would almost certainly have been avoided.

Visitors to Williamsburg, Virginia, which became Virginia's capital in 1689 when it was still a British colony and is today a living history park, will notice that the main street, running from the College of William and Mary at one end to the capitol building at the other end, is named Duke of Gloucester Street. The colony's House of Burgesses named it in honour of the then-living Prince

---

[141] *EHD, vol. VIII*, p. 130.

William in the hope and expectation that he would one day rule over the colony. Fate decreed otherwise. Instead of becoming famous as King William IV, the prince became an obscure footnote in history with his early death. Every year thousands of tourists stroll along DOG Street in Williamsburg, as the main street is popularly called, most without the slightest idea of who the Duke of Gloucester was.

Chapter 14
A Distant Branch: Sophia of Hanover

The Act of Settlement of 1701 declared that if William and Princess Anne had no issue, "the most excellent Princess Sophia, electress and duchess dowager of Hanover, daughter of the most excellent Princess Elizabeth, late Queen of Bohemia, daughter of our late Sovereign Lord King James the First of happy memory, be and is hereby declared to be the next in succession in the Protestant line to the imperial crown and dignity of the said realms of England, France [*sic*] and Ireland..." This right to succeed extended to "the heirs of her body being Protestants..."[142] Sophia was 70 years old at the time and 34 years older than Anne. But, unlike Anne, she was in robust good health and might well have outlived her. Who was this Sophia and how did she become the heir?

Sophia's connection to the British royal family went back generations. Her maternal grandfather was King James I. James's daughter, Elizabeth, married Frederick V, Elector of the Palatinate. In 1618, Protestant rebels in Bohemia broke away from the Catholic-ruled Holy Roman Empire and invited Frederick, one of the leading Protestants of his time, to come to Bohemia as its king. Perhaps foolishly, he agreed and he and Elizabeth moved to Prague, where he was crowned King of Bohemia in November 1619. However, his reign was brief as the powerful Holy Roman Empire was determined to reclaim its authority over Bohemia. One might say the Empire struck back. Imperial forces defeated the Protestant rebels at the November 1620 Battle of White Mountain, forcing Frederick to abdicate. These events precipitated the disastrous Thirty Years' War that devastated most of Germany, the main theatre of the war. They also earned

---

[142] *EHD, vol. VIII*, p. 132. It appears that Parliament still formally considered France part of the lands the British monarch ruled over. The French thought otherwise.

Frederick the sarcastic nickname, the Winter King; Elizabeth was called the Winter Queen.

Frederick and Elizabeth were forced to flee from Prague. Soon Frederick's home base in the Palatinate was also overrun by imperial forces and he went into exile in the Netherlands, where he lived until his death in 1632. Because he was related to the Dutch royal family, he was given the palatial Wassenaar Hof in The Hague as a residence. There, Sophia was born on 14 October 1630, the twelfth of thirteen children. Because she was also related to the Dutch royal family, the States of Friesland granted her a substantial annuity at her birth. When young, she was known as Sophia of the Palatinate. In 1648, as part of the Peace of Westphalia that finally ended the Thirty Years' War, her brother, Charles Louis, was restored to her father's former position as Elector of the Palatinate, with its capital in Heidelberg. The following year, Sophia moved to Heidelberg to live at her brother's court.

Sophia was a lively and highly intelligent woman. She was carefully educated in subjects such as mathematics and the classics, including Latin and Greek. She learned to speak several modern languages, including English. When she was young, there was talk of her marrying her English cousin, Charles, the son of the deposed (and executed) King Charles I. At this time, when Oliver Cromwell still ruled over England, Charles was living in exile and was not yet the restored King Charles II. The marriage never occurred. Instead, in 1658, Sophia married Ernest Augustus, the Duke of Brunswick-Luneburg, in Heidelberg. In 1692, he became the Elector of Hanover. As a result, Sophia is best known today as Sophia of Hanover and the dynasty she and her husband established is called the House of Hanover.

The marriage was not always happy. The stolid Ernest Augustus was not remotely Sophia's intellectual equal. He was also often unfaithful and absent. Nevertheless, Sophia seemed fond of her husband. She bore him seven children who survived into adulthood, six of them boys. She was actively engaged in raising her children and was especially close to her firstborn child, the future King George I. She also accompanied her husband during a lengthy stay in Italy in 1664-5.

When it came time for her oldest son to marry, her husband suggested George marry his cousin, Sophia Dorothea of Celle. At first, Sophia was against the idea, put off by the intended bride's commoner mother and other doubts about her worthiness. Eventually, she agreed and they were married. Sophia's doubts proved warranted. The marriage was a failure. Sophia Dorothea bore George two children, including the future King George II, but after that, George left her and lived with his mistress. Later, the two were divorced. In the meantime, Sophia Dorothea had a notorious affair with a Swedish count. George and his parents were livid. The count soon died, probably murdered. Sophia might have been involved in the count's murder, although she always denied it. Sophia Dorothea was imprisoned for the rest of her life, some thirty more years. She never saw her children again.

In addition to involving herself in her children's upbringing, Sophia developed a keen intellect. She befriended the great philosopher and mathematician Gottfried Leibniz when he was the court librarian in Hanover. A century later, Voltaire would brutally skewer Leibniz in his great satirical novel, *Candide*, for Leibniz's supposed (and misrepresented) philosophical view that ours is the "best of all possible worlds." But Leibniz possessed one of the most brilliant intellects of the age. He is best known for discovering differential and integral calculus simultaneously with, but independently of, Sir Isaac Newton. Sophia's intelligence and interest in all matters scientific and mathematical impressed even the great Leibniz. Beginning in 1676, he and Sophia engaged in a lifelong friendship that ended only with her death. Their prolific correspondence demonstrated the depth of her intellectual abilities and interests when it was published in the nineteenth century.

Sophia and her husband renovated and modernised their summer residence, Herrenhausen Palace, in their capital city of Hanover. She was the driving force behind the development of the palace gardens, among the most beautiful baroque gardens in Europe and a major tourist destination still today.

When the question of who would succeed Queen Anne became ever more pressing, attention turned to the Protestant Sophia as a possibility, even though many others, all Catholic, had a stronger dynastic claim. She did nothing to discourage the idea. Indeed, she eagerly pursued it. In September 1700, shortly after the death of Prince William, Sophia met with King William at Het Loo Palace in the Dutch city of Apeldoorn. The two were cousins on her father's side. Advantageously for Sophia, she could speak with William in Dutch, his native language. The question of the succession was a major topic of conversation. The meeting proved constructive for Sophia and her family. William supported her as the successor. The Settlement Act of 1701 soon followed. William died in

1702 and Sophia became Anne's heir presumptive. Because it was clear by now that Anne would never produce an heir, Sophia was in effect the heir apparent.

After she was designated Anne's successor, Sophia closely followed affairs in Great Britain to prepare to become its queen. She wanted to visit or possibly even reside in the country over which she might one day rule. Many British leaders thought a visit was a good idea to help transition from one monarch to another as smoothly as possible. But Queen Anne firmly opposed the idea. She wanted no rival court in her realm, no one eagerly awaiting her death. She especially wanted no one to make any adverse comparisons between Sophia who, although in her seventies, was still keen of mind and energetic of body and herself, sickly and infirm despite being three decades the younger. (Seventeen pregnancies, most of them failures, no doubt contributed to her ill health.) Anne supposedly prohibited all mention of Sophia in her presence. Sophia never saw the country that had designated her to rule over it.

Anne died on 1 August 1714, at the age of 49. But Sophia did not live long enough to fulfil her dream of becoming queen. Several weeks earlier, Anne wrote Sophia a letter stating that she and her family would never be welcome to come to England. The letter hurt Sophia and reportedly caused her to become ill. A few days later, Sophia was walking in her beloved gardens at Herrenhausen. A sudden rainstorm caused her to run for shelter. She collapsed and died a short time later. The date was 28 May 1714, just over two months before she might have become Queen of Great Britain. She was 83 years old. Sophia became another heir who never reigned.

Sophia was buried the next day at the Leine Palace in Hanover, the main residence of the House of Hanover. She joined her husband, who had been interred there many years before. Later her son, George I, would be buried with them. British air raids destroyed the palace during World War II. In 1957, Sophia's remains, as well as those of her husband and son, were removed to a mausoleum at the gardens of Herrenhausen Palace. The gardens she created and loved were the most fitting place for her reburial.

Unlike the stories of many heirs who never reigned, the timing of Sophia's death is not one of the major "what ifs" of history. Her son succeeded as King George I when Anne died. If Sophia had outlived Anne and become queen, she would have been, at the age of 83 years, the oldest person to be crowned in British history, possibly in world history. Her reign would obviously have been short and her son would soon have succeeded her as king. Thus, either way,

George would have become king and the House of Hanover would have been the ruling house. Little would have changed had Sophia had the brief queenship she ardently desired. But in a way, it is a shame that Britain never had the chance to add to its list of monarchs this woman of great intellect and drive.

Sophia left quite a heritage. Through her son, George I, all future British monarchs were descended from her. Through her daughter, Sophia Charlotte, who married the Prussian King Frederick I, all future kings of Prussia and emperors of Germany were descended from her.

Chapter 15
Frederick, Son of King George II

King George I was succeeded by George II, who was succeeded by George III, who was succeeded by George IV. Many people today assume the succession of the four Georges went from father to son. The assumption is incorrect. George III was the grandson, not son, of George II. In between was a prince named Frederick, the oldest son of the second George and father of the third George. Frederick lived to the age of 44, but he died too soon to become king and thus became, instead, another heir who never reigned.

Frederick was born in the German city of Hanover, the court of his great-grandmother, the Electress Sophia, on 1 February 1707 and given the German name Friedrich Ludwig. His parents were the future George II and Caroline of Brandenburg-Ansbach. Under the Act of Settlement of 1701, he was fourth in line to succeed to the British crown at his birth, after his great-grandmother, his grandfather and his father. When he was seven years old, his grandfather became King George I on the death of Queen Anne. His parents and most of his family moved to England, but the young Friedrich was left behind in Hanover to represent the family there. He was placed under the care of a grand-uncle. He would not see his parents again for another fourteen years.

Friedrich was educated in Hanover. An important part of his education was learning English. To help emphasise his future role in Britain, he was initiated into the Order of the Garter in 1716. As the representative of his family in Hanover, he presided over ceremonial events while growing up and often met visiting diplomats. Doing so helped prepare him for his anticipated eventual role as the British king. It might also have given him the habit of ruling on his own, a habit that would cause trouble later.

In 1722, when he was 15 years old, the prince was inoculated against smallpox at his mother's direction. Her decision to inoculate him was considered daring. In those days, smallpox was a scourge of Europe. It killed untold numbers of people, including many among the nobility and even royalty. As examples, two of Queen Anne's daughters had died of smallpox, as well as the heir of the French King Louis XIV. The disease would soon kill Tsar Peter II of Russia. It was an illness truly to be feared. But the practice of inoculation was then in its infancy and many considered it too dangerous. The idea of intentionally giving someone a case of the dreaded disease, even a mild case, was unsettling, to say the least. But Friedrich's mother, fearing for her family, studied the matter closely. She ordered six men who were condemned to be executed given a choice to be inoculated instead. Unsurprisingly, all chose to be inoculated and they were, using an early, primitive method called variolation. All survived. Based on this and other tests, Caroline decided that the risk of inoculation was less than the risk of acquiring the often-fatal disease. So, she ordered her children, including Friedrich, to be inoculated in the same way. The act of inoculating a boy slated to become king made Friedrich a pioneer in the fight against smallpox.

In 1727, Friedrich's grandfather, George I, died and his father became King George II. The next year, Friedrich was called to England, where he was reunited with his parents. In 1729, now using the Anglicised name Frederick (often shortened to Fred among his friends), he was created the Prince of Wales. He was now the direct heir apparent to the throne. He also became the chancellor of the University of Dublin, a position he proudly held until his death.

Frederick might have been reunited with his parents, but their relationship was never warm and soon became estranged. From the beginning of his residence in England, his parents made clear they preferred his younger brother, William, Duke of Cumberland. In fact, they seemed to despise their firstborn son. They were quoted as saying, "Our firstborn is the greatest ass, the greatest liar, the greatest canaille and the greatest beast in the whole world and we heartily wish he was out of it."[143]

The reasons for this estrangement are not entirely clear. The fact that Frederick's parents had not seen him for fourteen years and in the meantime had produced younger children who were close at hand, did not help their relationship. To some extent, Frederick had ruled in Hanover independently of his parents, which no doubt caused him to have his own ideas of how a realm should be governed, ideas that might have conflicted with his father's. He

---

[143] John Clarke and Jasper Ridley, *The Houses of Hanover and Saxe-Coburg-Gotha*, University of California Press (2000), p. 30.

became independent, some believed headstrong, when raised without his parents' presence. He was also viewed as a womaniser who liked to drink and gamble when he came to England.

Quarrels over money contributed greatly. In Frederick's view, the king never gave him enough. In this respect, Frederick's quarrel with his father resembled the quarrels in earlier days of Robert of Normandy with his father, William the Conqueror, and Henry, the Young King, with his father, Henry II. Money has long been a common source of family discontent, even, perhaps especially, among the rich. Robert and the Young King took their quarrels to the extent of military insurrection. (Chapters 1, 4.) Circumstances in eighteenth-century Britain were quite different. Military opposition was not then an option (and no reason exists to believe Frederick would have resorted to it had it been an option). Instead, Frederick eventually took his quarrel in another direction, a direction that *was* available in his time: political opposition.

During his early years in England, Frederick formed a close friendship with a court gossip, John, Lord Hervey. The two of them co-wrote a play that skewered the king and queen. It flopped. They also shared a mistress, Anne Vane. Anne gave birth to a son in June 1732. She named the son Fitz Frederick Vane. The prince was probably, but not certainly, the father. The friendship between Hervey and Frederick soon ended. Hervey went on to write scurrilous accounts of the quarrels between Frederick and his parents. He quoted his mother as once saying, when she observed Frederick walking by, "Look, there he goes— that wretch—that villain! I wish the ground would open this moment and sink the monster to the lowest hole in hell!"[144]

In these early years, Frederick came close to marrying a few times, but nothing came of the marriage negotiations. Finally, on 27 April 1736, at the age of 29, he married the 16-year-old Princess Augusta of Saxe-Coberg, the daughter of Frederick II, Duke of Saxe-Gotha-Altenburg. The wedding, held at St James's Palace, was a major event in British society. The great composer, George Frederick Handel, composed the anthem, *"Sing Unto God,"* for it and it was first performed on the wedding day. Handel also composed the opera *Atalanta* to celebrate the marriage, although it was not performed until two weeks after the wedding.

---

[144] Stephen Taylor, *Oxford Dictionary of National Biography, Princess Caroline of Brandenburg-Ansbach*, Oxford University Press (2004).

After the wedding, the king offered Frederick an allowance of 50,000 pounds a year (the equivalent of millions today). That seems like a princely sum, but Frederick still considered it inadequate for a crown prince. He took his financial quarrel with his father public, going so far as to have some of his friends introduce a measure in Parliament that would greatly increase his allowance. The measure failed, although it led the king to give the prince a moderate increase. His impudence (from the king's perspective) in going over his father's head and bringing Parliament into the quarrel greatly increased the acrimony between son and parents.

Although known for his premarital affairs as a young man, Frederick apparently settled down into domestic life after his marriage. The couple had many children, including the future King George III. He tried to be a much better father to his own children than his father had been to him. The circumstances surrounding the birth of the couple's first child exacerbated Frederick's breach with his parents. In June 1737, he told the king and queen that Augusta was pregnant, with a due date in October. In fact, the due date was in July. When Augusta was about to go into labour in July, Frederick ordered her removed from their home at Hampton Court and taken by carriage to St James's Palace. There, she gave birth to a daughter in secret. Only after the birth were his parents informed. Members of the royal family were supposed to be present at such births to act as witnesses and to guard against the switching of babies. Frederick's manoeuvring to ensure his parents were not present infuriated both the king and queen. He was banished permanently from the king's residence.

Frederick lived most of the rest of his life at a home called Leicester House. There, he established a court in opposition to his father's, with many prominent politicians attending. He particularly opposed the king's minister, Sir Robert Walpole, the Whig politician generally considered to be Britain's first prime minister. Frederick also opposed many of the measures in Parliament that the king favoured. He seemed to admire his cousin, the Prussian King Frederick II, later called Frederick the Great, for his relatively enlightened style of rule.

Queen Caroline died of a rupture in November 1737. When she was dying, she reiterated her hatred for her oldest son, reportedly saying that her one consolation in dying was that she would never again have to see Frederick. Frederick was not allowed to see her before she died and he was not invited to the funeral.

Frederick continued to preside over his own court in opposition. He was cultured, interested in music (he played the cello tolerably well), art (he accumulated a large collection), architecture and the natural sciences. One result of his patronage of the arts was the stirring patriotic song, *"Rule, Britannia!"* Frederick's friends Thomas Arne and James Thomson composed the music and wrote the words, respectively, as part of a masque (a form of entertainment popular at the time) about the Anglo-Saxon King Alfred the Great. The masque, including the song, was first performed at Frederick's country residence in 1740. Frederick liked being associated with the ninth-century king and British naval power. The masque has long since been forgotten; not so, the song.

Great Britain held general elections in 1741. Frederick actively campaigned against Walpole who, by this time, had been prime minister for some 20 years. He joined forces with a group of young politicians within Walpole's own party called the "Patriot Whigs"—formed initially to oppose Walpole—that included William Pitt, the Elder. The opposition managed to defeat Walpole in many boroughs, especially in small pocket boroughs. Pocket boroughs, sometimes called rotten boroughs, were boroughs containing few voters and often controlled by a single prominent person or family, but which returned members of Parliament the same as a borough with many voters. Frederick himself controlled several pocket boroughs, primarily in Cornwall. Although Walpole managed to retain a small majority in the new Parliament (he won a substantial majority of the boroughs containing many voters), the defeats in the election helped lead to his being forced out of office in February 1742.

The change in government had a beneficial effect for Frederick personally. It led to a formal reconciliation between him and his father. But Frederick was passed over as commander of the British forces raised to defeat the 1745 Jacobite rebellion in support of Bonnie Prince Charlie. The command went instead to his younger brother, William, Duke of Cumberland, whom some later called Butcher Cumberland for his show-no-quarter-take-no-prisoners policy against the Scottish rebels at the Battle of Culloden. (Chapter 12.) Later, Frederick continued to oppose some of his father's policies. In the general elections of 1747, Frederick's party lost and his political influence waned.

During these years, Frederick became interested in that most English of all sports—cricket. This interest might have been fuelled in part by the desire to show his future subjects that, although born and raised in Hanover, he had now become thoroughly English. Cricket's origins date back at least to the sixteenth century, but the sport became particularly popular beginning in the eighteenth century. Frederick's patronage, along with that of other members of the nobility, helped develop this popularity. He gambled on games and even played some himself. How good a player he was, has not been recorded. He was especially associated with the team of the County of Surrey, the forerunner of the Surrey County Cricket Club. His enthusiasm for the sport continued until his death.

Frederick did not live long enough to become king. He died under uncertain circumstances in 1751. It seems that in March of that year, he was hit hard by a cricket ball—or it might have been a tennis ball. The blow caused an abscess. He later caught a chill in the bitter March cold. It soon turned to pleurisy. The prince was moved to Leicester House. There he was bled by the doctors, a treatment that, as always, probably only made his condition worse. For a while, he seemed to be getting better, but the abscess burst, causing him to cough painfully. Around 9:30 in the evening of March 20, he "laid his head upon his pillow and without a convulsion sign or groan or the least movement—rattled in his throat and was dead in three minutes."[145] His wife and some friends were at his bedside. The general medical opinion at the time was that he died of pneumonia caused by a burst abscess in one of his lungs, but it might have been a pulmonary embolism that killed him. He was 44 years old.

After his death, his wife, Augusta, gave birth to their last child, Caroline Matilda, who was to become Queen of Denmark. On 13 April, Prince Frederick was buried with a minimum of ceremony in Henry VII's chapel at Westminster Abbey. Neither his father nor any of his brothers and sisters attended the funeral. As the great novelist Thackeray put it sardonically, Frederick's parents would have "no tears...when Prince Frederick died—their eldest son, their heir, their enemy."[146]

Frederick was reasonably likeable (except to his parents) and was reasonably well-liked (except by his parents). His death was mourned by his friends and the nation, although perhaps not as bitterly as that of some of the other heirs who died too soon to become the monarch. The fact that the succession was assured—Frederick left behind plenty of heirs—probably contributed to the relative lack

---

[145] Matthew Kilburn, *Oxford Dictionary of National Biography, Frederick Lewis, Prince of Wales*, Oxford University Press (2009).

[146] William Makepeace Thackeray, *The Four Georges*, The Book League of America, Inc. (1937), p. 45 (hereafter, Thackeray, *The Four Georges*).

of passion his death caused. An anonymous bit of doggerel that could pass as his epitaph might sum up the general feelings about his death:

> "Here lies Fred,
> Who was alive and is dead.
> Had it been his father,
> I had much rather.
> Had it been his brother,
> Still better than another.
> Had it been his sister,
> No one would have missed her.
> Had it been the whole generation,
> Still better for the nation.
> But since 'tis only Fred,
> Who was alive and is dead,
> There's no more to be said."[147]

Frederick left behind some monuments to remember him by. The city of Fredericksburg in Virginia in the United States was named for him, as were other, smaller towns. But otherwise, he has largely been forgotten. His early death did not cause history to take a greatly different path. The House of Hanover continued to rule over Great Britain. Frederick's son would have become King George III on his death, whenever it occurred. To all appearances, matters progressed rather seamlessly despite Frederick's failure to join the ranks of British monarchs. It appears that, unlike the case of many heirs who never reigned, his death did not significantly change the course of history.

But can we say this confidently? George III became king in 1760 at the young age of 22 years. Frederick would have been a mature 53 years old on the death of his father. Early in his reign, George III presided over the tumultuous years when Britain's American colonies began to protest what they viewed as Britain's heavy-handed and unfair policies towards them, protests that, when not resolved to the colonies' satisfaction, graduated to open warfare in 1775 and then to a declaration of American independence in July 1776. The former colonies effectively won their independence at Yorktown in 1781 and it was finally recognised for all time in the Treaty of Paris of 1783. Had Frederick lived

---

[147] Thackeray, *The Four Georges*, p. 86.

another, say, 30 years, thus surviving into his seventies, he, not the young, headstrong George, would have been king during this time. A mature Frederick might have handled matters differently and possibly more diplomatically. The colonists' journey under George's rule from loyal and proud English subjects with a few grievances—which they were at the outset—to ardent American patriots demanding and then winning total independence, all within two decades, might have gone a different route. As the very different evolution of the relationship between Britain and its Canadian colonies demonstrates, the actual historical events did not have to occur as they did.

As is the case with all of the heirs who never reigned, we will never know.

Chapter 16
Princess Charlotte of Wales

King George III reigned for some 60 years, longer than any British king and longer than any British monarch except for Victoria and Elizabeth II. He had numerous offspring, but as the eighteenth-century turned into the nineteenth-century, he had only one legitimate grandchild. The grandchild was Princess Charlotte of Wales, the daughter of the king's oldest son, the Prince of Wales, who was also named George. This George was destined to become King George IV on the death of his father. Charlotte seemed destined to succeed to the throne as Queen Charlotte on the death of her father.

The future George IV married his cousin, Princess Caroline of Brunswick, on 8 April 1795. The two disliked each other from the beginning and separated after only about three weeks of living as husband and wife. George later said they had had sexual relations a total of three times. But one of those times resulted in the birth of a healthy baby girl on 7 January 1796, which happened to be exactly nine months after the wedding minus one day. The couple named the girl Charlotte Augusta, after the child's grandmothers. Her paternal grandmother was George III's Queen Consort, Charlotte of Mecklenburg-Strelitz. Her maternal grandmother was Princess Augusta, a daughter of Frederick, the prince who had died too young to succeed his father, George II. The country celebrated the birth of the first heir of the next generation. Few seemed bothered that it was a girl rather than a boy. By this time, there had been plenty of queens regnant. The king was delighted to finally have a grandchild and was not a bit unhappy that it was a girl. The estrangement between Prince George and Caroline meant that George would likely not have any other children (he did not). So, Charlotte was the only heir to the throne after her father.

From the beginning, Charlotte's father limited the contact between the girl and her mother. Caroline was permitted no role in her daughter's upbringing and only given limited visitation rights. When Charlotte was young, both parents used her as a weapon against the other in their continual battling. "She became, inevitably, a pawn in a vast and complicated game, a fact of which she was well aware as soon as she was old enough to look about her." Her father, George, was never particularly popular. His shabby treatment of his wife contributed to his growing unpopularity. From the day she was born, however, Charlotte was popular, even beloved. The contrast between her and her father could hardly have been greater. He was strict and dour. As soon as she grew old enough to develop her own personality, she seemed to all to be a delightful girl, somewhat of a tomboy, not at all affected by her exalted status. "The impression one gets from all the early recorded stories of Charlotte is of a happy recklessness and a warm heart."[148] She became an accomplished horse rider and learned to play the piano well.

Although her father claimed to love her and probably did in his own way, her relations with him were strained. He greatly restricted her activities and contacts with the outside world. During much of her early childhood, she lived in her own, secluded, household without other family members or even close friends. As one biographer stated, she "lived in a household of her own, in the company of no one who was not paid to be there."[149] Charlotte was close to her grandfather, George III, who would soon lapse into insanity, but who loved his granddaughter while he still could. She greatly looked forward to the occasional times she could spend with him and bask in his unqualified love.

Charlotte did have one playmate for a while, the grandson of one of those who were paid to care for her. Many years later, he told a charming story that one day when Charlotte was visiting his family's home, a crowd gathered outside the house, hoping to catch a glimpse of her. She observed the crowd and playfully decided to join it. She snuck outside incognito through the garden gate. Charlotte mixed with the crowd without being recognised, exuding the same eager hope as the rest that they might view the fabulous princess. When she was tired of the game, she snuck back inside the house. Almost certainly, neither her father nor

---

[148] Thea Holme, *Prinny's Daughter: A Life of Princess Charlotte of Wales*, Hamish Hamilton (1976), pp. 5, 45 (hereafter Holme, *Prinny's Daughter*).

[149] James Chambers, *Charlotte and Leopold: The True Story of the Original People's Princess*, Old Street Publishing (2007), p. 16 (hereafter Chambers, *Charlotte and Leopold*).

King George ever learned of this escapade. The indulgent king probably would have laughed had he known. The strict father probably not.

As she grew older, some of her entourage considered Charlotte unconventional. She was a bit casual with her clothing and too much of a free spirit. She closely identified with the character of Marianne Dashwood in Jane Austen's first novel, *Sense and Sensibility*, which was published in 1811, when Charlotte was 15 years old. The character was 16 years old in the novel, around the same age as Charlotte when she read it. Marianne represented the "sensibility" part of the title (or, in more modern language, sensitivity) and she had strong romantic inclinations. This and other novels probably caused the young, sheltered princess to long for her own romance.

By the time Charlotte turned 14 and then 15 years of age, she had physically matured and was becoming a woman. She was still somewhat of a tomboy, very lively and some of her caretakers considered her coarse. One woman said she had "grown tall and very graceful," but that she was "forward, dogmatic on all subjects, buckish about horses and full of exclamations very like swearing."[150] "She was also warm-hearted and emotional and obviously attracted to men. The Regent conceived it his 'duty as a father' to ensure that she was kept firmly in hand, that she was closely watched from morning to night by those who had been appointed to supervise her upbringing."[151]

In 1810, when Charlotte was 14 years old, her beloved grandfather, the old King George III, now 72 years old, became hopelessly and finally insane. Charlotte had lost the one member of her family who always treated her well. Her father was named the Prince Regent early in 1811, effectively acting as king during his father's final incapacity. The new Regent arranged for a lavish ball to celebrate his new position. Charlotte, now 15 years old, hoped and anticipated that she would be invited. It would have been her first ball, her coming-out party. But, to her great disappointment, she was not invited. At the time, some believed the snub occurred because her father was concerned that his far more popular daughter might upstage him.

Even after he became Regent, Charlotte's father continued to restrict her activities and she lived in regal isolation. She chafed under the restrictions. As word got out of how the father was treating the daughter, his popularity suffered

---

[150] Chambers, *Charlotte and Leopold*, p. 36.

[151] Christopher Hibbert, *George IV: Regent and King*, Harper and Row (1973), p. 48 (hereafter Hibbert, *George IV: Regent and King*).

even more and hers grew. Most sympathised with Charlotte. These feelings distressed the vain Regent and added to his growing resentment of his daughter. The Regent made clear to her that only by marriage could she free herself from her isolation. She began to think about it.

The young Charlotte had various romances, some more or less real, some merely reputed. Some became public knowledge and the subject of gossip, much uninformed. Charlotte was early attracted to an illegitimate first cousin, then to a second illegitimate cousin, a lieutenant in the dragoons. With the connivance of her mother, Charlotte saw the lieutenant privately several times in the mother's home. It is unknown how far these trysts went. The Regent was furious when he heard of this. He was determined not to allow a repeat. But, much to the Regent's relief, in these early infatuations, Charlotte managed to avoid any talk of marriage and the public never heard the details of her private meetings with the lieutenant.

Charlotte also became interested in politics. And not just any politics, but progressive politics, sometimes verging on radical. She expressed great interest in the well-being of the common people, her future subjects, including the Irish. Her favoured political party was the Whigs. She was especially partial to a Whig leader, Charles Grey, the second Earl of Grey, a noted liberal politician, with whom she formed a personal friendship. (Although Earl Grey later became prime minister, his name is best remembered today for the tea named for him.) Her father had nominally been a Whig. But when he became Regent, the Tories were in power. When he did not move to replace the Tories with Whigs, Charlotte became angry. One evening, at the opera, she very publicly blew kisses in the direction of Earl Grey. A princess blowing kisses at a leader of the *opposition* created a sensation. It did not endear her to her father.

Charlotte's resistance to her father and the restrictions placed on her often led to tears on her part. Among those sympathetic with her and her political views was her good friend, the poet Lord Byron. He wrote a poem in her honour, called "To a Lady Weeping":

"Weep, daughter of a noble line,
A sire's disgrace, a realm's decay,
Ah! Happy if each tear of thine
Could wash a father's fault away!
Weep, for thy tears are virtue's tears,

Auspicious to these suffering isles,
And be each drop, in future years,
Repaid thee of thy people's smiles."[152]

Charlotte's political views and the people's belief, probably correct, that she sincerely cared for them rather than just herself, endeared her to them more and more over time. Everyone thought that, in her, they finally had a magnificent future queen after a century of the dull and mediocre Georges. Many eagerly anticipated the end of the reign of her ancient, insane grandfather and then that of her father, so she could finally become their queen and bring a new glorious era, perhaps one called the Charlottian Era, to Britain.

If Charlotte thought about her marrying, so did the Prince Regent. He considered the question of a husband for Charlotte something entirely for him to decide. Charlotte herself, he believed (or at least hoped), would have no say in the matter. In 1813, when she was 17 years old, he made his choice: William, the Hereditary Prince of Orange (who would later become King of the Netherlands). Such a marriage would bring great political advantage to Britain in northern Europe. Some of the Regent's advisors might have remembered the precedent set over a century before when an English princess married a Dutch prince and the two eventually reigned over Britain jointly as William and Mary.

The prince was willing. Not so much the princess. She was quite unimpressed when she first met him. She called him "Slender Billy." Later she softened her view of him and, for a while, found him marginally acceptable if uninspiring. But she did not want to leave Britain, the country she would one day rule over. "As heiress presumptive to the Crown," she wrote, "it is certain that I could not quit this country, as Queen of England still less. Therefore, the P of O must visit his frogs solo."[153] Charlotte's mother, Caroline, also opposed the marriage, as did most of the general population, who wanted Charlotte to have the husband of her choice. Charlotte turned to Earl Grey for advice. He advised her not to oppose her father publicly, but instead to be patient and see how matters developed.

Charlotte sometimes tried to deflect pressure to marry William by claiming an interest in another suitor, William Frederick, Duke of Gloucester. The press learned of this and had a field day speculating about whether she would marry

---

[152] Chambers, *Charlotte and Leopold*, p. 45.
[153] Chambers, *Charlotte and Leopold*, p. 76.

the "Cheese" (Duke of Gloucester, also called "Silly Billy") or the "Orange," also called Slender Billy. Eventually, Charlotte caved into her father's pressure to become engaged to the Prince of Orange. Or at least she said something sufficiently equivocal to her father that he became convinced she had agreed to marry the Dutchman. The Regent joyfully announced to the public and to the Prince of Orange that the two were engaged. Negotiations over the exact terms of the marriage commenced.

During these events, Charlotte met the man who was to become the true love of her life. Leopold was a German prince, the youngest of many children of Francis, the Duke of Saxe-Coburg-Saalfeld, a small duchy in Saxony. As a younger son of a duke, who would inherit essentially nothing, the impoverished Leopold had to make his own way in life. He was doing well. When he and Charlotte met, he was a lieutenant general in the Russian cavalry fighting against Napoleon in the seemingly endless Napoleonic Wars. He had personally led several cavalry charges and had been decorated for heroism.

With the wars finally seeming to come to an end, Leopold was in London, where he and Charlotte met briefly. He did not immediately sweep her off her feet, but they were attracted to each other. Leopold seemed kind, attentive and intelligent. Charlotte invited him to call on her. The next day, he took her up on the invitation and they visited for upwards of an hour. To avoid any possible misunderstanding as to the propriety of the visit, he wrote a letter to her father stating what he had done and explaining that his visit had been at her request. The letter made a favourable impression on her father, although the Regent did not consider a marriage between Leopold and his daughter remotely suitable. Leopold later had to leave England and matters continued as they were.

When the Prince of Orange insisted that his future wife would have to spend at least part of each year in the Netherlands, Charlotte broke off the engagement. Her outraged father responded by ordering her confined to her home. He permitted her to go to the theatre and opera occasionally, which she enjoyed (she had long loved music), but he ordered her to sit in the back of the box and to leave before the performance was finished. Charlotte responded as best she could. In a famous episode, to evade her confinement, Charlotte fled into the street. The long-sheltered princess had no idea of what to do. A man living nearby, not knowing who she was, kindly helped her find a hackney cab, which took her to her mother's house. There she directed her servants to pay the startled driver the exorbitant sum of three guineas. She consulted with her mother and

Whig politicians about what to do. They convinced her to return to her father, which she did. The escapade and the story of the runaway princess quickly spread throughout London. All sympathised with the princess and disliked the father even more.

Around this time, Charlotte's mother, Caroline, left the country, after a brief, rather tepid, farewell meeting with her daughter. Caroline never returned to England and mother and daughter never saw each other again. With her mother far away, Charlotte must have worried about the possibility that her parents would divorce and her father would remarry and produce a male heir. A male heir would supplant her as next in line to the British throne after her father. Fortunately for her, it never came to that. Instead, Caroline's absence eased Charlotte's strained relationship with her father. Over time, Charlotte became reconciled with her situation and, to some extent, with her father. Her father began to treat her kindlier and with more respect.

In September 1814, at her strong urging and on the advice of her doctors, who were concerned about the state of her health, Charlotte was permitted to visit the seaside. She wanted to go to the glamorous Brighton, but her father refused her that privilege. Instead, she travelled to Weymouth, meeting large, adoring crowds along the way that made abundantly clear how popular she was. She remained in Weymouth for several months, enjoying the scenery and the entertainments available to royalty.

Charlotte and her party did a lot of sailing while at Weymouth. One afternoon when they were sailing, they encountered a naval ship, the HMS *Leviathan*. She and her party were invited to come aboard to inspect the ship. When they were rowed next to the ship, a chair was lowered to allow the party to be carried comfortably on board. The rest of the party took advantage of the chair. But Charlotte would have none of that. She climbed up the rope ladder and clambered aboard, just like the sailors did. Those in the ship above cheered as they watched their princess, alone among her party, climb aboard on her own two feet. Onboard, she inspected the ship thoroughly, charming everyone present, then left the way she came—down the rope ladder.

Shortly before Christmas, she returned to London. Over the holidays, she and her father became closer. He was remarkably friendly towards her. He still hoped, however, that she would relent and marry William, the Prince of Orange. She refused, writing to a friend, "I remain firm & unshaken, & no arguments, no threats shall ever bend me to marry this detested Dutchman."[154] Eventually, George gave up on the Dutch connection and broke off negotiations with William. William turned his attention to other potential wives and the following summer, he became engaged to a Russian princess, whom he eventually married.

By early 1815, Charlotte had determined to marry Leopold, or "the Leo," as she called him. He was interested, but he was back fighting Napoleon on the continent, as the Corsican had returned from defeat and exile on the island of Elba to trouble Europe once again. Her father was also still unwilling to permit her to marry the penniless younger son of a minor German ruler. But Charlotte was determined. She wrote to her father, "I no longer hesitate in declaring my partiality in favour of the Prince of Coburg—assuring you no one will be more steady or consistent in this their present & last engagement than myself."[155] Matters stood at a stalemate for months. Finally, met with determined resistance from his daughter and with most of the royal family, as well as the rest of the country, taking her side—and after having received favourable reports on Leopold from British agents who had gotten to know him on the continent—the Regent yielded. He formally invited Leopold to come to England to meet with him and his daughter.

The invitation reached Leopold in Berlin as he was travelling back to Russia. Leopold immediately changed his plans and reversed direction. He arrived at Brighton in February 1816. The Regent, Charlotte and Leopold met and all went well. Charlotte and Leopold spoke at length of their plans and their future life together. They spoke in French, the second language of both, but the language they found mutually easiest in which to communicate. Even George had to admit that Leopold was a man of substance, a man who could make his daughter happy. Charlotte was ecstatic. She wrote to a friend, "I find him charming and go to bed happier than I have ever done yet in my life." She added, "I am certainly a very fortunate creature & have to bless God. A Princess never, I believe, set out in life (or married) with such prospects of happiness, real domestic ones like other people."[156]

The Prince Regent announced in the House of Commons on March 14 that Charlotte and Leopold were engaged to be married. The announcement was acclaimed by all. Many were relieved that the very public speculation and gossip

---

[154] Chambers, *Charlotte and Leopold*, p. 141.

[155] Holme, *Prinny's Daughter*, p. 210.

[156] Holme, *Prinny's Daughter*, p 213.

about her romances and the ongoing question of whom she would marry, would finally end. All looked forward to the wedding, to future heirs, and, especially, to their beloved princess becoming their queen one day they hoped would not be too far off. Parliament voted to purchase the Claremont House, a palatial mansion in Surrey, as a wedding present for them. The Regent commissioned Leopard a general in the British army.

Charlotte and Leopold were married on 2 May 1816. The wedding was held at the Prince Regent's London residence, the Carlton House. It was perhaps even a greater social event than the fabulous wedding between Edward, the Black Prince, and his cousin, Joan, the Fair Maid of Kent, back in the fourteenth century. (Chapter 6.) Large, adoring crowds cheered her as she rode in a carriage to the Carlton House. Charlotte's wedding dress was said to have cost some 10,000 pounds, a tremendous sum in those days (and not insignificant today). The dress had an embroidered chiffon overlay with a six-foot train held in place with a large diamond clasp. The bride wore a diamond-studded wreath and abundant diamond jewellery and accessories. The gaudiness and conspicuous consumption seem inconsistent with Charlotte's normally rather simple, unassuming personality. One suspects that others, not Charlotte, were the driving force behind the decision to have such an expensive dress and accoutrements. But Charlotte probably thoroughly enjoyed it, as any bride would. Leopold wore a scarlet British army uniform.

The wedding ceremony itself proceeded smoothly, for the most part. However, Charlotte was heard to giggle when Leopold vowed to endow her with all his worldly goods. She knew that she, not he, possessed the couple's worldly goods.

Charlotte and Leopold honeymooned at an uncle's residence in Surrey. The Regent visited them there. It was a friendly visit and the Regent was in a good mood, which added to her happiness. The couple returned to London and settled into a contented domestic life. Charlotte wrote that Leopold was "the perfection of a lover."[157] When she became overly excited, as she often did, he would admonish her by saying something like, "Doucement, mon Cherie." (Gently, my love.) She accepted the admonitions in good grace and soon started calling him Doucement. When they visited the theatre or opera, as they often did, the Coburgs, as they were known, were invariably applauded by the spectators. On one occasion, the company played "*God Save the King*," with verses added in

---

[157] Holme, *Prinny's Daughter*, p. 223.

honour of the couple, including this last one (readers may judge for themselves how well the words fit the tune):

"Long may the Noble Line,
When she descended, shine
In Charlotte the Bride!
Grant it perpetuate
And ever make it great;
On Leopold blessings wait
And Charlotte his Bride."[158]

As one biographer wrote, "It expressed the feelings of the English people. Charlotte was their hope, England's hope and after the long years of elderly, sick or debauched monarchs, the idea of being governed by this fair, young and apparently blooming girl, with her handsome husband who would doubtless sire a line of future kings, was immensely attractive."[159]

Early in their married life, Charlotte met Leopold's long time personal physician, Dr Christian Stockmar, a German physician who accompanied Leopold to Britain (and went on to have an influential career under later monarchs). At first, the doctor was unimpressed with the princess. But he soon changed his mind. He wrote in his diary, "She was handsomer than I had expected, with most peculiar manners, her hands generally folded behind her, her body always pushed forward, never standing quiet, from time to time—stamping her foot, without however losing my countenance. My first impression was not favourable. In the evening she pleased me more. Her dress was simple and in good taste."[160] The two soon become fast friends. He was devoted to her and she to him. She called him "Stocky."

Charlotte soon became pregnant, as producing an heir was a primary duty for a princess, even one slated to become queen regnant. But she became ill while at the opera and had to leave. It was later announced that she had miscarried. It was perceived as only a minor setback, however, as her doctors assured her she could still bear children.

---

[158] Holme, *Prinny's Daughter*, p. 225.
[159] Holme, *Prinny's Daughter*, p.225.
[160] Chambers, *Charlotte and Leopold*, p. 170.

In August 1816, the couple finally moved into the Claremont House, where they continued to live happily together. Charlotte had chosen well. Dr Stockmar wrote in his diary, "In this house reign harmony, peace and love—in short everything that can promote domestic happiness. My master is the best of all husbands in all the five quarters of the globe; and his wife bears him an amount of love, the greatness of which can only be compared with the English national debt." Leopold later wrote, "Except when I went out to shoot, we were together always and we <u>could</u> be together, we did not tire."[161]

Leopold and Charlotte spent the Christmas season with members of her family at Brighton, then returned to Claremont. They quietly celebrated her 21st birthday on 7 January 1817. Soon afterwards, she became pregnant again. Leopold proudly announced the pregnancy to her father and the world in April. He, she and her doctors were confident that this time she would produce a healthy heir.

The nation became wildly excited by the news that their princess would soon become a mother. The final end of the Napoleonic Wars after the Battle of Waterloo in June 1815 brought an era of unparalleled peace to Europe and Great Britain. This was a good thing in the long run. But in the short run, it caused substantial economic displacement, as thousands of no-longer-needed soldiers returned to Britain, many of them unemployed, and war industries, such as those making munitions, were dismantled. By 1817, Britain was in the midst of a severe recession. The country needed good news to provide hope for the future and this was it. Bookies took bets on what the child's gender would be. Economists calculated that the birth of a boy would raise the stock market by six per cent, the birth of a girl by a more modest two and a half per cent.

Charlotte's estimated due date was October 19. A medical team was formed to preside over pregnancy and birth. The team was led by Sir Richard Croft, a noted *accoucher* (a male midwife) with a track record of successful deliveries. Dr Stockmar declined to become a member of the delivery team formally. He was concerned that, as a foreigner, he would be blamed if anything went wrong. But he continued to observe events.

Prenatal care began in earnest that August. By this time, Charlotte had been having little exercise and had become overweight, a matter that greatly concerned Croft and his team. He put her on a strict diet and ordered a regiment that included daily exercise. These orders were probably beneficial. Less

---

[161] Chambers, *Charlotte and Leopold*, pp. 177, 178.

beneficial was another procedure Croft undertook. Following a treatment common in those days (and earlier; see chapters 13, 15), Croft ordered her bled periodically, an order that would horrify any modern obstetrician or midwife. It horrified even Dr Stockmar, who considered the practice of bleeding to be obsolete and misguided. Under this regimen, October 19 came and went. Day after day passed with no sign of the princess going into labour. Modern methods of inducing labour were not then available and Charlotte and her medical team could only wait and carry on with the regimen they thought best. A week after the expected due date passed, then a second week. Every day that passed worried the delivery team more, as the baby would be growing larger, making delivery even more difficult.

Finally, on 3 November, Charlotte went into labour. But progress was slow. The next day, witnesses to the expected royal birth, including the Archbishop of Canterbury, were called and began to arrive. But the day came and went without a birth. Croft tried to get Charlotte to exercise as much as possible, but he did not allow her to eat. She was growing weaker, as the labour extended into a nightmarish 48 hours. Charlotte bore it bravely. She promised one of the nurses, " 'I will neither bawl nor shriek,' and she did not do so."[162] The main problem, it seems, was that the baby, inordinately large after such a long pregnancy, was in the wrong position for delivery. Croft and other members of the medical team remained with Charlotte the whole time. To his everlasting credit, so did Leopold. He showed his devotion by staying at his wife's side and giving what encouragement he could. (Fathers did not commonly attend births in those days.)

The medical team included a doctor who was adept at using forceps. Croft had to make the agonizing decision whether to employ them. Use of forceps might or might not save a child and mother, but it might also do more harm than help. Forceps could damage the baby and maybe harm the mother in a way that would prevent her from having more children. Also, in the day before the use of antiseptic measures, forceps could cause a life-threatening infection. Croft decided against using forceps. The wisdom of the decision is still debated, although few suggest it was clearly wrong. Whether the use of forceps could have prevented what actually occurred will never be known.

Charlotte grew ever weaker from her ordeal. After substantial bleeding in her uterus, she finally delivered around 9 o'clock the evening of 5 November. Unfortunately, the baby, a nine-pound son, was stillborn. Frantic attempts to

---

[162] Hibbert, *George IV: Regent and King*, p. 98.

revive it failed. It had apparently died hours earlier. The foetus was presented for inspection to the witnesses. It appeared to be fully and normally formed.

The good news among the bad was that Charlotte seemed to be rallying. The bleeding appeared to have stopped. She accepted calmly the news that her son was stillborn and tried to console those about her. As one of her doctors reported, she bore it "with a Brunswick heart." (Her mother was a princess of Brunswick.) She was finally able to eat a bit. The witnesses went home, assured that the princess was resting peacefully. Leopold was told it was time for him to get some rest. Although he was naturally distraught over the death of his son, he retired. Dr Stockmar probably gave him a sedative to help him sleep. Croft also left to get some rest, leaving Charlotte in the care of experienced and capable nurses.

Around midnight, matters took a turn for the worse. Charlotte began vomiting, had difficulty breathing, started bleeding again and complained of pain in her womb. She drank some tea, then managed to sleep for a while. Croft was called back and, viewing her, became alarmed. He applied hot compresses to try to stop the bleeding and had her drink brandy and wine. He called for Dr Stockmar, who was also appalled at what he saw. Charlotte told him, "They have made me tipsy." After viewing Charlotte, Stockmar started to leave to try to rouse Leopold. He later reported, "I had just left the room, when she called out loudly, 'Stocky! Stocky!' I went back; she was quieter, but the rattle continued. She turned once more over on her face, drew her legs up and her hands grew cold..."[163] Soon it was all over.

Princess Charlotte of Wales, the fun-loving, high-spirited and yet serious, intelligent, conscientious, well-meaning, courageous, spunky and unpretentious girl who was so adored by so many, died shortly after midnight, 6 November 1817, at the age of 21. She would never be queen. Instead, she became just another heir who never reigned. There would be no Charlottian Era.

Exactly what Charlotte died of is debated today. It might have been postpartum haemorrhage. It might have been due to a pulmonary embolism. It might have been a combination of factors exacerbated by Charlotte's weakened condition after such a long labour. It hardly matters today exactly what killed her. It is clear that, more generally, she died of complications arising from childbirth, a common enough cause of death in those days.

The Prince Regent and the rest of the royal family were shattered when they learned of Charlotte's death. Her mother, Caroline, reportedly fainted when she

---

[163] Holme, *Prinny's Daughter*, p.240.

heard the news. Even the spurned suitor, the Prince of Orange, ordered a period of mourning in the Netherlands. The entire country was devastated. At a time of economic distress, when the people desperately needed good news to give them hope, they received the worse news possible. Their beloved princess was no more. The eagerly anticipated heir died before he was even born. The outpouring of grief probably exceeded that following the early death of any of the other heirs who never reigned and might have been matched only by that following the sudden death of Princess Diana 180 years later. Shops soon sold out of black cloth. Rather than gain six per cent, the stock market closed for two weeks of mourning. Other businesses also closed to honour the princess.

One Whig leader said it was "as if every household throughout Great Britain had lost a favourite child."[164] Even the great hero of Waterloo, the Duke of Wellington, was shaken. He said that Charlotte "would have behaved well," and that "her death is one of the most serious misfortunes the country has ever met with."[165] Lord Byron was in Venice when he heard the news. He is said to have let out a scream from his window that reverberated across the Grand Canal. It is unknown whether news of Charlotte's death ever penetrated the fog shrouding the insane George III's dim consciousness. If so, he too would have been devastated by the death of his beloved granddaughter.

Leopold mourned like no other. He lamented, "Two generations gone. Gone in a moment! I have felt for myself, but I have felt for the Prince Regent. My Charlotte is gone from the country—it has lost her. She was good, she was an admirable woman. None could know my Charlotte as I did know her! It was my happiness, my duty to know her character, but it was my delight!"[166] Dr Stockmar later wrote, "November saw the ruin of this happy home and the destruction at one blow of every hope and happiness of Prince Leopold. He has never recovered the feeling of happiness, which had blessed his short married life."[167]

Leopold was still in his twenties when Charlotte died. Despite his deep mourning, life continues, as the saying goes. Years later, he remarried and went on to have a brilliant career. In 1831, the citizens of the newly formed country of Belgium chose him to become the first King of the Belgians. Still today, the anniversary of his coronation, 21 July 1831, is celebrated as Belgium's National

---

[164] Holme, *Prinny's Daughter*, p. 240.

[165] Chambers, *Charlotte and Leopold*, p. 3.

[166] Chambers, *Charlotte and Leopold*, p. 201.

[167] Holme, *Prinny's Daughter*, p. 241.

Day. He reigned over that country for 24 years until his death. But he never forgot his first love. He named his only daughter Charlotte. (It is unknown how enthusiastic his second wife was to have her daughter named in honour of her husband's first wife.) On his deathbed in 1865, nearly half a century after Charlotte died, those gathered around his bedside to witness the death of their king heard his last words: "Charlotte… Charlotte."[168]

After lying in state, Charlotte was buried with her stillborn son in St George's Chapel at Windsor Castle on November 19. Her distraught father could not bear to attend the funeral. The public paid to have a beautiful marble statue erected and placed at her tomb. An obelisk in her honour was built on the grounds of the Red House Park in Sandwell in the West Midlands. It still stands today as a tribute to the princess who cared more for her future subjects than she did for herself and who died trying to perform her duty of producing an heir.

The events of early November 1817 have been called a triple tragedy. The first two victims are easy to identify: Charlotte and her stillborn son. But who was the third? After Charlotte's death, people started placing the blame, as people do when a seemingly preventable tragedy has occurred. The autopsy performed after she died revealed no evidence of negligence. Neither Leopold nor the Prince Regent ever blamed Sir Richard Croft. Instead, they publicly exonerated him. Modern opinion largely absolves him of blame. Bleeding Charlotte during her pregnancy was certainly harmful. But the consensus today (although not universal) is that he did everything he could to save both the mother and the child utilizing the methods then available and that his decision not to use forceps to force an earlier delivery was at least defensible. (However, Charlotte's death ignited a public debate and led to the increased use of forceps and other methods of early intervention in the future.)

The general public was not so generous. Justly or unjustly, many blamed Croft for Charlotte's death. He was, after all, the leader of the medical team that had failed Charlotte, as well as the new heir to the throne, the royal family and the entire nation. Among those who blamed Croft was Croft himself. One day in February 1818, at a patient's home, he slouched in a tall chair, placed a pistol in his mouth and fired a bullet through his brain. The back of the chair caught the blood and brains. The bullet went through the wall. Croft died instantly. Supposedly, his lifeless left hand fell onto an open book containing

---

[168] Chambers, *Charlotte and Leopold*, p. 232.

Shakespeare's play, *Love's Labour's Lost*. The open page contained the line, "Fair Sir, God save you! Where is the princess?"[169]

This story has an epilogue, one that, perhaps, makes it a bit less unbearable. Charlotte's death left King George III with no legitimate grandchildren, thus threatening a succession crisis after the king's offspring died one by one. The king's children were called upon, in the newspapers and elsewhere, to produce another grandchild. His fourth son, Edward, then 50 years old, unmarried and living with his mistress, heeded the call. He dismissed the mistress, looked around for a suitable wife, found one in Leopold's older sister and married her. A year and a half after Charlotte died, the couple gave birth to a child who would later inherit the throne. They gave the child a name that resonates around the world still today and that designates an entire era of British history: Victoria.

---

[169] Chambers, *Charlotte and Leopold*, pp. 1-2.

Chapter 17
Prince Albert Victor, Known as Eddy

When George III finally died at the age of 81 in 1820, his son, the Prince Regent (Charlotte's father), followed him as King George IV. George IV died without an heir ten years later, in 1830. (This means that, had she lived, Princess Charlotte would have been 34 years old when she succeeded her father and became queen.) Because George III's second son, Frederick, had died childless in 1827, George III's third son succeeded as King William IV. William died, also childless, in 1837. George's fourth son, Edward, had already died by then. Thus, Edward's daughter, Victoria, became queen. As everyone knows, hers would be a long and glorious reign, a time known as the Victorian Era. Her oldest son, Edward, succeeded her as King Edward VII in 1901. Edward's oldest son was Prince Albert Victor.

This prince's full name was Albert Victor Christian Edward, but he was known to his family and friends as "Eddy." He seemed destined to become King Albert in his turn when first his grandmother and then his father died. But he died before either of them and thus became the final British heir who never reigned. Instead of becoming King of the country with the largest and richest empire in the world, he became the least understood and the most misunderstood prince the country has ever produced. People still do not know what to make of him. Many believe, without proof, that he was mentally deficient and homosexual. (Today, we would use the word "gay" to describe someone who was homosexual, but the word did not have that meaning in the nineteenth-century.) Of the few who remember him today, most think of him in a macabre way that is entirely unfair to his memory.

Eddy was born on 8 January 1864, at Frogmore House near Windsor Castle. He was some two months premature, but he managed to survive infancy. His mother was Alexandra of Denmark, who would become queen consort when her

237

husband became King Edward VII. Eddy's first two names were in honour of his paternal grandparents, Queen Victoria and her consort, Prince Albert of Saxe-Coburg and Gotha. At his birth, his title was His Royal Highness Prince Albert Victor of Wales. The following March, he was christened at Buckingham Palace. Among his godparents was his great-great-uncle, the aged Leopold I, King of the Belgians—the same Leopold who had married the doomed Princess Charlotte nearly half a century earlier. (Victoria was the daughter of Leopold's older sister. (Chapter 16.))

Less than a year and a half after his birth, Eddy's younger brother, George, was born. Because of the proximity of their ages, they were raised and educated together when young. They became attached to each other, although they quarrelled a lot, as siblings do. When Eddy was seven years old, John Dalton was appointed as the boys' tutor. George was always considered the more capable of the two and probably for a good reason. To many, Eddy seemed dull and lethargic. He had difficulty learning and even reading. He might have been partially deaf. He also had an abnormally long neck, which forced him to wear long collars, giving him the nickname, "Collars-and-Cuffs."

One historian has written, "'Dear,' 'good' and 'kind' were the adjectives most usually employed in reference to Prince Eddy by his relations… Even his nearest and dearest, who were naturally bent on making the best of poor Eddy, could not bring themselves to use more positive terms. Prince Eddy was certainly dear and good, kind and considerate. He was also backward and utterly listless. He was self-indulgent and not punctual. He had been given no proper education and as a result, he was interested in nothing. He was as heedless and as aimless as a gleaming goldfish in a crystal bowl."[170] After a few years, when their parents considered separating the brothers, the tutor, Dalton, advised against it. He told the parents that "Prince Albert Victor requires the stimulus of Prince George's company to induce him to work at all."[171] On the other hand, most people who knew the prince came to like him. "Everyone agreed that Eddy was good-looking, sweet-natured and charming."[172] Some ascribed his dullness to Dalton's

---

[170] James Pope-Hennessy, *Queen Mary, 1867-1953*, Alfred A. Knopf (1960), pp. 177-8 (hereafter Pope-Hennessy, *Queen Mary*).

[171] Stanley Weintraub, *Victoria: An Intimate Biography*, Truman Talley Books (1987), p. 420 (hereafter Weintraub, *Victoria*).

[172] Andrew Cook, *Prince Eddy: The King Britain Never Had*, Tempus Publishing (2006), p. 52 (hereafter Cook, *Prince Eddy*).

uninspiring tutelage. Eddy, along with George, did manage to learn Danish, although he struggled with other languages at a time when most of the European nobility could speak multiple languages.

In 1877, Eddy contracted typhoid fever. Unlike his forebear Prince Henry, who also contracted typhoid fever after swimming in the Thames (chapter 11), Eddy survived the illness. Dr William Gull treated the prince during his recovery, for which Queen Victoria gave him great credit. She awarded the doctor with a baronetcy and made him one of her own physicians. When Eddy was well enough, he and George, accompanied by Dalton, were placed aboard the HMS *Britannia*, a training ship moored at Dartmouth. Their education continued on the ship. Again, George was the better pupil and, often, had to look after his older brother. Then came what the queen and Eddy's parents, as well as the government and general public (all of whom despaired of making anything out of him), hoped would be a turning point in his young life.

In 1879, the brothers were sent on a three-year around-the-world tour of the British Empire aboard the HMS *Bacchante*. The ship travelled extensively, visiting most provinces in Britain's widespread empire—including such places as the Falkland Islands, Australia, Fiji, Singapore and Egypt, as well as other exciting places such as the Holy Land and Greece. In Japan, the brothers received blue and red dragon tattoos on their arms and had an audience with the Emperor. During the tour, on his sixteenth birthday, Eddy was commissioned a midshipman. The tour, it was hoped, would expand the prince's horizons and bring him out of his lethargy. It seemed, however, to have had no such effect. He seemed interested in very little. Eddy was eighteen years old when the ship returned to England. It was time again to try to figure out what to do with him. He and George were sent to Lausanne in Switzerland for several months in the hope they would learn German and French, but with limited success.

The year after the *Bacchante* returned to England, Eddy and his younger brother parted ways. George remained in the navy. In 1883, despite his apparent intellectual limitations, Eddy was sent to study at Trinity College in Cambridge, although he was never expected to take any examinations. Before his arrival in Cambridge, he made a pilgrimage to Balmoral Castle in Scotland, where his grandmother, Queen Victoria, awarded him with the Order of the Garter.

In Cambridge, he was given a new tutor, James Stephen. Stephen's character has also been questioned. Some suspected, then and still today, that he was homosexual and that he was a bit too fond of the prince. This has never been proven. Although Stephen found his pupil kind and sympathetic and not entirely without intelligence, he also came to believe he could not be educated to the point necessary for a future king. He wrote, "I do not think he can possibly derive much benefit from attending lectures at Cambridge... He hardly knows the meaning of the words *to read*."[173] However, one of Eddy's instructors observed that, although he could not read well, he could learn by listening and that he absorbed what he heard. If so, this might mean he was suffering from some form of dyslexia or similar learning disability for which he was never properly treated.

Speculation abounds over whether the prince had any sexual experiences while at Cambridge and, if so, what kind. This is the time, some believe, that Eddy's homosexual tendencies first became manifest. For a prince in the liberated sphere of Trinity College, willing sexual partners, both male and female, would have been readily available. Nothing is known for certain, but this period was one of the happier times of Eddy's life. Interacting with people of intelligence and sophistication probably helped to develop his personality. He particularly enjoyed playing whist (a forerunner of the modern game of contract bridge), at which he was said to be quite capable. And the prince was not always lethargic. Because he was never *forced* to excel at anything, it depended on what interested him. "He who so notoriously reacted with 'indolence and inattention' could spend long evenings concentrating on the complexities of whist and furiously energetic afternoons playing hockey or lacrosse because these things mattered to him."[174] He also loved hunting.

Some allege that around this time, Eddy contracted some form of syphilis or gonorrhoea, either on the world tour or at Trinity College, although this, too, has never been proven. In the summer of 1884, Eddy was sent to Heidelberg to try to improve his knowledge of the German language. He appears to have been well-liked by the German students.

In 1885, Eddy left Cambridge. He later received an honorary degree from the institution but never a real one. In April, he accompanied his parents on a state visit to Ireland, where he became interested in the question of home rule for the Irish. The following July, he was gazetted to the Tenth Royal Hussars cavalry regiment, known as the Prince of Wales's Own. He was promoted to captain in 1887 and major in 1889, although it is doubtful that he earned either promotion rather than simply received it because of his birth. For a while, he received some

---

[173] Cook, *Prince Eddy*, p. 103.

[174] Cook, *Prince Eddy*, p. 109.

training at Aldershot in Hampshire, but his military performance was mediocre at best. Indeed, for much of the time, his military activities were virtually non-existent. During this time, he took up the sport of polo. He also performed some of the public engagements royals were expected to perform. In June 1887, he was present for the opening of the Hammersmith Suspension Bridge across the Thames in London. In August 1889, he was part of a delegation that met the German, Kaiser Wilhelm II, on a state visit to Britain. Thus, matters continued for the prince, as he (and others) struggled to prepare him for the exalted role he was expected to play from birth.

In July 1889, a scandal broke out in London. The police discovered an all-male prostitution ring on Cleveland Street that had a prominent clientele. Today, this would not cause much of a stir. But section 11 of the Criminal Law Amendment Act of 1885 made "gross indecency" between two men, even if consenting, a crime punishable by up to two years of imprisonment at hard labour, as Oscar Wilde would learn a few years later. The prostitutes revealed to the police the names of their clients. Eddy was not among those named. But the man responsible for running the horse stables of Eddy's father, Lord Arthur Somerset, *was* named. When questioned by police, Somerset supposedly implicated Eddy as one of the clients. It has been charged that Somerset—or his solicitor—named Eddy to take the heat off of Somerset. Naming Eddy as a suspect might cause the entire matter to be covered up. In the event, the scandal was, indeed, hushed up. Neither Somerset nor any of the other high-ranking individuals identified as clients on Cleveland Street were ever prosecuted.

Rumours existed then that Eddy had, in fact, been a client of the Cleveland Street brothel and that the Prince of Wales himself intervened to put a stop to the investigation to protect his son. Some believe this today, although there is no evidence to support either rumour. It is possible that Eddy had visited the Cleveland Street brothel, although, if so, one would expect that the prostitutes would have identified him; they identified other high-ranking men. Eddy might have been homosexual or bisexual. But, as with so much else regarding this prince, nothing has ever been proven. Whatever the true facts, the scandal and the rumours harmed his standing in public opinion. "He had not been completely taken up by contemporaries of his own class, so nobody knew how he spent his time and it is this widespread ignorance of his true nature that allowed gossip to thrive."[175]

---

[175] Cook, *Prince Eddy*, p. 186.

In October 1889, the prince embarked on a seven-month tour of India, the so-called jewel in the British crown. The tour had been planned since the spring. As a prospective Emperor of India, as well as King of England, he was entertained lavishly by the various maharajahs who recognised British suzerainty. He had many adventures, generally in luxurious circumstances. Ceremonial elephant rides were common. He spent Christmas at Mandalay. The prince shot many wild animals for sport—tigers, lions, deer, cheetahs, leopards, peacocks and many more—a practice generally condemned today but then considered great fun. He visited the Taj Mahal. A woman he met on tour later claimed he fathered her son. He denied it, and, once again, nothing was proven.

After Eddy returned to England, he was made the Duke of Clarence and Avondale in a ceremony conducted on 24 May 1890, Queen Victoria's birthday. By this time, he was in his mid-twenties. It was time to find a wife.

The first prospective bride was a cousin, Princess Alix of Hesse and by Rhine. Alix was the daughter of Queen Victoria's second daughter, Alice. Victoria thought Alix would make a fine future queen and Eddy proposed to her. But Alix had a mind of her own. She did not like the prince and she turned him down. Victoria was astonished and irritated, declaring that "she refuses the greatest position there is!" Later, Alix married Nicholas II, destined to become the last Tsar of Russia. Changing her name to Alexandra and her religion to Russian Orthodox, she went on to have an eventful life in Russia, living during World War I and the Russian Revolution of 1917. Taken prisoner during the Revolution, she was shot to death, along with her entire family, in July 1918 in the remote city of Yekaterinburg, east of the Ural Mountains. One wonders whether she ever regretted turning down the British Prince during the grim days of her imprisonment so far from anywhere.

After Alix, came a true love affair, one that undermines the view of Eddy as homosexual. Princess Hélène of Orleans was the daughter of Prince Philippe, Count of Paris, the current pretender to the French throne. Philippe and his family were living in exile in England. Eddy and Hélène met and got to know each other at the home of Eddy's sister, Princess Louise. They fell in love, or at least all reports so indicate. Hélène was a true beauty and was considered extraordinarily intelligent. She may have been dazzled by Eddy's position in life, but it also appears she truly loved him. They decided to get married. But there was a major obstacle. Hélène was Catholic. Under the Act of Settlement of 1701, no future king could marry a Catholic and remain heir. (Chapter 12.) But the couple was determined. In August 1890, Eddy and Hélène travelled to Balmoral Castle and met with his grandmother, the now 71-year-old Queen Victoria. The queen was impressed with Hélène, believed the couple was truly in love and sympathised with their situation. She said she would try to help them but warned there would be difficulties.

Hélène volunteered to convert to the Church of England so she could marry Eddy. Doing so would present difficult legal questions under the Act of Settlement. Could a future king marry a *former* Catholic? What would it take for her to fully convert? Would Catholics recognise any conversion? Would Parliament? For his part, Eddy offered to renounce his right to the succession if necessary, so he could marry her. (That Hélène did not object suggests she did love the man and not just the position.) He wrote to his brother: "You have no idea how I love this sweet girl now and I feel I could never be happy without her."[176]

The legal questions never had to be resolved because another obstacle appeared. Hélène's father refused to agree either to his daughter's converting to another religion or to her marrying the English Prince. Hélène travelled to Rome and asked Pope Leo XIII to intervene on her behalf. The Pope refused. Realizing she could not go against her father's wishes, she wrote to Eddy, releasing him from his marriage proposal to her and advising him to marry a Protestant princess. The pair's dream had come to an end. Victoria's support was not enough. Hélène had to look elsewhere. In 1895, she married Prince Emanuele Filiberto, the Duke of Aosta and became the Duchess of Aosta, a far cry from the exalted position to which she had aspired. She died in 1951 in Italy.

After two possible brides for the prince had gone by the wayside, Victoria essentially took over. She found another bride for Eddy. Princess Mary of Teck, known as May, was the daughter of one of Victoria's cousins. The queen and Eddy's family essentially told him to marry her, even though the two barely knew each other. When they met, however, they seemed to get along well. In December 1991, to Mary's "great surprise," as she later reported, Eddy proposed to her.[177] To everyone's satisfaction, Mary said yes. The wedding was set for 27 February 1892. Both seemed happy and they eagerly anticipated the wedding. Eddy was also being considered for the post of Viceroy in Ireland, a position that would take him and his new wife to Dublin and help prepare him for his future

---

[176] Pope-Hennessy, *Queen Mary*, p. 186.

[177] Pope-Hennessy, *Queen Mary*, p. 198.

role as king. Although largely symbolic, the posting would have been a formal position that mattered. He had never held a position that actually meant something. Things were definitely looking up for the prince. But then fate intervened.

Beginning in 1889 and continuing off and on for the next few years, an influenza epidemic swept through Europe and much of the rest of the world, killing some 1,000,000 people worldwide. Among those who fell ill of the disease was Eddy himself. He missed his birthday party, held on 8 January 1892, at Sandringham House, a royal residence in Norfolk, because of illness. He developed pneumonia and grew increasingly worse. Eventually, his doctors despaired for him. The end came on 14 January. He died around 9:35 that morning. In his final delirium, he was heard to shout, "Hélène! Hélène!" The young man who had the world at his feet lived only a week beyond 28 years. Many of his family, including his intended bride, Mary, were at his bedside when he died. Mary wrote to Queen Victoria, "Never shall I forget that dreadful night of agony and suspense as we sat round His bed watching Him getting weaker & weaker."[178]

The outpouring of grief was genuine, if not as great as that following the death of Princess Charlotte 75 years earlier. The Prince of Wales, Eddy's father, wrote to the queen, "Gladly would I have given my life for his, as I put no value on mine… Such a tragedy has never before occurred in the annals of my family and it is hard that poor little May should virtually become a widow before she is a wife." Younger brother George, who had now become the heir to the throne, also mourned the death of his brother and great friend. He wrote, "It is only now that I have found out how deeply I did love him and I remember with pain nearly every hard word and little quarrel I had with him and I long to ask his forgiveness but alas! It is too late now."[179] His mother was especially shattered. She preserved Eddy's room just as he had left it as a shrine to his memory, with a fire burning in the grate and his soap and hairbrushes in their accustomed spot. Among those who mourned was his former love. Princess Hélène later told Queen Victoria, "I loved him so much. And it was probably foolish of me, but I couldn't help it. He was so good."[180]

---

[178] Pope-Hennessy, *Queen Mary*, p. 215.

[179] Cook, *Prince Eddy*, p. 272.

[180] Cook, *Prince Eddy*, p. 279.

Eddy was buried near St George's Chapel at Windsor Castle on 20 January after a long and sombre funeral. "The following day, *The Times* would devote thirteen and a half unbroken broadsheet columns to the services and messages of 20 January, when the whole country mourned the death of a young man who had been so widely liked."[181]

During the period of mourning, Princess Mary and George got to know one another and they liked what they saw. Queen Victoria thought that if Mary would have made a good queen for Eddy, she would now make a good queen for George. Much as, after the death of Prince Arthur, his wife, Catherine of Aragon, married his younger brother, Henry (chapter 9), George married Princess Mary himself. He eventually succeeded to the throne and Mary became the ever-popular Queen Mary, the grandmother of Queen Elizabeth II. She died in 1953, 85 years of age and is also buried at St George's Chapel.

Posterity has not been kind to Eddy's memory and in at least one respect unfairly so. We turn first to the unfair respect. Of the few who remember Eddy today, most probably think of him in connection with the notorious London killer Jack the Ripper. There was no contemporary, or even near contemporary, suggestion that Eddy had anything to do with the Ripper's crimes. But, beginning in 1962, long after everyone connected with the prince or the Ripper had died, people began to claim he was the killer. Over the next few decades, "nonfiction" books (in reality fiction), novels, movies and television series have supposed that he was either Jack the Ripper or in conspiracy with him. The suppositions were based on no evidence that was ever actually produced, but instead were based on a good deal of speculation and, even more, pure imagination, mixed, it seems, with the desire to sell books.

In actual fact, Eddy, a royal prince whose whereabouts were generally well documented, was far away when the murders were committed. For example, on the date of two of the murders, Eddy was with his family and other dignitaries, including Queen Victoria herself (who noted in her journal that she had lunch with him that day), at Balmoral Castle in Scotland, 500 miles or 800 kilometres from London. As one biographer wrote, "The fact that on each and every occasion a Ripper murder took place Eddy was not only out of London, but was attending functions in front of large numbers of people, seems to have escaped the attention of many writers determined to place him in the Ripper frame."[182]

---

[181] Cook, *Prince Eddy*, p. 274.

[182] Cook, *Prince Eddy*, p. 9.

Eventually, those determined to connect Eddy with the murders realised they could no longer credibly claim he was the Ripper himself. So, they converted to a conspiracy theory. Eddy might not have been Ripper, but he was associated with him and the murders were committed on his behalf. Because the whereabouts of those people who were not royalty were not as well documented as were Eddy's whereabouts and because every possible suspect or witness was long dead, it was harder to disprove, and thus easier to assert, that someone else connected to the prince was Jack the Ripper. One of several suspects named was Dr William Gull, the physician who had treated Eddy when he contracted typhoid fever and became Victoria's personal physician. He was 71 years old and in ill health when the murders were committed, which alone casts doubt on whether he could have been the killer. Another suspect was James Stephen, Eddy's tutor at Trinity College. Various mutually inconsistent conspiracy theories have been postulated. One popular theory is that Eddy impregnated one of the victims and the royal family commissioned the murders to cover it up. Among those supposedly involved in some of the suggested conspiracies was Queen Victoria herself.

Serious historians have thoroughly debunked such conspiracy theories.[183] The author of a book presenting one of the theories publicly challenged Queen Elizabeth II to make the royal archives on Prince Victor Albert available to him, expecting (and no doubt hoping) to be refused so he could claim the royal family was hiding the truth. But a Buckingham Palace spokesperson stymied him by offering him full access to the archives. The author rejected the offer, leading, a historian credibly states, "to the inevitable conclusion that his challenge had been made to publicise his book." As the same historian summarises, "Ripper and Royalty have been the perfect combination for the sensation seekers despite the ridicule that has been heaped upon the resulting theories."[184]

The time has come to relegate such lurid and sensational, but unsupported, conspiracy theories to the realm of fantasy and no longer give them credence. Prince Albert Victor was not Jack the Ripper, he was not associated with Jack the Ripper and neither he nor the royal family had anything to do with the murders.

---

[183] For example, Donald Rumbelow, *The Complete Jack the Ripper*, Virgin Books (2013), pp. 211-247 (hereafter Rumbelow, *The Complete Jack the Ripper*).

[184] Rumbelow, *The Complete Jack the Ripper*, p. 247.

But many people then and still today believe Eddy's early death was a good thing for Britain. One historian wrote that Eddy's limited abilities made him "the best contemporary argument for a monarchy shorn of responsibility."[185] Others, especially more recently, have been less certain of Eddy's incapacity to have been at least a decent king. His mental abilities do, indeed, seem to have been limited, although he never seems to have been pushed to excel or to develop his mind to its full potential. If, as it appears, he learned to play the difficult mind game of whist well, he had some mental abilities. He also had good, perhaps excellent, people skills. Most of those who got to know him genuinely liked him. And he would have had the same queen his brother actually had—Mary of Teck, a great helpmate to her husband. A recent biographer, who has sought to rehabilitate Eddy's memory, summarised his life: "Prince Eddy was just twenty-eight when he died and had met thousands of people and travelled around the world. Yet he had made no mark on history. He had not yet done anything remarkable or even reprehensible. He appeared to be, as one writer put it, 'spotless' when he died and because goodness is dull, he was easily forgotten."[186]

By the nineteenth-century, the United Kingdom had become a constitutional monarchy. Others in the government, from the prime minister down, wielded the actual power, not the monarch. As king, Eddy would have had limited ability to influence events, just as his brother, when he became George V, had in actual fact. But perhaps, with his sympathetic demeanour and good people skills, he could have gotten along better than his brother did with England's nemesis in the early twentieth-century, his cousin, Kaiser Wilhelm II of Germany. Maybe things would have developed differently and possibly, just possibly, for the better.

It is fruitless to speculate whether the unfortunate series of events that brought the United Kingdom into World War I in the summer of 1914 and the tragic events that followed, would have played out differently under King Albert I. Probably not. But this biographical sketch of the final heir who never reigned will end with a common refrain: We will never know.

---

[185] Weintraub, *Victoria*, p. 3.

[186] Cook, *Prince Eddy*, p. 278

Conclusion

Prince Albert Victor Christian Edward was the most recent British heir who never reigned. His brother became King George V in his place in 1910. When George died in 1936, his oldest son became King Edward VIII. This king reigned only briefly before abdicating the throne in December of the same year so he could marry the "woman I love," the twice-divorced American Wallis Simpson. He was succeeded by his brother, George VI, the second successive younger brother named George to become king. When this George died in 1952, he was succeeded by his daughter, the current Queen Elizabeth II. Elizabeth is now the longest-reigning monarch in British history, having passed Victoria's record of 63 years in 2015. Elizabeth is well on the way towards breaking the European record of just over 72 years set by France's Sun King, Louis XIV (reigned 1643-1715). As everyone knows, her heir apparent is her oldest son, Charles, the Prince of Wales.

Because of Elizabeth's long reign, Charles has long since shattered the record for the longest wait for a British heir to the throne. He was three years old when his mother became queen and he has been the heir apparent ever since. Currently, he is an heir who has not yet reigned. Over the years, due to various familial scandals and so-called crises, such as his well-publicised divorce from Princess Diana, followed by her tragic death in Paris in an automobile accident as she was fleeing the paparazzi, some have speculated that he might never become king. Some suggest he might be passed over in favour of his (and Diana's) oldest son, Prince William, the Duke of Cambridge, or perhaps that the monarchy would be dispensed with altogether. But this is all pointless speculation. Assuming, as is probable, that Charles survives his mother, he will and certainly *should*, succeed her as King Charles III.

When he does, he will have avoided joining the ranks of heirs who never reigned.

The foregoing conclusion was written before Queen Elizabeth II's death in

September 2022. Her death ensured that Charles, now King Charles III, would not become another heir who never reigned. The question now becomes, what about Prince William, the new Prince of Wales?